ESSAYS ON

The Monetary History of the United States

BY

CHARLES J. BULLOCK, Ph.D.
ASSISTANT PROFESSOR OF ECONOMICS IN WILLIAMS COLLEGE

GREENWOOD PRESS, PUBLISHERS
NEW YORK

Copyright © 1900 by Macmillan

First Greenwood Reprinting, 1969

Library of Congress Catalogue Card Number 69-18301

PRINTED IN UNITED STATES OF AMERICA

92517

TO

Augustus H. Buck

PROFESSOR OF GREEK IN BOSTON UNIVERSITY

THIS BOOK IS DEDICATED

AS A MARK OF GRATITUDE AND AFFECTIONATE REMEMBRANCE

BY HIS FORMER PUPIL

THE AUTHOR

92517

PREFACE

THE three essays in this volume are based upon
a part of the materials that the author collected
some years ago, when lecturing upon the monetary and financial history of the United States.
They are now published in the hope that they will
prove to be of some value to students and investi-
gators in this field. The author desires to make
grateful acknowledgment of the constant aid received from his wife, who has devoted several
months to the work of gathering materials and
assisting in the preparation of the book.

CHARLES J. BULLOCK.

WILLIAMSTOWN, MASS.,
August, 1900.

CONTENTS

PART I

PART II

CONTENTS

PART III

THE PAPER CURRENCY OF NEW HAMPSHIRE

PART I

*THREE CENTURIES OF CHEAP MONEY
IN THE UNITED STATES*

CHAPTER I

INTRODUCTION

At the present day, after all the discussion that has occurred upon the subject, it is certainly difficult to present anything that is wholly new or original concerning the monetary problems that have vexed the United States. But it may prove worth our while to undertake to review and interpret familiar historical events in the light of certain primary facts, the full significance of which has seldom been appreciated in sufficient measure. These facts are, first, that a strong movement in favor of cheap money has existed continuously in this country from the earliest period of colonization; and, second, that the persistence of such an agitation has been due, more than to any other single cause, to the constant spread of settlements westward over large areas that have long remained thinly populated. With the growth of numbers, the rise of manufacturing and commercial industries, and the increase of wealth, the desire for a cheap currency has gradually diminished; but this has no sooner taken place in the more populous states than the old phenomena have reappeared in newly settled districts, while any localities that have remained sparsely peopled and devoted chiefly to agricultural pursuits have always furnished a favorable field for the old propaganda.

Back of all the strivings for an inexpensive medium of exchange, each generation of our people has always heard the complaint that our supply of money has been insufficient;[1] and this cry has invariably furnished an unmistakable indication of the underlying cause of the agitation. "No complaint," wrote Adam Smith, in 1776, "is more common than that of a scarcity of money. Money, like wine, must always be scarce with those who have neither wherewithal to buy it, nor credit to borrow it. Those who have either, will seldom be in want either of the money or of the wine which they have occasion for."[2] In the

[1] One of the earliest of these complaints is found in a resolution of the General Court of Massachusetts in the year 1641. It is so typical of similar complaints of later times that a part of it may well be quoted here : "Whereas many men in the plantation are in debt, and heare is not money sufficient to discharge the same, though their cattle and goods should bee sould for halfe their worth, as experience hath shewed upon some late executions, whereby a great part of the people in the country may be undone, and yet their debts not satisfied, . . ." The Court then proceeded to grant relief to insolvent debtors. Mass. Recs., I. 307. John Winthrop wrote that the merchants had brought over "great store of provisions" in 1640, "so as now all our money was drained from us." Winthrop, N. Eng., II. 7.

[2] Smith, W. of N., II. 9. A year or two later John Witherspoon wrote : "The cry with many is, we must have paper for a circulating medium, as there is such a scarcity of gold and silver. Is this just? No. They mistake their own poverty, or the nation's poverty, for a scarcity of gold and silver ; . . ." Works, IX. 45.

INTRODUCTION

United States an enterprising and resolute people has been engaged, for nearly three centuries, in occupying and developing a vast area of free land. While natural resources have abounded, each newly settled district has always experienced a lack of the capital needed to bring the soil under cultivation, to supply means of communication, and to develop manufacturing enterprises.[1] This want might have been little felt by a less progressive people; but with us it has been a real and serious obstacle, which has been removed only by the slow growth of wealth and numbers. In order to possess a sufficient supply of metallic money, a nation must convert a portion of its capital into a stock of gold or silver coins or bullion, a process that is expensive, even under the most favorable circumstances. In the United States, prior to the discovery of mines of the precious metals, gold and silver could be obtained only through exchange with foreign countries; and the acquirement and maintenance of an abundant metallic currency was made especially difficult by the poverty of our people in all sorts of capital. The difficulty was intensified still further by the sparseness of settlement and the economic isolation of households and communities, a circumstance which made the

---

[1] This was well stated by Governor Ward of Rhode Island, in 1740: "And as the first settlers were not of the wealthiest sort, nor over-stocked with servants, the greatest part of their money was unavoidably swallowed up in procuring provisions, clothing, and utensils for husbandry and labor, to subdue and cultivate the soil." Recs. of R. I., V. 8.

monetary circulation sluggish and increased the volume of currency required for the transaction of a given number of exchanges. The accumulated products of our industry were more often converted into other things than money. Each person usually desired to employ in production or exchange whatever gold or silver might come to him; for he had many uses for other kinds of capital, and could ill afford to keep on hand a stock of money that appeared to be an idle investment. Therefore it happened that supplies of the precious metals secured in trade tended to move out of the colonies in exchange for other things that were felt to be more necessary. This fact explains the circumstance, so often bewailed by writers of the seventeenth and eighteenth centuries, that the balance of trade was commonly against the colonies, so that gold and silver seemed to take to themselves wings, and to fly out of the country.

It may be said that it would have been better for the people to have retained enough metallic money to furnish an adequate medium of exchange, and this is undoubtedly true. But the matter did not appear in this light to the individual colonist, who would usually expend his own coins for things that were felt to be immediately desirable, and would leave to some patriotic neighbor the task of accumulating a stock of money that appeared to be idle capital. In the colonial period, the usual outcome was that the attempt to maintain a specie currency was abandoned, and some less expensive medium was substituted. In later times, the poorer and less populous regions of the country have experienced a similar scarcity of gold or silver, and have been equally desirous of finding some form of currency that would be easier to obtain. The continued growth of new commonwealths in the West has served to perpetuate the conditions under which an agitation for cheap money was sure to remain with us.

It is the purpose, then, of this first essay to review the entire monetary history of the United States in the light of the facts just stated, and to show that all the varied currency experiments with which our people have been vexed for nearly three centuries have been, first and fundamentally, efforts to secure a cheap medium of exchange. While it is not claimed that this thesis is entirely novel,[1] it is believed that the essay is the first systematic effort to supply a unitary interpretation of the leading facts in the history of American currency. The second and third essays contained in this volume are primarily investigations into subjects about which little has been known hitherto.

---

[1] Professor Sumner has appreciated this fact very clearly. See Currency, 5–6 ; Banking, 1–3; also article in First Century, 238–259. In the last-mentioned work he says that " the monetary history of the United States from the first colonization until now is a history of experiments with cheap substitutes for money." Professor F. J. Turner has well shown the similarity between the present silver movement in the West and similar agitations of earlier days. *Atlantic Monthly*, LXXIX. 441–442.

But, since North Carolina and New Hampshire remained, up to the very close of the colonial period, sparsely settled farming communities in which manufactures and commerce were of slight importance, they offer a favorable field in which to test the thesis which the first essay seeks to establish. Thus a real unity of purpose may be traced throughout this book, in which, as in most collections of essays, no formal unity is to be expected.

CHAPTER II

WAMPUM AND BARTER CURRENCY

THE first immigrants brought into the colonies little or no money, since they were poor men and needed other forms of capital. Some years were to elapse before the new plantations were to develop any extensive foreign commerce, by means of which specie was finally secured; and a scarcity of currency was experienced in the very first years of settlement. Accordingly in Virginia, as early as 1619, tobacco was made receivable at three shillings per pound; while in New Netherland and Massachusetts the settlers utilized peltry as a medium of exchange.[1] In trading with the Indians the colonists learned to use wampum, the common Indian currency, and they soon began to employ this in their dealings among themselves. Thus commenced in this country the quest for cheaper substitutes for metallic money.

For the Indians, wampum had been a satisfactory currency.[2] It was manufactured largely at

[1] Bruce, II. 498–499; Ripley, 110; Fernow, 298; Felt, 11, 12, 14.
[2] On wampum currency, see Weeden, I. 32–46; Bruce, II. 520–521; *Amer. Nat.*, XVII. 468; Fernow, 297–299; Docs. of N. Y., I. 269, 365.

7

the eastern end of Long Island, where were found "the cockles whereof wampum is made." Much labor and patience were required for its production, and "an Indian's utmost manufacture amounted only to a few pence a day." But the English settlers, with their iron implements, were able to increase the output greatly, especially after they settled upon Long Island near "the mine of New Netherland." As a result, the wampum depreciated, so that, in 1649, Massachusetts had to prohibit its receipt in payment of taxes, although it was allowed to remain a legal tender for private debts until 1661. In counterfeiting and otherwise deteriorating this rude medium, the Indians seem to have learned a few lessons from the white men, for we find that complaints came to the commissioners of the New England Confederation that "the Indians abused the English with false badd and unfinished Peage."[1] Troubles growing out of the depreciation and counterfeiting of this currency became especially serious in New Netherland, which seems to have received much bad wampum from New England as well as a bountiful supply directly from the cockle-shell mints operated industriously by the English on Long Island. In 1641, complaints were made that "very bad wampum is at present circulating here, and payment is made in nothing but rough unpolished stuff which is brought hither from other places," so that "the good, polished Wam-

[1] Hazard, II. 124.

8

pum, commonly called Manhattan Wampum, is wholly put out of sight and exported." Then we hear of a plague of bad wampum " of Stone, Bone, Glass, Muscle-Shells, Horn, yea even of Wood and Broken Beads." Washington Irving had an undoubted basis of fact for his humorous description of the trials of the Dutch with the enterprising Yankees, for we find wampum greatly depreciated in 1659, " in consequence of the great importation of Wampum from New England, which barters therewith, and carries out of the country not only the best cargoes sent hence, but also a large quantity of Beaver and other Peltries," so that the people of New Amsterdam " remain with a chestful of Wampum, which is a currency utterly valueless, except among New Netherland Indians only." [1] In spite of all such disturbances, however, this rude money continued to be used more or less in New York as late as 1701.

As time went on, other forms of barter currency multiplied in the colonies. Yet Maryland and Virginia clung to the use of tobacco, which long remained the principal medium of exchange, even after its value had fallen from three shillings to twopence per pound.[2] In nearly all the plantations, beaver and other kinds of peltry were util-

[1] For these references to New Netherland, see O'Callaghan, 26, 115, 434.

[2] Scharf, I. 273, 278, 280, 282 ; II. 35–36 ; McMahon, 224–225, 283 ; Ripley, 110, 111, 131–132 ; *Hist. Mag.*, II. 42–43. In Virginia the burgesses frequently insisted upon having their own wages paid in coin. Ripley, 132.

ized extensively as currency, since furs, like tobacco, " were in demand in Europe, and could always, without much loss, be converted into coin or its equivalent." In the Carolinas, rice and tar were used for a similar purpose. Massachusetts, in 1631, made corn a lawful tender for all debts, except in cases where beaver or money should be specified.[1] In addition to the commodities already mentioned, we find that the various colonies, at one time or another, authorized the payment of public or private debts in wheat, oats, barley, peas, bacon, pork, beef, fish, flax, wool, sugar, brandy, whiskey, and even musket balls.[2] West of the Alleghanies, in Tennessee and Kentucky, Mr. Roosevelt tells us that a similar barter currency was in use during the last decade of the eighteenth century; and, as late as 1885, the *Bismarck Tribune* reports that gopher tails were at that time employed as money in some sections of Dakota.[3]

The use of these forms of " country pay," or "specie," as, singularly enough, it was sometimes

---

[1] For the Carolinas, see Hawks, II. 163 ; Douglass, Discourse, 317 ; Stat. of S. C., II. 37 ; Col. Recs. N. C., IV. 920. For Massachusetts, see Felt, 16. " It is further ordered, that corne shall passe for payement of all debts at the usuall rate it is solde for, except money or beaver be expressly named." Mass. Recs., I. 92.

[2] On these barter currencies, see Bronson, 5–13 ; Weeden, 101, 119, 128, 142, 170, 178, 196 ; Fernow, 298 ; *Hist. Mag.*, II. 43–44 ; Bruce, II. 521 ; Douglass, Discourse, 315–317.

[3] Roosevelt, III. 160–161 ; IV. 113–114, 232–233 ; Andrews, 119.

called, occasioned great trouble for public officials. Attempts were made to regulate prices in order to keep the currency from fluctuating so much as to be useless.[1] In Massachusetts the collectors of taxes were continually involved in the most ridiculous difficulties.[2] Payment of the public dues in the lankest cattle available became so common that the General Court had to enact, in 1658, that no man should discharge the rates with "leane cattle."[3] Ten years later the mere cost of transporting the commodities received for taxes amounted to ten per cent of the entire assessment, and a further loss of five per cent was incurred through shrinkage and deterioration. Accordingly, in 1694, the government was obliged to discontinue the payment of taxes in such a currency.[4] The experience of other colonies did not differ greatly from that of Massachusetts. Obviously enough, the employment of such cheap substitutes served to expedite the exportation of such gold or silver coins as found their way into the country, and to delay the accumulation of a sufficient stock of metallic money. The precious metals could not

---

[1] Weeden, 97, 99, 115, 118, 132.

[2] Thus a Springfield constable had to transport to Boston one hundred and thirty bushels of peas received in payment of province taxes. This required eight trips to Hartford, and two from there to Boston. In passing the falls of the Connecticut a part of the cargo was spoiled by the water, and the collector had to petition the General Court for relief. Felt, 53.

[3] Mass. Recs., IV. 348.

[4] Felt, 38, 40, 45, 54 ; Douglas, Fin. Hist., 49-50.

well compete with puny cattle and bad grain as a
medium for the settlement of public or private
debts.[1]

[1] In 1749, the Governor of North Carolina complained of the
losses caused in that province by receiving commodities for taxes.
He said that it was "a stated rule that of so many commodities
the worst sort were only paid." Col. Recs. N. C., IV. 920.

CHAPTER III

SILVER AND GOLD CURRENCIES

IN spite of the initial poverty of the colonists and the influence of the rude barter currencies, the increase of industry and commerce gradually brought into the more prosperous of the plantations a considerable amount of specie, of which a portion was retained in circulation. In the seventeenth century this consisted chiefly of Spanish silver money; but in the eighteenth, gold coins, mainly from the Brazilian mines, appeared in no small numbers.[1] Nevertheless

---

[1] The relative quantities of gold and silver that found their way into the colonies have not been made the subject of special investigation. But see Chalmers, 5, 8, 10, 15. In 1676 Edward Randolph wrote from Massachusetts : "There is a reasonable quantitie of silver money in the colony, but no gold." See Hutchinson's Coll. Papers, 498. In the seventeenth century gold was much scarcer than silver throughout the world. The world's annual gold product, which was only $3,885,000 at the time of the discovery of America, averaged but $5,662,000 between 1600 and 1620. The silver mines of South America, however, had increased the world's annual silver product from $1,954,000 in 1500 to an average of $17,579,000 between 1600 and 1620 ; and Spanish silver money had become common in all parts of the globe. For these statistics see Rep. Prec. Metals, 1896, 346–347. The gold product increased but little during the seventeenth century. In 1677 the Brazilian mines began to be systematically operated, and

13

complaints of the scarcity of coin and the alleged impossibility of keeping it in circulation remained so common, and have been accepted so complacently by most historians, that it will be necessary to present a little of the evidence that proves the presence of a moderate amount of specie in the colonies.

As early as 1639, Winthrop noted in his "Journal" the arrival of a bark which brought "much wealth in money, plate, indico and sugar." [1]   This trade continued until, thirteen years later, Massa-

by 1700 were contributing largely to the world's stock of gold.   As a result, the annual production of gold increased greatly between 1700 and 1760, as is shown in the following table : —

Years.	Average Annual Product in Thousands of Marks.	
	Brazil.	All Other Countries.
1681–1700	4,185	25,849
1701–1720	7,673	28,095
1721–1740	24,692	28,535
1741–1760	40,734	27,928

See Soetbeer, 109–110.   For an account of the Portuguese gold coinage, based on the product of the Brazilian mines, see Del Mar, 128–132.   This enlarged output of the yellow metal furnished the American colonies with gold coins in the eighteenth century.   The increase of the gold output relatively to that of silver is shown in the following table : —

Years.	Average Annual Product in Thousands of Dollars.	
	Gold.	Silver.
1581–1600	4,905	17,413
1681–1700	7,154	14,210
1721–1740	12,681	17,924
1741–1760	16,356	22,162

[1] Winthrop, N. Eng., I. 307.   Cf. Bradford, 441.

14

chusetts established its celebrated mint in order to recoin its circulating medium into a uniform silver currency. In 1671, Ogilby wrote of Maryland, "yet there wants not, besides English and other foraign Coyns, some of his Lordship's own Coyn."[1] In Virginia, Mr. Bruce finds abundant evidence of considerable accumulations of money and plate toward the close of the seventeenth century; and Dr. Ripley has reached the conclusion that a good deal of metallic money was always in circulation, especially in the tidewater districts.[2] In the year 1698, Gabriel Thomas reported that silver was plentiful in the vicinity of Philadelphia.[3] Two years later, John Fysack wrote concerning Carolina, Pennsylvania, New York, and New England: "There is now in the Plantations a great quantity of Spanish money Plate and Bullion and would be more if returns were answerable."[4] In 1740, Dr. Douglass stated: "Before Paper-Money took Place in New England, Silver abounded in Currency as much and perhaps more, than in many of our Colonies."[5] Ten years later, when Massachusetts returned to a specie basis, its trade prospered as never before; and Franklin, who was an advocate of paper money, was obliged to admit that the resumption of a silver currency had

[1] Chalmers, 5.

[2] Bruce, II. 504, 506, 507; Ripley, 118, 119, 131.

[3] Gouge, 5. See also statement of William Fishbourne, in 1739. Watson, Annals, I. 75.

[4] Chalmers, 12.

[5] Douglass, Discourse, 338.

met with popular approval.[1] This is only a tithe of the evidence that might be presented upon this point.

With the appearance of the Spanish and other coins, began the process of clipping the money. This was practised extensively in the West Indies, whence the colonies on the mainland secured the larger part of their supply of specie; and it continued until the Spanish piece of eight was often reduced in weight by as much as one-third.[2] The light weight coins naturally drove the "broad" pieces of eight out of the country, but the colonists may have condoned the practice, since the cheaper money was more readily retained in circulation. For it was difficult to keep even the clipped money in the country so long as the barter currencies were in vogue. A shilling in "country pay" was always at a discount when compared with a shilling in silver, and this discount amounted to thirty or forty per cent.[3] A full weight dollar

[1] See his examination before Parliament in 1766. Works of Franklin, III. 426–427. In 1767, while opposing Parliamentary prohibition of paper money, Franklin had to admit the beneficial effects of resumption in New England. *Idem*, IV. 84–85.

[2] " As the said Silver Coins went by Tale, and were not mill'd, they were clipped to such a Degree, that the Exchange to England varied in Proportion, . . ." Ashley, 51. See especially Douglass, Discourse, 301 ; Docs. of N. Y., IV. 1133–1135 ; *Yale Rev.*, VII. 263, 409 ; Felt, 35, 59, 60 ; Bronson, 20–22 ; Fernow, 303–305.

[3] In 1704, a traveller reports that the price of a knife was 12*d*. in "country pay" and 6*d*. in coin. Mr. Bronson finds that the barter currency was always at fifty per cent discount in Connecticut. Bronson, 22–23. Cf. *Yale Rev.*, VII. 248, 259.

of 17½ dwts. would not remain in circulation by the side of a barter shilling; and it could be clipped down to 12 dwts., or even less, before it would cease to be dearer than "country pay." Thus the practice of clipping coins became practically universal in spite of stringent laws that were designed to prevent it.[1]

Since the colonies, until the Revolution, retained the English denominations of pounds, shillings, and pence for their money of account, it became necessary to establish rates at which the Spanish and other foreign coins should be received. In the seventeenth and eighteenth centuries, the silver pound sterling was the standard, or "rating," money of England. This equalled, from 1600 to 1816, 1718.7 grains of fine silver; so that the shilling contained 85.93 grains of pure metal.[2] In the seventeenth century, the Spanish dollar, or piece of eight, has been variously estimated at 385 to 388.5 grains of fine silver, a weight which would have made it equivalent to about 4s. 6d. in English money.[3] In 1704, Newton's assay at the English mint gave the coin an official rating of 386.8 grains of pure metal, and fixed its value at 4s. 6d., a valuation which it retained during the next eighty

[1] Bronson, 21 ; Fernow, 303 ; *Yale Rev.*, VII. 264. In South Carolina the penalty for clipping was at one time death without benefit of clergy. Stat. of S. C., II. 72–73.

[2] McCulloch, 318–319 ; Ruding, I. 12, 357.

[3] This subject has been treated exhaustively by Professor Sumner in *Amer. Hist. Rev.*, III. 607–619. Cf. Chalmers, 390–394, 402–403 ; Del Mar, 105–111.

years, although its fine contents gradually diminished.[1] This customary rating of the dollar made the pound sterling worth $4.444; and, so long as the colonies valued the coin at 4s. 6d., the colonial pound remained the same as the pound sterling.

But as early as 1642, Massachusetts raised the rating of the dollar to 5s., and Connecticut took similar action the following year.[2] In 1645, Virginia rated this coin at 6s., but this valuation was lowered to 5s. a decade later.[3] Thus began the depreciation of the colonial metallic currencies. In 1652, Massachusetts established a mint, and began to coin shillings that were $22\frac{1}{2}$ per cent lighter than the sterling standard.[4] Upon this basis, the dollar would have been worth a little less than 6s. Between 1671 and 1697, no fewer than nine colonies began to advance the piece of eight,[5] and by 1700 great diversities existed in the ratings given to this coin in different localities.

[1] Chalmers, 414; *Amer. Hist. Rev.*, III. 613–615.

[2] Mass. Recs., II. 29; *Yale Rev.*, VII. 247–248; Conn. Recs., I. 86.

[3] Hening, Stat., I. 308, 397; Ripley, 112, 114.

[4] On the New England mint, see Felt, 30–35; Hutchinson, Hist., I. 164–165; Watson, 2–6; *Yale Rev.*, VII. 249 *et seq.;* Hickcox, Coinage, 1–13; Crosby. The New England shilling had fine contents of 66.6 grains. *Yale Rev.*, VII. 252.

[5] In 1671, Maryland rated the dollar at 6s. Arch. of Md., II. 286. In Mass. and N. Y., pieces of eight that were of full weight were, in 1672, advanced to 6s. Mass. Recs., IV. Part II. 533; Fernow, 300. For other instances referred to, see Papers of N. H., I. 448, 480; Belknap, I. 201; *Yale Rev.*, VII. 261, 263; Bronson, 20; Leam. and Spicer, 285, 295, 517; Min. of Penn., I. 558; Scharf, II. 35; Bruce, II. 507–511; Ripley, 115–119; Stat. of S. C., II. 72, 94, 163, 165.

Virginia, after having advanced the dollar to 6s. in 1683, allowed it to pass at 5s. a few years later. South Carolina fixed a rate of 5s. for a light coin weighing 12 dwts., with an addition of $3\frac{1}{2}d$. in value for every additional pennyweight. In New York, a dollar weighing 15 dwts. passed at 6s., while one weighing 17 dwts. was rated at 6s. 9d. Pennsylvania, and possibly West Jersey, gave the piece of eight the highest rating, valuing it at 7s. 6d. for a coin of 17 dwts. gross contents. In the other colonies 6s. had become the prevailing valuation of the dollar.[1] By this time the evils of these diverse and fluctuating currencies had become so great as to call forth complaints to the English authorities, who had already directed colonial governors to refuse assent to laws that tampered with the currency.[2] Accordingly a royal proclamation

[1] For Virginia, see Ripley, 116–118 ; Bruce, II. 510–511. For South Carolina, Stat. of S. C., II. 178 ; Carroll, II. 258. The rating of 5s. for a dollar weighing 12 dwts. would give a rate of 6s. $5\frac{1}{2}d$. for a dollar weighing 17 dwts., allowing $3\frac{1}{2}d$. for each additional dwt. Cf. Stat. of S. C., IX. 779. For New York, Fernow, 301. For Pennsylvania, Shepherd, 402–404 ; Docs. of N. Y., IV. 1047, 1059, 1134. For West Jersey, a law of 1693 rated a 17 dwt. coin at 7s. This was done in order that the coins might have the same rating that prevailed in Pennsylvania. See Leam. and Spicer, 517. It seems possible that the actual usage in West Jersey may have followed that of Pennsylvania in 1700. In Maryland there is a contemporary statement that the dollar was rated at 4s. 6d. in 1697. See Ripley, 115 ; Bruce, II. 511. This seems to be an error, since it conflicts with the acts passed by Maryland in 1686 and 1708, rating the dollar at 6s. See Scharf, II. 35.

[2] Chalmers, 10–15 ; Bruce, II. 509–510 ; Docs. of N. Y., IV. 1047, 1059 ; Fernow, 301 ; Ripley, 116 ; Smith, N. J., 240.

was issued in 1704, and an express act of Parliament was passed in 1707, requiring that the Spanish piece of eight should not be rated at more than 6s., and other coins at more than corresponding values.[1] But this law was almost universally evaded. The West Indian colonies, noting that the act specified only silver coins, proceeded "to give independent ratings (by weight) to the gold coins of Spain," and thus adopted a gold standard of value which could be depreciated at will without any violation of law.[2] Upon the mainland the colonies before long began to rate silver *by the ounce*, and thus the depreciation continued. In accordance with the rating of 6s. fixed by Parliament for the dollar, an ounce of silver should have been valued at 6s. 10.65d.[3] But the colonies usually[4] began to rate silver at 7s. or 8s. per ounce, and soon placed it at even higher figures.[5] Thus

[1] Chalmers, 14–16, 414–415 ; *Yale Rev.*, VII. 406–410 ; Douglass, Discourse, 301–302 ; Ashley, 50–63.   [2] Chalmers, 15.

[3] See Sumner, in *Yale Rev.*, VII. 407. The sterling value of silver was 5s. 2d. per ounce. The law of 1707 allowed a rating one third higher than this. Cf. Chalmers, 14.

[4] Maryland passed a law in 1708 in compliance with the act of Parliament. Scharf, II. 35. Until 1733, when the colony issued paper money, this valuation was retained. Douglass, Discourse, 315. Virginia in 1710 rated the ounce of silver at 6s. 3d., which was even less than Parliament had allowed. Ripley, 127. But in 1727 silver was raised to 6s. 8d. *Idem*, 130. See Douglass, Discourse, 316. Here it continued, and was, therefore, always a little below the rate fixed by Parliament.

[5] Belknap, III. 225 ; *Yale Rev.*, VII. 407–412 ; Felt, 60; Weeden, 387 ; Conn. Recs., V. 157 ; Phillips, I. 19, 61, 106, 111 ; Fernow, 306 ; Douglass, Discourse, 311, 312.

it became necessary for all people that handled any considerable quantity of money to have scales for ascertaining the weight of the coins. Finally, it is to be remembered that, during the first half of the eighteenth century, most of the colonies issued a paper currency whose depreciation soon brought them down to a paper money basis; so that the valuations which the English authorities gave to specie were a matter of small moment.

In 1750, when Massachusetts retired her paper currency and resumed a specie basis, Spanish dollars weighing 17 dwts. were rated at 6s., and silver was rated at 6s. 8d. per ounce.[1] This was a return to the rates fixed in the Parliamentary enactment of 1707. A somewhat similar process went on in other colonies that redeemed or repudiated their redundant paper currencies, but the rates finally given to the dollar were not uniform. New Hampshire, Rhode Island, Connecticut, and Virginia rated the dollar at 6s.[2] South Carolina and Georgia adopted valuations of 4s. 8d. and 5s.

[1] *Yale Rev.*, VII. 412–413 ; Felt, 121, 127 ; Weeden, 674–676 ; Acts of Mass., III. 430, 480, 494. These rates for the dollar and the ounce of silver are not equivalents, since, with the dollar at 6s., an ounce of silver would have been worth about 6s. 10.65d. But, as a matter of fact, few, if any, dollars were of full weight, *i.e.* 17½dwts. gross contents. With silver at 6s. 8d. per ounce, the dollar should have had fine contents of about 377.4 grains, and this corresponds well with what information we have concerning the contents of the dollar. On this basis, the shilling would contain 62.9 grains of fine silver.

[2] Papers of N. H., IX. 66 ; Potter and Rider, 99 ; Bronson, 74 ; Ripley, 132–133 ; Writings of Jefferson, VII. 409.

respectively.[1] In Pennsylvania, New Jersey, Delaware, and Maryland, the dollar passed for 7s. 6d.[2] Finally New York and North Carolina settled upon a rating of 8s.[3] These valuations were retained until the state currencies were superseded by a national system after 1789. The resulting confusion that attended interstate dealings can easily be imagined.

The result of this process was a gradual and progressive depreciation of the colonial currencies, as compared with the sterling standard.[4] When the Spanish dollar, which was worth 4s. 6d., was rated at 5s., the colonial pound was reduced to $4.00, or 1547 grains of fine silver, and £111 of colonial money equalled £100 sterling. With the dollar advanced to 6s., the colonial pound fell to $3.33, or 1289 grains of pure metal, while £133⅓ of colonial currency equalled £100 sterling. A rating of 7s. 6d. for the piece of eight reduced the colonial pound to $2.66, or 1031 grains of silver;

[1] Stat. of S. C., IV. 543 ; Dip. Corr. of Rev., XII. 91. In South Carolina until 1783 the dollar was rated at 32s. 6d., a valuation that was fixed by the depreciation of the paper money. Ramsay, II. 164.

[2] Phillips, I. 26–27 ; Acts of N. J., 7 ; Laws of Md., 1781, Chap. 16 ; Laws of Del., II. 731–732 ; Dip. Corr. of Rev., XII. 91.

[3] In 1738, silver was current in New York at 9s. 3d. per ounce. Douglass, Discourse, 312. Two years later it fell to about 9s. Docs. of N. Y., VI. 169. In 1756, Smith wrote that since the last war silver had been valued at about 9s. 2d. Smith, N. Y., 333. This last rating of silver would make the dollar worth 8s., and it remained thenceforth at that figure. See Hickcox, Bills of Credit, 50. For North Carolina see Williamson, II. 115 ; Dip. Corr. of Rev., XII. 91.

[4] On this general subject, see Adler.

and made £166⅔ of colonial currency equal to
£100 sterling. Finally, when the dollar was
valued at 8*s.*, the colonial pound amounted to
$2.50, or 967 grains of fine metal; while £177$\frac{7}{10}$
of colonial money was equivalent to £100 sterling.[1]

The chief reason for the progressive depreciation of the colonial coin currencies was the fact
that the colonists believed that specie could be
more easily retained within their borders, or at-
tracted from neighboring plantations, by raising
the rates at which it should be received. Before
1635 Rice Vaughn wrote: "If we do observe those
States which do soonest and most raise their Money,
we shall find that they do most abound with Money;
and that Trades and Manufactures do most flour-
ish there." [2] This expedient of raising the value
of money, so often employed in Europe, was likely
to be favored in a new country, where the poverty
of the settlers made it difficult to accumulate a
large stock of specie. Moreover, since it lightened
the burden of debts whenever past obligations
were not specifically excepted from its operation, it is easy to see why such a measure should
have found support from certain classes of people
in the colonies. Many of the acts for raising the
value of the coins state that the purpose is the

---

[1] See note by editor, in Douglass, Discourse, 300–301. All of
these comparisons may be found carefully tabulated in Wright. See
also Adler.

[2] Chalmers, 5, 7.

"Encouragment of those that shall bring monys into this Province," or some similar object.[1] The royal proclamation of 1704 alleges "the indirect Practice of Drawing the Money from one Plantation to another," as a cause for the imperial regulation of the colonial currencies; and Franklin, in 1767, assigns a similar motive for the policy of overvaluing specie.[2] Of course, in the long run, an increase of prices rendered nugatory all attempts to increase the volume of money in this manner.[3] Equally futile were the numerous prohibitions placed upon the exportation of gold and silver,[4] which, of course, had the same general purpose in view.

If more materials were available, it would be interesting to examine at length the attempts of the several colonies to regulate the rates at which gold and silver coins should circulate concurrently.

[1] Arch. of Md., II. 286; Stat. of S. C., II. 163, 178; Hening, Stat., I. 308; Papers of N. H., I. 448; Mass. Recs., V. 351; Felt, 36; Shepherd, 402. See also two interesting petitions asking that coins should be raised, in Cal. Va. Papers, I. 53–54; Docs. of N. Y., IV. 1134.

[2] Chalmers, 414; Works of Franklin, IV. 81–82. In North Carolina and New York, the increase in the rating of the dollar to 8s. has been attributed to the influence of the paper currencies. See Williamson, II. 115; Smith, N. Y., 332–333.

[3] Franklin, in the passage just referred to, well states the result of this "weak practice," as he termed it: "The balance of trade carried out the gold and silver as fast as it was brought in, the merchants raising the price of their goods in proportion to the increased denomination of the money."

[4] See Felt, 16, 35, 36; Bronson, 17–18; Weeden, 382; *Yale Rev.*, VII. 257, 264; Fernow, 305; McMahon, 226; Bruce, II. 506.

As it is, we may find it worth while to consider the subject briefly. It has been shown that gold coins came into the colonies in much larger numbers after 1700 than had formerly been the case. In Pennsylvania, between 1700 and 1739, there were at least seven changes in the rates at which gold and silver were receivable, and the ratio varied from 14.70 : 1 up to 16 : 1.[1] In South Carolina a statute enacted in 1695 practically established a ratio of 13 : 1; while six years later a ratio 15 : 1 prevailed.[2] Virginia established a ratio of 16 : 1 in the year 1714, but this was changed to 15 : 1 thirteen years later. In 1782 a ratio of 16 : 1 was reëstablished.[3]

In 1736 Massachusetts issued bills of credit of a "new tenor" which were declared to be "equal in value" to certain weights of gold and silver, from which a ratio of 14.84 : 1 may be computed.[4] Thir-

---

[1] Phillips, I. 19, 27. In 1709, the ratio adopted was so favorable to gold that Philadelphia merchants stated that "our payments were mostly made in gold, New York and Britain gradually exhausting our silver." Proud, II. 161. The ascertainment of the exact ratios established by colonial statutes is commonly a work of some difficulty, because the colonists, in some cases at least, "disregarded the difference in fineness of the metals, and derived the ratio from the gross weights." See *Yale Rev.*, VII. 413. In most cases the computations here presented are necessarily based upon a comparison of the gross weights. In some cases, however, where Professor Sumner's computations are used, the ratios are based upon a comparison of the fine contents of the coins.

[2] Stat. of S. C., II. 195, 178; Carroll, II. 258.

[3] Hening, Stat., IV. 51, 52, 218, 219, XI. 117, 118; Ripley, 127, 130.

[4] *Yale Rev.*, VII. 411.

teen years later, the acts providing for resumption
of a specie basis rated gold and silver coins in such
a manner that it is difficult to compute the ratio.[1]
But in 1752 treasury bonds were made payable in
silver or gold at a ratio of 15.38 : 1.[2] Gold was not
legal tender at this time, although it was current
in the province at about the rates specified in a
statute of 1750.[3] In 1758 a large amount of gold
was received from England in payment of subsi-
dies voted by Parliament, so that the legislature
could declare four years later that "gold is now
become by far the greatest part of the medium of
trade in this province." Meanwhile the relative
value of silver in Europe had risen so that an ounce
of gold, which in 1756 was equivalent to 14.94
ounces of silver, would exchange for only 14.14
ounces of the white metal in 1760. Under such
conditions, foreign obligations naturally were met
by shipping silver out of the province.[4] In 1762 an
act was passed making gold legal tender at a rate
of about 4.22 grains for a shilling. Since the silver coins in actual circulation passed at 62.9 grains

[1] *Yale Rev.*, VII. 413–414. Taking the value of a shilling in
the gold coins that received the most favorable rating, and the
value of a shilling of the silver currency then in circulation, we
obtain a ratio of 14.94 : 1.

[2] *Yale Rev.*, VII. 414. Taking the fine contents of the silver
coins in actual circulation, Professor Sumner computes a ratio of
14.52 : 1.

[3] One writer claimed that the act of 1750 made gold a legal tender. *Yale Rev.*, VII. 414. But Hutchinson entertained the opposite opinion. Hutchinson, Hist., III. 98.

[4] Soetbeer, 129; Hutchinson, Hist., III. 99.

for a shilling, this law established a ratio of 14.905.[1] This ratio would probably have overvalued gold sufficiently to enable it to drive silver out of the province if silver had remained at the value which it held in 1760. But, as it proved, the white metal fell in value so that in 1762 it required 15.27 ounces to purchase one ounce of gold; while, for the next few years, the ratio between gold and silver remained at about 14.8 : 1. As a result, the act of 1762 did not drain the province of its specie; although its immediate effect was, as the legislature probably intended, to depreciate the standard of value about $4\frac{3}{4}$ per cent.[2] Finally it may be noted that the ratings of gold and silver adopted in Massachusetts in 1750 seem to have been followed fairly closely in New Hampshire, Rhode Island, and Connecticut; so that a ratio of slightly less than 15 : 1 may be said to have prevailed in New England.[3] This undervalued silver, which in every year from 1740 to 1790, with only five exceptions, was worth more than one-fifteenth as much as gold.[4] Yet the divergence of the legal from the market ratio was not great enough to drain these colonies of their silver coins, although silver was probably the metal more commonly

[1] Acts of Mass., IV. 515, 516; *Yale Rev.*, VII. 417.

[2] *Yale Rev.*, VII. 418.

[3] Acts of Mass., III. 495 ; Papers of N. H., VII. 77–78, 282, 296 ; Conn. Recs., X. 339 ; Potter and Rider, 99. All of these acts rate silver at 6s. 8d. per ounce, and gold at about £5 per ounce.

[4] Soetbeer, 129.

employed in the payment of foreign debts.[1] Perhaps the coins in actual circulation were clipped to such an extent that the lighter silver pieces would stay in circulation longer than the heavier gold pieces, in spite of the overvaluation of the yellow metal.

[1] In Canada during the eighteenth century silver was overvalued, and the problem of currency legislation was to keep gold in circulation. In the West Indies, on the other hand, gold was overvalued, and even the fractional silver coins tended to disappear from circulation. See Chalmers, 20–21.

CHAPTER IV

COLONIAL PAPER MONEY

Soon after the colonies commenced to advance the ratings of their current coins, there began a series of attempts to establish private banks. It must be remembered that, during the entire colonial period, the word "bank" meant simply a batch of paper money, a conception that has disappeared only gradually during the present century as the functions of deposit and discount have assumed greater importance in modern banking. During the seventeenth century, more especially during its closing decades, public and private credit had been developed in the countries of northern Europe upon a scale that was previously unknown. Naturally enough the real nature and precise limitations of the great agency thus created were not clearly understood. It was perceived that credit increased enormously the control over capital enjoyed by a person or a company; but it was not realized so readily that credit is not the same as capital, and that capital cannot be directly created by credit, although its efficiency may be greatly increased. John Law's projects, the Mississippi Scheme in France, the English Land Bank Scheme, and the South Sea Bubble were no isolated phenomena: many other fallacious enterprises grew out of the misunderstandings that prevailed concerning the nature and proper uses of credit. Theories and plans of a paper currency began to appear in England as early as 1650, when William Potter published "The Key of Wealth, or A new way for Improving of Trade." Other schemes followed, all of which proposed to find some other medium than metallic money for a basis of paper credit. For this purpose deposits of merchandise or pledges of land were commonly suggested.[1] In England the existence of more settled industrial conditions and the possession of a larger supply of capital facilitated the growth of sounder views concerning the true nature and proper basis of credit, but these lessons were not learned until much sad experience had been gained from unsafe banking ventures; while, as late as the period of restriction from 1797 to 1819, all the forces of unreason had to be most vigorously combated before it was generally admitted that the premium on bullion was due to the depreciation of the paper currency, and not to an alleged scarcity of gold.[2] In the American colonies, however, the economic conditions were precisely the reverse of those which prevailed in the mother country; and all circumstances favored the persistence of erroneous ideas.

[1] On these banking schemes in England, see Rogers, 1–88; Dunbar, in *Q. J. E.*, II. 482–490; Trumbull, 6–7.

[2] Macleod, II. 30–50.

At some time previous to 1652, "paper bills" seem to have circulated in some parts of Massachusetts, and there is a record of projects "for raiseing a Banke."[1] William Potters's "Key of Wealth," or some similar publication, may have come to the attention of Governor John Winthrop, of Connecticut; for, in 1661, he is found to be entertaining "some proposalls concerning a way of trade and banke w^{th}out money."[2] A few years later, the Rev. John Woodbridge submitted a project "for erecting a Fund of Land, by Authority, or private Persons, in the Nature of a *Money-Bank* or *Merchandise-Lumber.*"[3] In 1671, 1681, and 1686, private banks were actually established in Massachusetts; and bills were issued, probably upon the security of "such Real Estates of Lands, as also personal Estates of goods and Merchandizes not subject to perishing or decay."[4] These projects, however, proved to be short lived. In them can be distinctly traced the influence of theories that were then prevalent in England.[5] In 1690, Massachusetts, followed shortly by other colonies, emitted its first public bills of credit.

---

[1] Felt, 33 ; Proc. Ant. Soc., 1866, 35–36 ; Weeden, 318.

[2] Trumbull, 8–9 ; Weeden, 318–324.

[3] Trumbull, 4–7, 9–11 ; Weeden, 328–329 ; Douglas, Fin. Hist. 44–45.

[4] Proc. Ant. Soc., 1866, 38–39 ; Felt, 46–47 ; Douglas, Fin. Hist., 45–47 ; Trumbull, 11–14 ; *Q. J. E.*, XI. 70–75.

[5] This is shown by Trumbull, 6–9. It is interesting to note that, in the middle colonies, Thomas Budd in 1685 projected a bank of commodities. Budd, Good Order, 40–41.

Such issues soon became so common as to divert attention, in a great measure, from private banking enterprises. Yet in 1700, 1714, 1733, 1739, and 1740, private banks were projected in Massachusetts, and were finally suppressed with great difficulty.[1] In some cases, however, these associations actually placed a considerable quantity of their bills in circulation. The great Land Bank of 1740 issued about £35,000 of notes, and made a most vigorous struggle to maintain its existence.[2] In New Hampshire, Connecticut, and South Carolina, associations were formed, between 1732 and 1738, for the purpose of engaging in similar ventures; and at a later date we hear of other attempts in Pennsylvania and Virginia.[3] But Parliament interfered, in 1741,[4] by extending to the colonies the provisions of the " Bubble Act," which had been passed twenty-one years earlier in order to suppress such swindles as had occurred during the time of the South Sea Company.

The paper money that so long cursed the American colonies was issued by acts of the several legis-

[1] Felt, 55, 65–67, 88–89, 97; Hutchinson, Hist., II. 188–189, 341; Sumner, Banking, 6–9; Q. J. E., XI. 75–91, 136–143.
[2] Hutchinson, Hist., II. 352–355; Felt, 97–109; Douglas, Fin. Hist., 127–129; Sumner, Banking, 9–11; Weeden, 486–491; Q. J. E., XI. 148–157; Proc. Ant. Soc., April, 1896.
[3] Papers of N. H., IV. 685; Felt, 91–92; Bronson, 42–43; Q. J. E., XIII. 71–84; Douglass, Discourse, 310, 317; Shepherd, 433; Phillips, I. 27–28, 199; Sumner, Banking, 8, 9, 11.
[4] Stat. at Large, 6 Geo. I. c. 18, 14 Geo. II. c. 37. Cf. Sumner, Banking, 10.

latures. Massachusetts had led the way, in 1690, with an issue of bills that were used to defray the expenses of a disastrous military expedition.[1] Her example proved contagious; and, by 1712, New Hampshire, Rhode Island, Connecticut, New York, New Jersey, North Carolina, and South Carolina had issued quantities of bills of credit in order to meet the outlays occasioned by Queen Anne's War.[2] In subsequent years bills were emitted as a regular means of defraying the current expenses of government; and, as the volume of paper accumulated, a great depreciation ensued. Sooner or later all the plantations were deeply involved in the mazes of a fluctuating currency, for the burdens attending the various wars of the eighteenth century were so great as to induce even the most conservative colonies to resort to this easy method of meeting public obligations.[3] Virginia suc-

[1] Hutchinson, I. 356–357 ; Felt, 49–52 ; Weeden, 330, 379–381 ; Proc. Ant. Soc., Oct., 1898.

[2] South Carolina (1703); Stat. of S. C., II. 210, IX. Appendix. New Jersey, New York, New Hampshire, and Connecticut (1709) ; Phillips, I. 59 ; Hickcox, Bills of Credit, 13 ; Fernow, 313 ; Papers of N. H., III. 410–411 ; Bronson, 30–31. Rhode Island first issued paper in 1710, and North Carolina in 1712 ; Potter and Rider, 7–10 ; Arnold, II. 39–41 ; Col. Recs. of N. C., II. p. IV., IV. 576. On all these colonies, see Douglass, Discourse, 302–318.

[3] Papers of N. H., V. 722, 740–742, 812–813 ; VI. 506–507 ; Hutchinson, Hist., II. 390–391 ; Douglas, Fin. Hist., 118–119 ; Potter and Rider, 100 ; Bronson, 63–64 ; Hickcox, Bills of Credit, 36, 39, 42 ; Fernow, 324–333 ; Phillips, I. 22–25, 73–76 ; Shepherd, 427–432 ; Scharf, II. 37 ; Iredell, Laws, 115, 157, 192, 198 ;

cumbed last, in 1755, but made large issues in the ensuing years.[1]

A second excuse for issuing bills of credit was found at an early date. In 1712, South Carolina created a public loan bank, and issued bills that were loaned to its citizens at interest, upon real or personal security. This expedient was followed sooner or later by nearly all of the other colonies.[2] Rhode Island easily distanced all competitors in the readiness and facility with which she created loan banks; while Pennsylvania, New Jersey, and

Col. Recs. of N. C., VI. 1308–1309 ; Stat. of S. C., IV. 114. Dr. Douglass called paper money "a great promoter of expeditions." Douglass, Summary, I. 310.

[1] Ripley, 154–157; Phillips, I. 194–196. Georgia issued her first bills in the same year. Stevens, I. 399.

[2] Stat. of S. C., II. 389, III. 232 ; Ramsay, II. 162–163. Massachusetts issued money on loan in 1714, Rhode Island in 1715, and New Hampshire in 1717. Felt, 67, 77, 84 ; Hutchinson, II. 189 ; Potter and Rider, 11 ; Arnold, Index, " Banks " ; Papers of N. H., V. 620, 684–688. Pennsylvania and New Jersey created loan banks in 1723. Phillips, I. 13, 63 ; *Annals*, VIII. 50–126 ; Mulford, 327. Delaware issued bills upon loan at about the same time. Laws of Del., I. 97. North Carolina adopted this expedient in 1729, Connecticut and Maryland in 1733, New York in 1737, and Georgia in 1755. Col. Recs. of N. C., IV. 419, 476 ; Bronson, 44 ; Scharf, I. 280; Hickcox, Bills of Credit, 25 ; Stevens, I. 399. Virginia was the only colony that did not resort to this method of issuing bills. Even there, only the governor's veto prevented such action in 1755. See Phillips, I. 195. Pennsylvania, Maryland, and Georgia issued their first paper money in this form. In 1739, Douglass wrote that Delaware had issued paper " upon the same footing as Pennsylvania." Douglass, Discourse, 315. Land and plate were the favorite forms of security upon which these public loan banks were issued. On the loan banks in general note Douglass, Summary, II. 99, 365, Discourse, 302–317.

Delaware followed a more conservative course than most of the other plantations.

The abuses attending both forms of paper currency were usually of the most flagrant sort. Bills were issued for the payment of current expenses or extraordinary outlays, and taxes would be voted for the purpose of redemption. Then subsequent assemblies would extend the period during which the paper money should be current, or would neglect to levy sufficient taxes for its withdrawal.[1] Thus the currency tended always to accumulate, and its depreciation increased. Sometimes a legis-

[1] Papers of N. H., III. 564–565, IV. 72 ; Potter and Rider, 19 ; Fernow, 317, 320, 327, 330 ; Shepherd, 423, 430 ; Phillips, I. 20, 61 ; Stat. of S. C., IX. 767, 769, 773. By the year 1731, South Carolina had piled up a debt of £106,000 that represented bills issued many years previously. These were then exchanged for new bills, and continued in circulation without any provision for their redemption. Stat. of S. C., IX. 778–779. Subsequent statutes, of which the last was passed in 1769, provided for the continued circulation of these bills. Douglass had good reason for remarking that South Carolina had been "notoriously guilty of breach of public faith." Discourse, 317. He could with propriety say : "By this unnatural Contrivance they oblige Posterity to supply the Extravagances of their Parents and Ancestors, instead of the common and natural Instinct of Parents providing for their children." He said that piling up a debt in this manner was "really analogous to the Negroes in Guinea, who sell their Progeny into Slavery, for the sake of raising some ready Pence." Discourse, 338, 343. Thomas Paine called attention to the manner in which one assembly would incur debts that were bequeathed to subsequent assemblies, and said : "The amount, therefore, of paper money is this, that it is the illegitimate offspring of assemblies, and when their year expires, they leave a vagrant on the hands of the public." Paine, II. 181.

lature would resolve that the bills in circulation should not exceed a certain sum, but such a declaration would prove utterly worthless.[1] In almost every colony the first issues were to remain current for a short time only, and were to be redeemed speedily by taxes; but the periods were gradually lengthened to twelve, sixteen, or twenty-five years.[2] Laws were often passed providing for the emission of new bills to replace worn or mutilated issues. Then the new money would frequently be placed in circulation without withdrawing and cancelling the old,[3] while bills that had been withdrawn for the original purpose of destroying them would often be reissued for current expenses.[4] In some colonies it happened that paper issued upon loan would not be repaid at the stated periods, and interest payments were commonly in arrears. When this occurred, the legislature would frequently extend the time of the loans, and sometimes a large part of both principal and interest

[1] Thus when Massachusetts issued her first bills, it was resolved that the issues should not exceed £40,000. Felt, 51. But when the issues of legal tender notes ceased in 1748, the sum of £2,466,000 was outstanding. Douglass, Summary, I. 528. In 1749, the amount was £2,200,000. Hutchinson, II. 392.

[2] Felt, 63 ; Douglas, Fin. Hist., 117 ; Bronson, 37 ; Fernow, 315 ; Annals, VIII. 72 ; Ripley, 154, 156.

[3] Bronson, 35–37 ; Stat. of S. C., II. 256, IX. 767, 772, 773.

[4] Bronson, 51, 59, 71 ; Annals, VIII. 57, 58 ; Douglass, Discourse, 312. In New York it was found in 1748 that the treasurer, instead of destroying bills that were supposed to be cancelled, reissued them " for his own benefit or for the benefit of his friends." Docs. of N. Y., VI. 534 ; Fernow, 326.

would never be repaid.[1] In this respect Rhode
Island was probably the worst offender. Her loan
banks were placed in the hands of a few favored
persons, called "sharers," who happened to
possess the requisite "pull." The "sharers"
then proceeded to lend out the money at a rate
of interest that was, for the first ten years, five
per cent higher than that which they were obliged
to pay to the colony. In some cases the fortunate
"sharers" would sell their privileges for premiums
that sometimes amounted to as much as thirty-five
per cent. The results of such performances can
readily be imagined.

Although the colonial bills of credit were not
always made a legal tender, they were usually
given a forced circulation. Most of the advocates
of paper money would have agreed with the New
York legislature that bills not legal tender were
useless.[2] The direst penalties — fines, imprison-

[1] Many colonies experienced difficulty in collecting interest and
principal. Felt, 70 ; Bronson, 59 ; Shepherd, 419 ; Iredell, Laws,
117–118 ; Docs. of N. Y., VII. 204. In Rhode Island interest was
often defaulted. Potter and Rider, 16, 34, 35. Once, when a loan
became due, it was extended for ten years without interest. *Idem*,
19. In 1741, in only six towns, 539 lawsuits were begun for the
collection of loans. *Idem*, 56. In 1759, when the affairs of the
loan office were settled up, £50,269 was found to be unpaid and
uncollectable. *Idem*, 96. This was nearly eleven per cent of the
principal of the nine loan banks that had been issued. *Idem*, 135–
138. For an account of the speculation in "sharers'" privileges
see Douglass, Discourse, 308–309.

[2] Fernow, 329. When Connecticut bills were made legal tender
only at their current value in specie, the debtor party secured the
repeal of the law in three years. Bronson, 63.

ment, and confiscation — were imposed upon those evil-disposed persons who should dare to discriminate in favor of specie; but such forcing laws were as ineffectual in supporting the credit of the paper money as they have proved in all other cases.[1] When older issues had depreciated hopelessly, "bills of a new tenor" were often emitted; and these were sometimes followed by others of a newer tenor. Thus it happened that issues of the "old tenor," "middle tenor," and "new tenor" circulated concurrently at different rates of depreciation, the legislature usually undertaking to fix the relative values of the three classes of currency.[2] In order to prevent depreciation some of the issues bore interest, but this was a provision that was readily repealed by subsequent assemblies.[3]

As has always been the case, the appetite for paper money increased with the issues of bills of credit. Complaints of the scarcity of money almost invariably followed each emission, and one pretext after another was found for issuing larger

[1] The influence of the tender laws of Virginia is well described by Burnaby, 31–32.

[2] Felt, 92, 107 ; Bronson, 56, 59, 63, 65 ; Papers of N. H., V. 143, 145, 621, 623 ; Potter and Rider, 53–56. In Massachusetts, one shilling of the new tenor was declared equal to three of the old tenor. In Rhode Island the proportion was one to four. Douglass mentions " old tenor, middle tenor, new tenor first, new tenor second." Douglass, Summary, I. 493.

[3] Felt, 57, 75 ; Hickcox, Bills of Credit, 14 ; Ripley, 156 ; Stat. of S. C., II. 712, 713, IX. 766 ; Douglass, Summary, II. 254.

quantities of paper.[1] Trade was said to be decay-
ing, public buildings had to be constructed, fortifications were needed, and dozens of other things
must be done by setting the printing presses at
work. The experience of the colonies demon-
strates conclusively the impossibility of satisfying
the desire for "more money" by issuing a paper
currency. Depreciation commenced at an early
date, and tended to increase as time went on. In
New England sterling exchange was 133 in 1702,
a rate corresponding exactly to the rating of the
dollar at 6s. In 1713, it rose to 150, and had
reached 550 by the year 1740. The climax was
reached in Massachusetts and Connecticut in 1749
and 1750, when exchange was quoted at 1100,
indicating a depreciation of nearly 9:1. In
Rhode Island, the old tenor bills finally sank to
23 for 1. In the middle colonies the depreciation

---

[1] In Rhode Island, says Mr. Bates, one emission of bills "only
created the demand for the next." Bates, 33. When Connecticut
had issued enough paper to cause a depreciation of fifty per cent,
complaints of a scarcity of money became so numerous that the
legislature once more made taxes payable in produce. Bronson, 38,
56. The same thing occurred in Massachusetts. Felt, 76. Hutchinson describes these complaints of the scarcity of money in Massachusetts. Hutchinson, History, II. 211, 340, 341. In Virginia,
in 1776, when the state had issued £350,000 and Congress had
emitted $10,000,000, "freeholders" petitioned the legislature for
more currency. Phillips, I. 200. For such complaints of a lack
of money in the time of superabundant issues of paper, see Bates,
33–35; Potter and Rider, 33–34; Hutchinson, History, II. 197,
210, 295; Bronson, 32; Shepherd, 414; Fernow, 321; Phillips, I.
69, 70, 74, 76, 77.

never reached such figures. In Pennsylvania exchange once reached 180, while the par of exchange for specie was not higher than 166½. In Maryland exchange rose from 133 to 250. In North and South Carolina the paper currencies finally sank to one-tenth the value of sterling.[1]

Such fluctuations in the standard of value wrought intense hardships. In 1741, Governor Shirley stated in his message to the Massachusetts legislature : " A creditor who has the misfortune of having an outstanding debt, of the value of 1000 pounds sterling, contracted anno 1730, can now receive no more in our courts of judicature . . . than the value of about 650 pounds sterling." Between 1741 and 1749 exchange rose from 550 to 1100, so that, as Douglass said, " Every honest man not in debt lost about one-half of his personal estate."[2]   A widow who had had an income of £3 found by 1748 that this was reduced to about one-eighth of its original value.[3]   Clergymen's salaries suffered a corresponding reduction, so that Massachusetts passed an act allowing them to receive bills of credit " only at their real value."[4]   Harvard College is said to have lost £10,000, and the Scotch Charitable Society of Boston suffered sixty-six per

[1] For New England in general, see Douglass, Summary, I. 494; Wright, LXI. For Rhode Island, Potter and Rider, 100. For the middle colonies, Douglass, Summary, I. 494, II. 365. For the Carolinas, Ramsay, II. 168; Douglass, Summary, II. 494.

[2] Douglass, Summary, I. 497, II. 14.

[3] Minot, I. 84.

[4] Felt, 79.

cent loss upon the repayment of some of its investments.[1] Under such conditions of demoralization,
it is not strange that the legislature of Massachusetts complained of "universal infectious corruption" in the conduct of public affairs, and that
Hutchinson observed that "the morals of the people depreciate with the currency."[2]

In 1749, when the currency had depreciated to
nearly one-eleventh of its nominal value, Massachusetts succeeded in redeeming it at a rate of $7\frac{1}{2}$
shillings of paper for one shilling of specie.[3] This
was accomplished with the aid of a grant of
money which Parliament had voted in order to
recompense the colony for its expenditures during
King George's War.[4] Efforts were made to secure
the coöperation of the other provinces of New
England, but without immediate result. Connecticut finally adopted a plan similar to that followed

[1] Douglass, Discourse, 366; *Q. J. E.*, XI. 143.

[2] Douglass, Summary, I. 500; Hutchinson, History, II. 391.
Douglass has described very well "The Mischiefs arising from a
large Paper Currency." He shows, for instance, that wages
changed less rapidly than prices, so that laborers suffered from the
disturbances caused by paper money. He states that in 1712, when
silver was at 8s. per ounce, wages were 5s. a day; while in 1739,
when depreciation had driven silver up to 29s. per ounce, wages
were only 12s. a day. See Discourse, 322–325.

[3] The act provided that 45s. old tenor should be exchanged for
one dollar. With a dollar rated at 6s., this gives a ratio of $7\frac{1}{2}$: 1.

[4] Hutchinson, I. 392–395; Douglass, Summary, II. 15–16; Felt,
118–122, 131; Weeden, 674–677; Douglas, Fin. Hist., 131–133.
Shortly before this action was taken, the currency had fallen into
such a wretched condition of depreciation, that people were driven
to barter. Minot, I. 84.

by Massachusetts, and decided to retire her currency at the rate of $8\frac{5}{6}$ for 1. Some years later, New Hampshire made a tardy provision for at least a part of her paper issues ; and Rhode Island exchanged her bills for treasury notes, or allowed them to be paid for taxes at a high rate of depreciation.[1] The opponents of resumption in Massachusetts predicted that such a policy would deprive the people of a circulating medium, and ruin all branches of trade. The result was that a specie currency was restored and industry prospered. Prior to this time, Newport had controlled the importation of West India goods into some parts of Massachusetts. This trade at once passed over to Boston and adjoining ports, and Rhode Island paid the penalty for her obstinate adherence to a fluctuating paper currency.[2]

[1] Felt, 118; Bronson, 67–73; Papers of N. H., V. 565–568, 574, VI. 225, 226, VII. 58, 65, 145; Belknap, II. 425 ; Potter and Rider, 67, 80, 97.

[2] It seems probable that the resumption of a specie basis was attended with some temporary inconvenience. A private letter from Boston, of the date of June 17, 1750, says : "Trade is quite dead, the Town is dull and still as on a Sunday; full of Goods, but no Money to buy; . . ." *Mag. of Amer. Hist.*, II. 627. Douglass refers to a similar situation in 1750. Summary, II. 88. A threatened uprising of the paper money men resulted in a passage of a stringent riot act. Felt, 129–131. But all such difficulties were merely temporary, for the colony certainly enjoyed great subsequent prosperity, while the trade of Rhode Island languished. Weeden, 676, 736; Potter and Rider, 24, 68. The French and Indian War and the confusion attending the controversy with Great Britain were injurious to trade, but yet the colony prospered until the Revolution. Hutchinson could write in 1771 : "Commerce

During this carnival of fraud and corruption, interference by an act of Parliament had often been invoked. English merchants had sometimes complained to the Board of Trade concerning the losses to which the dishonest American currencies had subjected them. The instructions of colonial governors frequently directed that consent should be refused to the passage of laws for the emission of paper money.[1] The governors often opposed most vigorously all attempts to issue a depreciating currency, and violent contests with the legislative bodies not infrequently ensued. In Massachusetts, the governor's salary was refused when he could not be induced to consent to such measures; and in South Carolina, no acts passed the assembly for four years on account of a deadlock over the subject of paper money.[2] Such occurrences were by no means peculiar to these two colonies, and the

never was in a more flourishing state. The Massachusetts province was, in this respect, the envy of all the other colonies; and while the other colonies, by encouraging a delusive paper medium of trade, had banished silver and gold, the Massachusetts had drawn them, not only from several of the other colonies on the continent, but from Jamaica, and more or less, every year, from Spain and Portugal, and had obtained the name of the silver money colony." History, III. 350. See also II. 395-396.

[1] In 1720, instructions to this effect were sent to all the governors, and such instructions were commonly repeated during the next forty or fifty years. Docs. of N. Y., V. 539; Papers of N. H., III. 814 ; Col. Recs. of Penn., III. 261 ; Greene, 163; Hutchinson, II. 339 ; Felt, 76, 81, 84 ; Phillips, I. 15, 51-55.

[2] Hutchinson, II. 298 ; Greene, 173 ; Whitney, 113-114 ; Winsor, V. 328-329 ; Ramsay, II. 165.

political party that stood for popular rights, as against the prerogative of the royal or proprietary governor, regularly included all the advocates of paper currencies.[1] When threats or open defiance failed, the assemblies were accustomed to resort to bribes in order to accomplish their purpose.[2] Finally, in 1751, Parliament passed an act prohibiting any of the New England colonies from emitting bills of credit and making them legal tender; but permission was given to issue treasury notes that should be redeemed at the end of brief periods from the proceeds of taxation, and should not be given a forced circulation.[3] Such a wholesome restriction was immediately denounced as

---

[1] The New Jersey assembly refused supplies for two years on account of the governor's rejection of various measures, among which was a bill for issuing more paper. Mulford, 346 ; Pap. of Morris, 213-226, 250, 270, 274, 310, 314-320. In New York, the right to limit the time of revenue bills was used to extort consent to issues of bills of credit. Docs. of N. Y., V. 805. The Massachusetts legislature refused to provide for the debts of the province because Governor Belcher would not issue paper money. Felt, 86. See also Shepherd, 424-428 ; Fernow, 323 ; Williamson, II, 65 ; Felt, 69, 76-79, 110.

[2] Scharf, II. 35-36 ; Douglass, Summary, II. 14, 365 ; Phillips, I. 72 ; Pap. of Morris, 216; Williamson, II. 81. The Massachusetts legislature reduced the salary of Governor Shute, who was unfriendly to the projects of the paper money men ; while Governor Shirley, who proved more pliant, had his allowances and perquisites increased. Douglass, Summary, I. 492, II. 17-18.

[3] A number of writers had invoked interference by Parliament. See Douglass, Discourse, 311 ; Ashley, Memoirs, 61-63. The House of Commons first considered the question in 1740, when it directed the colonial governors to refuse assent to laws for the

" destructive of the liberties and properties of his Majesty's subjects " in the colonies; but, in 1764, Parliament passed another act which imposed a similar regulation upon all the other plantations, and required that outstanding bills of credit should be gradually retired.[1]

This legislation put an end to probably all further issues of legal tender bills.[2] But " treasury notes " or " orders " or bills of still other names, receivable at the provincial treasuries, were extensively employed until the time of the Revolution. The New England colonies made a regular practice of issuing treasury notes that were redeemed by taxes within short periods, and usually bore interest. Similar issues under various names can be found elsewhere.[3] In 1769, Maryland succeeded in emitting $318,000 of bills upon loan,

emission of legal tender bills. Journ. of H. of C., XXIII. 527–528. Four years later, a bill prohibiting further issues was introduced. *Idem*, XXIV. 658. For the act of 1751, see Stat. at Large, 24 George II. c. 53.

[1] Stat. at Large, 4 George III. c. 34. For Franklin's efforts in opposition to this measure see Works of Franklin, IV. 11, 79–94. In 1773, an explanatory act specified that treasury notes could be made receivable at the provincial treasuries. Stat. at Large, 13 George III. c. 57.

[2] The writer has been unable to find any legal tender issues after 1763 except one in South Carolina. Stat. of S. C., IV. 312, 313. But this was merely a reëmission of old legal tender notes that had been outstanding for many years.

[3] Papers of N. H., VI. 506–507 ; Felt, 31 ; Bronson, 81–84 ; Potter and Rider, 94, 100, 209 ; Shepherd, 433 ; Ripley, 157, 161 ; Stat. of S. C., IV. 323.

and a larger issue followed in 1773.[1] In 1771, New York created another bank of £120,000, but the bills were made legal tender only at the treasury; and finally, upon the eve of the Revolution, Pennsylvania and New Jersey attempted to reëstablish their loan offices.[2] In 1774, therefore, there must have been a considerable amount of paper in circulation in America. Pelatiah Webster estimated the "circulating cash" of the thirteen states at $12,000,000 at this time.[3] He thought that one-half or three-fifths of the currency of Pennsylvania was made up of paper, and believed that this proportion was not exceeded in other states.

Under the political conditions that prevailed in the colonies, it was inevitable that the question of paper money should get into politics. In Massachusetts, this occurred in 1713, when banking projects were being agitated,[4] and eight years later Dr. Trumbull tells us that the paper money party had become identified with the "popular" or "liberal" party.[5] This was natural, since the governors and their councils often combated vigorously all measures that tended to depreciate the currency. Sometimes the governors undoubtedly opposed a paper medium because they had a

[1] Laws of Md., 1769, c. 14; 1773, c. 26.
[2] Hickcox, Bills of Credit, 45-46; Phillips, I. 29, 76; Fernow, 334-335.
[3] Webster, 142.
[4] Hutchinson, Hist., II. 188.
[5] Trumbull, 30. Cf. Hutchinson, Hist., II. 394.

just appreciation of its evils; at other times they seem to have been concerned chiefly with the prospect that their fixed salaries would inevitably be paid in bad money; and, often enough, they received from England explicit instructions that were intended to leave them no opportunity to exercise their own discretion.[1] In colony after colony, party lines came to be drawn upon this sole issue; and when opposition was encountered from the governors or councils, deadlocks frequently ensued. Public disturbances were often aroused by these controversies over paper money, and a factional and disorderly spirit was engendered.[2] There can be no doubt that the debtor class, as a rule, accorded an active support to the inflationist party; and conducted a persistent agitation for a cheap currency with which existing debts could be more easily paid. Even Franklin was unable to deny, in 1764, the truth of the allegation that in some colonies, at least, paper money had been issued " with fraudulent views " through the influence of the debtor classes.[3] Douglass wrote, in 1749: "The Parties in Massachusetts Bay at present, are not the Loyal and Jacobite, the Governor and Country, Whig and Tory, or any religious sectary denominations, but the Debtors and the

---

[1] Sometimes the council proved more strenuous than the governor in opposition to issues of paper, and stood out against the inflationists even when the governor had yielded. See Greene, 77–78, 163.

[2] This subject has been treated sufficiently in a previous note; but see, in addition, Douglass, Discourse, 331–332.

[3] Works of Franklin, IV. 89.

Creditors. The Debtor side has had the ascendant ever since anno 1741, to the almost utter ruin of the country."[1] He said: " Paper-money-making assemblies have been legislatures of debtors, . . . ;"[2] and as much has been admitted by several of the historians of colonial affairs.[3] It is probable that Thomas Paine did not overdraw the picture when he wrote:[4] "There are a set of men who go about making purchases upon credit, and buying estates they have not wherewithal to pay for; and having done this, their next step is to fill the newspapers with paragraphs of the scarcity of money and the necessity of a paper emission, then

[1] Summary, I. 535.

[2] *Idem*, I. 310. Elsewhere he says: "Men are chosen into the legislature and executive parts of their government, not for their knowledge, honour, and honesty, but as sticklers for depreciating . . . the currency, by multiplied emissions: this year, 1750, the parties amongst the electors of assemblymen were distinguished by the names of paper money makers, and the contrary." *Idem*, II. 87; cf. I. 314. Referring to the journal of the house for August 17, 1747, he says that complaints sent to the legislature concerning depreciation were "referred to committees consisting of the most notorious depreciators." *Idem*, II. 14. Cf. Discourse, 330, 371-372.

[3] See Hutchinson, Hist., II. 295, 353. In 1740, a majority of the representatives elected in Massachusetts were subscribers to the land bank scheme, and at another time several of the leading representatives were notorious debtors. In Rhode Island, the evidence is perfectly clear. In 1731, the paper-money party secured complete control. Bates, 36–37; Potter and Rider, 26, 30, 82; Arnold, II. 53; Recs. of R. I., V. 312. On other colonies see Weeden, 490; Bronson, 42, 77; Fernow, 321; Ripley, 160; Williamson, II. 81; Col. Recs. of N. C., IX. 76.

[4] Paine, II. 178.

to have a legal tender under pretence of supporting its credit, and when out, to depreciate it as fast as they can, get a deal of it for a little price, and cheat their creditors; and this is the concise history of paper money schemes."

There is evidence that, as time went on and the lessons of sad experience were learned, the leading merchants and propertied classes in the colonies began to appreciate fully the evils of the fraudulent paper currencies. As early as 1714, a town meeting in Providence protested against further issues of paper.[1] At about the same time in the assembly of New York, the members from New York City opposed an increase of the bills of credit.[2] In 1717, merchants of South Carolina protested against the policy of the inflationists in that colony.[3] Three years later, Thomas Hutchinson and other leading citizens of Boston urged the legislature to emit no more bills upon loan, and to retire outstanding issues as soon as practicable; while, at the same time, Salem instructed her representatives to oppose further measures of inflation.[4] In 1723, "Gentlemen and Merchants of Philadelphia" pointed out to the legislature the danger attending the use of paper money;[5] while

[1] Arnold, II. 53.   [2] Fernow, 318.
[3] Ramsey, II. 164; Carroll, II. 147–148.
[4] Felt, 72, 73.
[5] Shepherd, 406–409; *Annals*, VIII. 52–53; Proud, II. 152–162. The merchants seem to have drawn their arguments from Pollexfen's Discourse of Trade, Coin, and Paper Credit, a copy of which was in the library of James Logan, one of the objectors.

Franklin has written concerning the Pennsylvania issues of 1729: "The wealthy inhabitants opposed any addition, being against all paper currency, from an apprehension that it would depreciate, as it had done in New England, to the prejudice of all creditors." [1] In 1731, merchants of Newport protested against renewed emissions of bills of credit in Rhode Island.[2] In Massachusetts, Hutchinson tells us [3] that, when the land bank of 1740 was under consideration, "men of estates and the principal merchants in the province abhorred the project. . . ." At nearly the same date, Douglass said that "they who call out loudest for this Paper Medium, are not our large Traders."[4] In 1750, leading citizens of Rhode Island sent to the King a remonstrance against the conduct of the paper-money party, stating that the landholders of the colony had mortgaged their lands as security for the loans extended by the province, and now found it to their interest to increase the volume of paper in order that they might pay their debts with worthless currency.[5] Two years later twenty-five merchants and traders of Hartford presented to the Connecticut legislature the following interesting petition for relief: "As the medium of trade

[1] Works of Franklin, I. 152.
[2] Records of Rhode Island, IV. 457–461.
[3] Hutchinson. Hist., II. 354.
[4] Discourse, 330.
[5] Records of Rhode Island, 311, 330, 334; Potter and Rider, 82–84.

is that whereby our dealings are valued and weighed, we cannot but think it ought to be esteemed of as sacred a nature as any weights and measures whatsoever, and in order to maintain justice, must be kept as stable; for as a false weight and a false balance is an abomination to the Lord, we apprehend a false and unstable medium is equally so, as it occasions as much iniquity, and is at least as injurious."[1] Finally, Pownall has left us the following explicit statement: "The majority of the men of business and property in the Colonies have ever heretofore wished to have the assemblies restrained by act of Parliament, from the power of giving the sanction of a legal tender to their paper money."[2]

At this point it may prove interesting to review briefly the arguments that were advanced in the eighteenth century for and against government paper money. The first issue of bills of credit in Massachusetts called forth a pamphlet, written probably by Cotton Mather, in defence of paper money;[3] and the controversies that ensued during the next eighty or ninety years resulted in a veritable deluge of writings dealing with the subject. Nearly thirty pamphlets appeared between 1714 and 1721; and, in 1728, government issues of paper were

[1] Bronson, 71.
[2] Pownall, I. 198.
[3] Quotations from this pamphlet are given by Trumbull, 15–18. Mather held that money "is but a Counter or Measure of men's Properties." He favored a paper currency, "an abiding Cash," since "no man will carry it to another Country."

defended in a master's thesis at Harvard College.[1] The flood of publications continued until the close of the century, when it was thought that the Federal Constitution had finally barred the door to further issues of bills of credit.[2]

The advocates of paper currency always claimed that it was the only means by which a sufficient circulating medium could be secured, and many historians have accepted this plea with discreditable complacency. The opponents argued, on the other hand, that an adequate stock of specie always existed until it was displaced by a cheaper form of money; and that complaints of a scarcity of silver were never so common as they always became after repeated emissions of bills of credit.[3] When, for instance, the inflationists in Massachusetts were endeavoring to secure larger issues of paper, in 1712, Judge Sewall answered, in his speech in the legislature: "I was at making the first bills of

[1] Weeden, 485; Proc. Mass. Hist. Soc., XVIII. 124, 125.

[2] Trumbull gives copious extracts from many of these pamphlets. Other extracts may be found in *Q. J. E.*, XI. 70–91, 136–160. Lists of scores of such publications may be found in Thomas, II. 370 *et seq.*; and Douglas, Fin. Hist., 138–146. Especially valuable is Winsor, V. 170–176. See, finally, a reprint of a pamphlet by Hutchinson, in Proc. Mass. Hist. Soc., Feb., 1899.

[3] Douglass, Discourse, 338; "A Countryman's Answer," quoted by Felt, 74. In a protest of five members of the Rhode Island legislature, in 1740, against the issue of more paper, are found the following words: " In respect to trade, this bank will probably so far depreciate the whole paper currency, that we shall have, in reality, a less medium of exchange, and all complaints of scarcity of money greatly increased." Recs. of R. I., IV. 580. Cf. Hutch-

credit in the year 1690. They were not made for want of money; but for want of Money in the Treasury."[1] Dr. William Douglass argued in 1740: "The more a Country grows in good Trade, the more *true Medium* of Trade it acquires."[2] At a later date, John Witherspoon, Pelatiah Webster, and Thomas Paine voiced similar opinions.[3] These writers always insisted, as Douglass had done in 1740, that "a trading Country must have regard to the universal commercial Medium, which is Silver; or cheat, and trade to a Disadvantage."[4] Like Paine, they inquired: "But why, since the universal custom of the world has established money as the most convenient medium of traffic and commerce, should paper be set up in preference to gold and silver?"[5] Frequently, the advocates of bills of credit argued that a large paper currency would stimulate trade, and thus lighten the weight of the taxes that would ultimately be levied for redeeming the bills issued.[6] Douglass

inson, Hist., II. 197, 210, 340–341. Douglass argued that the emission of a depreciating paper currency "does not add to the real Medium, but rather diminishes from it." Discourse, 329. Forty years later, Pelatiah Webster made the same contention. Webster, 6. Writing in 1739, Douglass says that, with £630,000 of paper circulating in New England, "Money was never so scarce and Debts worse paid." Discourse, 333. Cf. also *Idem*, 341.

[1] Coll. Mass. Hist. Soc., Fifth Series, VI. 366.

[2] Discourse, 342.

[3] Witherspoon, Works, IX. 45, 50 ; Webster, Essays ; Writings of Thomas Paine, II. 132–187. See especially, Writings, II. 179.

[4] Discourse, 294.   [5] Paine, II. 178.

[6] Hutchinson, Hist., II. 219, refers to these arguments.

replied that inflation caused extravagance and speculation ; and Paine retorted : " Paper money is like dram drinking ; it relieves for a moment by deceitful sensation, but gradually diminishes the natural heat, and leaves the body worse than it found it." [1] When the inflationists urged that magnificent public improvements could be undertaken by means of government issues,[2] Douglass reminded them that some one must ultimately pay for all such indulgences.[3] Again, when depreciation set in, and specie rose to a premium, the friends of paper always claimed that the bills of credit had not deteriorated, but that silver had risen in value on account of the demands of persons who desired to export bullion. To this effect Franklin wrote in 1729: " I need not say anything to convince the judicious that our bills have not yet sunk, though there is and has been some difference between them and silver ; because it is evident that the difference is occasioned by the scarcity of the latter, which is now become a merchandise, rising and falling like other commodities as there is a greater or less demand for it or as it is more or less

[1] Discourse, 340–341, 365 ; Paine, II. 183–184.

[2] See quotations given by Felt, 65, 72. Governor Ward, defending Rhode Island's issues, argued that the money had been expended for public buildings, fortifications, and the like. Records of Rhode Island, V. 8–14. Cf. Hutchinson, Hist., II. 219, 295.

[3] " The unthinking Part of our People do not consider, that every emission of Paper Credit called Money, is laying a heavy Tax upon us, which in Time will contribute to our Misery." Discourse, 343, 344.

plenty." [1] Douglass replied : " The repeated large
Emissions of Paper Money are the Cause of the
frequent rise of the Price of Silver and Exchange."
This, he argued, was equivalent to saying that the
bills had depreciated. Under such conditions, the
premium on silver must follow, " the same as the
Tides do the Phases or Course of the Moon." [2]
After the depreciation of the paper had gone to
such lengths that it could no longer be denied, its
advocates always advanced, with the greatest complacency, the suggestion that the fall in the value

[1] Works of Franklin, I. 376. In 1764, Franklin repeated
this argument, and at greater length. Works, IV. 89–91. He
said that soon after the emission of the first paper in Pennsylvania,
" a difference soon arose " between silver and paper, due to the demand
for silver for export. In 1721, when exchange had risen from 133
to nearly 270, the Massachusetts house of representatives thought
that a prohibition of selling bullion at more than 8s. per ounce
would remedy the difficulty, and that depreciation would not have
taken place at all if such a measure had been adopted at the very
start. Felt, 77. In 1740, Governor Ward of Rhode Island, and in
1750 the legislature, attributed the depreciation to the pernicious
practice of merchants in offering a premium for silver, " to the
injury and oppression of many poor widows, orphans, and others."
Potter and Rider, 74, 161, 188. This was in the face of a rise in
exchange from 133 to 550 in 1741, and 1100 in 1749. The solici-
tude of a legislature of paper-money inflationists for widows and
orphans is most interesting.

[2] Discourse, 325. Hutchinson said of a bill prohibiting silver to
be sold above proclamation rates : " Such an act can no more be
executed than an act to stop the ebbing and flowing of the sea."
Hist., II. 222. See Writings of Paine, II. 179. In 1723, a petition
of Philadelphia merchants argued as follows : " But, from hence a
sure rule may be taken, in relation to paper, that by so much as the
value of the public bills sink, by so much will gold and silver rise,
in proportion to their intrinsic worth." Proud, II. 162.

of the bills of credit had operated as a gradual and insensible tax upon the community; so that no great harm had been done after all. To this optimistic view it was readily replied that such a tax was the most unjust and harmful method ever devised for meeting public expenditures. It taxed only those who were so situated that they could not avoid it, and benefited sharpers, speculators, and dishonest debtors. It devoured the estates of widows and orphans, paralyzed legitimate business undertakings, and wrought untold injury to public and private morals.[1] Yet the advocates of a depreciating currency still insisted that bills of credit were a necessity, and that government should assume its proper duty of supplying money directly to the people. No better answer has ever been given than is found in the following words of William Douglass:[2] "In all Countries excepting in Paper Money Colonies, the People support the Government: it is absurd to imagine that a Government finds Money for its People, it is the People who by their Trade and Industry, provide not only for their own Subsistence, but also for the Support of Government. . . ."

This chapter of our monetary history presents a sufficiently dark and disgraceful picture. But certain important facts still remain to be noted before we pass from the subject of provincial paper currencies. For eighty years the people of

[1] Douglass, Discourse, 322–325 ; Webster, 30–32.
[2] Discourse, 342–343.

the colonies were schooled in the belief that bills of credit furnished a proper and convenient means of defraying public expenditures, ordinary as well as extraordinary. Such issues of paper would depreciate, and could ultimately be wholly repudiated, or could be redeemed at a fraction of their face value. Under such circumstances, there inevitably developed a strong disinclination to permit taxation to be practised on any scale commensurate with the public needs.[1] The habit of paying taxes readily and regularly is not easily acquired, while it is lost with the utmost facility. The colonists, for three generations, were trained in a bad school of public economy ; and had learned lessons

[1] In Massachusetts, in the first half of the eighteenth century, the policy of the legislature was "the abandonment of the constantly increasing current expenses of the government, to be met by larger and larger issues of bills of credit." Douglas, Fin. Hist., 121. During a long term of years, only one budget provided for current expenses. Cf. Hutchinson, II. 339. Pennsylvania, although more moderate in her issues of paper prior to 1775, is found, on the very eve of the Revolution, yielding to the "temptation to overcome instant wants by means of larger sums payable in the future." Phillips, I. 28. Cf. Shepherd, 427. At the close of the colonial period, Virginia, which had been far more conservative than most of the colonies in her financial policy, was in a condition which Mr. Bancroft describes as follows : "Virginia was, moreover, unprepared for war. Its late expedition against the Shawnee Indians had left a debt of a hundred and fifty thousand pounds ; its currency was of paper, and it had no efficient system of revenue." Bancroft, Hist., IV. 144. With such conditions prevailing in the larger and more populous colonies, it is easy to conceive of the situation elsewhere. Professor Sumner has described admirably the tardy and inadequate development of colonial taxation. Sumner, Financier, I. 11–34.

that were soon to bear bitter fruit. It is not at all remarkable that, in the Continental Congress of 1775, members are reported to have entertained strong objections to burdening their constituents with taxes, when it was possible to send to a printer and obtain a wagon load of money, one quire of which would pay for the entire sum needed to prosecute the struggle for independence.[1] In opposing the attempts of Parliament to levy taxes upon them, the colonies were contending not only against "taxation without representation," but also against taxation in any form. They were quite as certain that it was impracticable to secure representation in that body, as they were that Parliament ought not to tax them without their consent.[2] Finally, as a matter of simple historical fact, there can be little doubt that the acts of 1751 and 1764, which suppressed further issues of bills of credit, contributed not a little to the final breach with the mother country. In 1744, when Parliament was considering the advisability of prohibiting colonial issues of paper money, the New York assembly resolved that such a measure would be contrary to the constitution of Great Britain, incompatible with the rights and liberties of Englishmen, and likely to

[1] Webster, 7–8.

[2] The declaration of rights, adopted by the Stamp Act Congress in 1765, maintained that taxes could not be imposed upon the colonists without the consent of their representatives, and that the colonies, "from their local circumstances," could not be represented in Parliament. Niles, 457. Professor Sumner has stated the matter very clearly. Sumner, Financier, I. 25.

subject America to the absolute will of the Crown.[1] The action finally taken by Great Britain aroused the most bitter feelings of resentment ; and the law of 1764 was enacted at a time when the minds of Americans were excited over the Stamp Act, and the wisdom of the restrictions imposed upon the paper currencies was the less likely to be admitted. In 1766, when he was examined before the House of Commons, Franklin gave it as his deliberate opinion [2] that one reason for the impatience and disrespect which the colonies were manifesting toward Parliamentary authority was " the prohibition of making paper money." Too little attention has been given to this fact by most American historians.[3]

[1] Hickcox, Bills of Credit, 32 ; Winsor, V. 203. Similar declarations were made in other colonies. See Felt, 81, 115 ; Bronson, 68 ; Pap. of Morris, 221.

[2] Works of Franklin, III. 418. Cf. IV. 106.

[3] Mr. Felt seems to be the first writer to appreciate this fact. Felt, 132.

CHAPTER V

CONTINENTAL PAPER MONEY

THE story of our Revolutionary paper money supplies the next chapter in the experience of the United States with a cheap medium of exchange.[1] With the inception of the struggle against Great Britain, the colonies were confronted with the problem of raising the supplies necessary for the prosecution of the war. In the spring and early summer of 1775, revolutionary assemblies or conventions were convoked in various provinces, and preparations were made for the public defence. With the restraining influence of the royal governors and the acts of Parliament removed, it was practically certain that issues of paper would be renewed. The disinclination to pay taxes, which had been fostered by eighty years of false financial methods, inevitably asserted itself in a refusal to meet by heavy taxation the burdens incurred in a war that was caused in large measure by opposition to the taxing power of Parliament.

The Continental Congress has often been blamed for resorting to the disastrous expedient of issuing paper money, but the financial policy of the Revo-

[1] On this subject much has been written. See bibliography in Bullock, 122. Since this bibliography was written, two other accounts of the continental currency have appeared. See White, 134-148 ; Holt, in *Sound Currency*, V.

lution was practically settled by the provincial assemblies. Congress did not convene in Philadelphia until May 10, and did not determine to issue bills of credit until June 22.[1] Meanwhile, Connecticut had decided in April to emit paper money; and Massachusetts had adopted a similar measure seven days before Congress assembled.[2] Before the month of May had expired, Rhode Island pursued a similar course; and, in June, New Hampshire, Pennsylvania, and South Carolina followed suit.[3] During the next few months all the other colonies, without a single exception, decided to provide the sinews of war by means of bills of credit.[4]

Although the Continental Congress was a revolutionary assembly which might conceivably have attempted to assume all the authority of a strong national government, it is almost certain that such a course would have resulted in the downfall of that body. It was in reality a consultative assemblage, whose powers were limited by the wishes of the several colonies. In order to exist and to maintain any respect for its authority, Congress had to be governed by the temper of its constituents; and, in respect to the proper financial policy,

[1] Journ. of Cong., June 22, 1775.

[2] Conn. Recs., XIV. 432 ; Force, II. 782.

[3] Recs. of R. I., VII. 321 ; Force, II. 659, 1168 ; Ramsay, II. 171. For South Carolina, Force mentions no issue before November 15. See Force, IV. 55.

[4] Force, II. 1551, III. 113, 197, 575, 1240 ; Laws of Del., I. 571-586 ; Laws of Md., 1780, c. 22, note.

the wishes of the people of America had already
been indicated with sufficient clearness by the
action of the various provincial assemblies.[1] These
bodies had commonly pledged the half or the whole
of their estates for the preservation of their sacred
liberties, but they had shown a uniform determina-
tion to raise money by sacrificing only the estates
of those people who were helpless to avoid the
losses of a depreciating currency. It is perfectly
true that the expenses of any war must, apart from
help secured in foreign countries, be defrayed out
of the annual produce of the industry of a people;
and that taxation is the safest, surest, and wisest
method of meeting such expenditures. But the
hands of Congress seem to have been bound by its
lack of authority and the manifest desires of the
people. The New York assembly, and probably
some others, had conveyed to the men gathered
in Philadelphia explicit statements of their sen-
timents;[2] and the actions of various provincial

[1] For a somewhat different view see Bronson, 146–156.

[2] The New York provincial congress, as early as May 26, sent to
the New York delegates at Philadelphia a letter stating that, since
it would be impossible to conduct the war without paper money,
the council was about to consider that subject, and would communi-
cate the results of its deliberations as soon as possible. Force, II.
1255. The New York council appointed a committee, of which
Gouverneur Morris was a member, to consider the subject of a
paper currency. Sparks, Morris, I. 38. This committee reported
in favor of a continental currency on May 30, and its report was
adopted and forwarded to the delegates in Philadelphia. Force,
II. 1262–1264, 1281. New Hampshire also expressed its desire for
paper money. Papers of N. H., VII. 483.

congresses in actually issuing paper were more significant than any words.[1]

Thus the Continental Congress and the individual colonies, or states, undertook to carry on the struggle for independence by the aid of bills of credit. The dangers of such a course were fully appreciated by many men, but the temper of the great body of the people could not be mistaken. Recent historians have investigated with great care and entire fairness the extent and character of the opposition which the revolutionary movement encountered from many of the most intelligent and respectable persons in America, and have assured us that earlier writers have failed to do justice to the strength and honesty of that party which considered separation from the mother country to be unnecessary and undesirable.[2] With the history of colonial paper currencies before us, it is reasonable to believe that the fear of reckless issues of bills of credit was certainly one cause for the hostile attitude assumed by a large portion of the conservative, propertied classes.[3]

[1] How well Congress understood the disposition of the colonies, and the limits of its own authority, is well shown in some "Observations on the Finances of America," which were sent to Franklin in 1778. The "Observations" pointed out that, since America had "never been much taxed" and the war was "upon the very question of taxation," "the laying of imposts, unless from the last necessity, would have been madness." Sec. Journ. of Cong., II. 118.

[2] See Tyler, I. 293–315 ; *Amer. Hist. Rev.*, I. 24–25 ; Sumner, Hamilton, 48–51, 53–61.

[3] Even John Adams was afraid of what the debtor class would

Congress began by issuing $6,000,000 of paper money before the close of 1775, and urged the states to redeem their respective quotas of the bills by imposing taxes.[1] But the states refused to resort to taxation, except for inconsiderable sums, and continued to emit increasing amounts of their own paper. After unsuccessful efforts to raise revenue by such expedients as a lottery and a domestic loan,[2] larger continental issues had to be emitted. In 1777, Congress began to make requisitions upon the states for money that was to be raised by taxes which only the states could impose; but these requests met with such a partial compliance that further issues of paper were placed in circulation. Several years elapsed before the states instituted effective systems of taxation, and little assistance was secured from this source.[3] Loans and subsidies furnished by France brought considerable sums into the federal treasury; but more and more paper was emitted, the amounts of the issues increasing as the depreciation of the currency progressed. By the end of 1779, Congress had issued $241,500,000 of the continental bills of credit; while the states had gradually increased their emissions to more than $200,000,000.[4]

do if power should pass completely into its hands, " for half the nation are debtors." Works of Adams, II. 420.

[1] Bullock, 125.

[2] *Idem*, 166–167, and references there given.

[3] *Idem*, 151–164 ; Sumner, Financier, I. 11–34, II. 64–80 ; Bolles, I. 190–205.

[4] Bullock, 125–130. The estimate of the amount of paper

At the opening of 1781, a dollar in paper was worth less than two cents in specie, and the currency soon afterward sank in value to such an extent that it became practically worthless.[1]

Congress knew, as is shown by its resolution adopted Nov. 22, 1777, that "when a quantity of money of any denomination exceeds what is useful as a medium of commerce, its comparative value must be proportionately reduced."[2] But the unwillingness of the states either to levy taxes themselves, or to allow Congress to do so, seemed to leave no alternative but to continue the conti-

issued by the states is from Schuckers, 127. The figures have been considered too large by some writers. See Knox, 10. But the writer has collected sufficient data to justify the statement given by Schuckers.

[1] Until 1779, the depreciation was fairly gradual. Late in 1775 and early in 1776 committees of safety and other similar bodies took measures to force unwilling persons to accept the money. Force, III. 1799, IV. 887, 888, 896, 941, 942, 1211, 1284. By May, 1776, the depreciation of the paper has been clearly established. Sumner, I. 49–50. The last half of 1776 saw a continuous depreciation, until, by the opening of 1777, a depreciation of thirty-three per cent was acknowledged by law in Pennsylvania. Phillips, I. 33. A year later four dollars in paper were equal to no more than one dollar in specie ; and by January, 1779, the rate was eight for one. During 1779, the currency rapidly declined to one-fortieth of its nominal value. Bullock, 133. After 1780, it sometimes circulated at rates of five hundred or one thousand for one. Webster, 502 ; Elliot, III. 472. Finally barbers' shops were papered with it, and suits of clothes were made out of it. Breck, 19.

[2] Journ. of Cong., Nov. 27, 1777. Many of the leading Americans understood this perfectly. John Witherspoon and Pelatiah Webster are notable examples. See also the extracts given by Sumner, Financier, I. 43–44, 95–97.

nental issues. When the bills began to depreciate, the states were requested to declare them a legal tender for all debts; and this recommendation was willingly accepted. Legal tender laws were passed, and every possible effort was made to force the circulation of the paper.[1] Price conventions were held, and these assemblages made futile attempts to regulate prices.[2] General Washington was authorized to seize whatever supplies might be required for his army, and to compel the owners to sell their goods at reasonable prices.[3] All such methods were as idle as attempts to violate the natural laws of money have always proved to be. Persons who refused to sell their lands, houses, or merchandise for nearly worthless paper were stigmatized as misers, traitors, forestallers, and enemies of liberty;[4] but prices continued to rise, as the inflation of the currency proceeded apace. Stores were closed or pillaged, and merchants were mobbed, fined, or imprisoned;[5] but such action merely drove men out of business, and

[1] Felt, 169–170; Papers of N. H., VIII. 144; Bronson, 90, 95; Hickcox, Bills of Credit, 50; Mulford, 439; Laws of Md., 1777, c. 9; Laws of Del., II. 599; Col. Recs. of N. C., X. 194–196; McCall, II. 127, 134; Phillips, I. 31, 32, 78, 199.

[2] Sumner, Financier, I. 53–66, 72–78; Bolles, I. 158–167; Bronson, 92; Potter and Rider, 168–171.

[3] Journ. of Cong., Dec. 27, 1776; Bullock, 128.

[4] Force, III. 1799; Felt, 168; Phillips, I. 78; Col. Recs. of N. C., X. 194–196; Sumner, I. 61.

[5] Some of the penalties imposed upon " depreciators" were fines, forfeiture of debts or goods for which paper was tendered, confiscation of property, imprisonment, and disqualification for holding

tended to produce a real scarcity.[1] Even Washington failed to appreciate the true cause of the rise in prices, and bitterly condemned those who were guilty of what he called "forestalling" and "engrossing."[2] Yet men like John Witherspoon labored to show him that, "Fixing the prices of

public offices and prosecuting suits at law. Phillips, I. 32, 80, II. 129–132; Bronson, 90–92, 122; Hening, Stat., IX. 147; Laws of Md., 1777, c. 9; Laws of Del., II. 599; Breck, 23–24.

[1] A letter from Boston, written in June, 1777, says: "We are all starving here. Since this *plaguey* addition to the regulating bill, people will not bring in provision, & we cannot procure the common necessaries of life." And, in 1779, the same person wrote: "We are likely to be starved thro'out Boston. Never such a scarcity of provisions." Coll. of Mass. Hist. Soc., Sixth Series, IV. 124, 152. See also p. 139. For a similar complaint see Pickering, I. 242.

[2] Many laws were passed against these offences. Bronson, 91; Mulford, 463; Sumner, Financier, I. 50, 53, 54, 57–59, 62–64, 77. Washington denounced "the monopolizers, forestallers, and engrossers," wishing that they might be hunted down as "pests of society" and "hanged upon a gallows five times higher than the one prepared for Haman." Writings of Washington, VII. 282. But Washington himself had been guilty of discriminating against the paper money. In September, 1777, he advised John Parke Custis to take care that the rent of a tract of land "shall have some relative value, to secure an equivalent for the land and slaves." He expressed a willingness to receive paper money, but at "equal value to its intrinsic worth at the time of fixing the rent." *Idem*, VI. 90–91. The next year he advised Custis not to sell land faster than he could reinvest the purchase money in other lands. Exchanging lands for paper might be eventually "a means of giving away the estate." *Idem*, VII. 214–216. In August, 1779, Washington decided to "receive no more old debts" at "the present nominal value of the money." The law, he thought, "never was nor could have been intended to make a man take a shilling or sixpence in the pound for an honest debt." *Idem*, VIII. 20.

commodities has been attempted by law in several states among us, and it has increased the evil it was meant to remedy, as the same practice has done since the beginning of the world." [1] And Pelatiah Webster insisted that the "utmost effect" of forcing laws "was like that of water sprinkled on a blacksmith's forge"; [2] but the tender acts were not repealed until after the paper had become practically valueless. [3]

The misery and iniquity wrought by the depreciating currency were beyond all description. The rise of prices encouraged the most demoralizing speculation, while the sudden acquisition of unearned and undeserved wealth by rascals and sharpers stimulated the most wanton and shameful extravagance. [4] Washington has drawn a correct picture of the conditions, the cause of which he did not originally understand : "If I were to be called upon to draw a picture of the times and of men,

[1] See letter to Washington, in Witherspoon, Works, IX. 150. In his " Essay on Money," Witherspoon held that the laws making paper a legal tender " are directly contrary to the first principles of commerce." Works, IX. 41.

[2] Webster, 129.

[3] It was not until 1780, when the paper was worth only one or two cents on the dollar, that Congress advised the states to amend or repeal their tender laws. Journ. of Cong., March 20, 1780.

[4] General Greene wrote that luxury and dissipation were very prevalent in Philadelphia, and called them " the common offspring of sudden riches." Mr. Stone has written, " Philadelphia soon became the centre of speculation and of the pursuit of private gain." *Penn. Mag.*, III. 362, 376. In general, see Greene, Hist. View, 160; Belknap, 146–147 ; Breck, 28 ; Sumner, Financier, II. 136–137.

from what I have seen, heard, and in part know, I should in one word say, that idleness, dissipation, and extravagance seem to have laid fast hold of most of them; that speculation, peculation, and an insatiable thirst for riches seem to have got the better of every other consideration, and almost every order of men; . . ."[1] The paper money opened the door to the most shameful frauds upon all who were so unfortunate as to be in the position of creditors. Dishonest debtors were enabled to pay their debts in worthless currency. Witherspoon wrote, "For two or three years we constantly saw and were informed of creditors running away from their debtors, and the debtors pursuing them in triumph, and paying them without mercy."[2] Many persons lost a large part or the whole of their fortunes.[3] Guardians of trust funds were enabled to acquit themselves of their obliga-

[1] Sparks, Writings of Washington, VI. 151.

[2] Witherspoon, Works, IX. 36. In Rhode Island, in 1786, stories were told of creditors "leaping from rear windows of their houses or hiding themselves in their attics," in order to escape debtors. Potter and Rider, 120.

[3] McKean lost £6000 by depreciation. *Amer. Hist. Rev.*, II. 99. William Livingston was worth £8512 prior to the paper money era. He lost a large part of this by having debts paid in worthless paper. Sedgwick, 158. Richard Henry Lee found that, in 1779, he was receiving as rent for four thousand acres of good land a sum of money that would not purchase four barrels of corn. Lee, II. 45–46. Jefferson offered to repay a personal loan with currency depreciated to one-fourth of its nominal value. Some years later, however, he caused payment to be made in full. Ford, Writings of Jefferson, II. 181–182. Jonathan Amory received for debts money worth only one-sixth of its nominal value. Weeden, 799. Cf. also

tions by paying widows and orphans in paper that was worth only the smallest fraction of its nominal value.[1] Pelatiah Webster could well say of this iniquitous currency that it had "polluted the equity of our laws; turned them into engines of oppression and wrong; corrupted the justice of our public administration; destroyed the fortunes of thousands who had most confidence in it;" and had gone far "to destroy the morality of our people."[2] Memories of those times were burned into the minds of all honest men who witnessed

p. 803. The rich were often impoverished, while the poor acquired sudden riches. Wells, III. 75. In 1786, the superior court of Rhode Island heard twenty bills in equity brought by people who sought to discharge mortgages with worthless paper. The legal tender bills were brought into the court by the sackful. Bates, 144. Mr. Breck, who took the most favorable view possible concerning the currency, wrote: "Old debts were paid when the paper money was more than seventy for one. Brothers defrauded brothers, children parents, and parents children. Widows, orphans, and others were paid for money lent in specie, with depreciated paper, which they were compelled to receive." Breck, 28. See, finally, Bolles, I. 179–180.

[1] In Philadelphia, a guardian invested the fortune of his ward in real estate at some time prior to the Revolution. In 1779, when seventeen paper dollars were worth only one in specie, he proposed to pay the principal of the estate in continental paper at its nominal value. Phillips, II. 158. Benjamin Greenleaf, judge of probate in Essex County, Mass., has left us a most interesting statement of the injustice wrought by a depreciated currency, in the settlement of estates. Q. J. E., IX. 243–246.

[2] Webster, 175, 176. Mr. Breck has written: "The morals of the people were corrupted beyond anything that could have been believed, prior to the event. All ties of honor, blood, gratitude, humanity, and justice were dissolved." Breck, 28.

them; and never during their lifetime did the national government again resort to such a villanous agency of fraud and corruption.[1]

For a long time Congress had refused to admit that depreciation had taken place, and had repeatedly pledged the public honor, its sacred honor, and several other kinds of honor, that the currency would certainly be redeemed at its face value.[2] Insinuations that the paper would be repudiated were indignantly rejected as "derogatory" to the honor of that body; while, as late as September 13, 1779, Congress declared, in a public address: "A bankrupt faithless republic would be a novelty in the political world, and appear among respectable nations like a common prostitute among chaste and respectable matrons." We are, therefore, at no loss for forcible language in which to describe the action that was taken only six months after this solemn declaration was sent to the various states. On March 18, 1780, when one dollar of the paper was worth only one or two cents, Congress adopted a plan for redeeming it at one-fortieth of its nominal value.[3] It may be true

[1] Of course the continental paper called forth many discussions of the subjects of money and credit. We have often referred to Witherspoon, Webster, and Paine. Various discussions may be found in the *Amer. Mus.*, II. 23–73. See also the references in Sumner, Financier, I. 79–80, 88–89.

[2] Journ. of Cong., Dec. 26, 1775 ; Dec. 28, 1776 ; Nov. 22, 1777; Dec. 29, 1778 ; Jan. 2, 1779 ; Jan. 13, 1779; Sept. 13, 1779.

[3] Bolles, I. 135, 207 ; Sumner, Financier, I. 85–87 ; Bullock, 136–138 ; Journ. of Cong., March 18, 1780.

that there was good reason for despairing of the ability of the Confederation ever to redeem the bills of credit at par; and it is certain that such a course would not have repaired the losses that had been suffered by most of the original holders of the bills. Nevertheless the resolution of 1780 was just what Witherspoon called it, "The first and great deliberate breach of public faith" and "an act of bankruptcy."[1] Congress probably justified its action, as Jefferson did in 1786, by claiming that the "former offers to redeem this money at par" were "relinquished by the general refusal to take but in progressive depreciation."[2] Yet this does not alter the simple fact that thirty-nine for-tieths of the paper was absolutely repudiated. Franklin might say, as he did in 1779, that "there is some advantage to the public in the depreciation, as large nominal values are more easily paid in taxes, and the debt by that means more easily extinguished."[3] But such a complacent view was merely indicative of a loose sense of moral obliga-tions. As a matter of fact, the credit of the United States received a shock from which it was slow to recover.

Congress next proceeded to issue "bills of a new tenor," to the amount of about $4,000,000; but these quickly depreciated. They were exchanged, in 1790, for the new public stocks created when

---

[1] Witherspoon, Works, IX. 118, 131.
[2] Ford, Writings of Jefferson, IV. 154.
[3] Works of Franklin, VI. 345.

the national debt was at length funded.[1] The old bills gradually disappeared from circulation, and specie quickly took their place.[2] This was the end of the continental paper currency, of which only a small part was funded, in 1790, at one cent on the dollar.[3] David Ramsay was pleased to write that the money "gently fell asleep in the hands of its last possessors." Mr. White has very properly emended this by saying : " A truer figure of speech would be that it passed out of the world like a victim of delirium tremens."[4] After the close of the war, the paper-money mania broke out once more in 1785 and 1786. This movement was most distinctly an agitation carried on by and for the debtor classes of the country, and is thoroughly typical of the struggles of the inflationists of the colonial period.[5] Seven of the states at this time emitted bills of credit,[6] and in all of the others there was

---

[1] Bolles, I. 138–139, 141; Phillips, II. 170–172; Bullock, 137–138.

[2] Webster, 75 ; Writings of Jefferson, IV. 154 ; Writings of Madison, I. 48 ; Chastellux, II. 30.

[3] Elliot, Fund. System, 12. Of the bills circulating in 1780, $119,400,000 were paid in by the states under the act of March 18, 1780. State Papers, Finance, I. 54, 58–59.

[4] Ramsay, II. 181 ; White, 146.

[5] This paper-money movement of 1785 has been carefully studied by Libby, 50–69. Cf. Bancroft, VI. 167–176.

[6] Rhode Island, New York, New Jersey, Pennsylvania, North Carolina, South Carolina, and Georgia. Bates, 118–148 ; Arnold, II. 520–537 ; Potter and Rider, 117–132 ; Fernow, 342 ; Phillips, I. 34, 84, 85 ; Iredell, Laws, 551 ; Stat. of S. C., IV. 712–713 ; Ramsay, II. 184–185 ; Stevens, II. 374.

a strong party which favored such a policy.[1] In Massachusetts, the agitation started by the debtor classes resulted in Shays's Rebellion, and order was not restored without considerable difficulty. Perhaps the baldest and most shameless declaration ever issued during an agitation for paper money may be found in the following resolution, which was adopted in the Hampshire county convention in 1786:[2] " Voted, that this convention recommend to the several towns in this county that they instruct their representatives to use their influence in the next general court to have emitted a bank of paper money, *subject to a depreciation, making it a tender in all payments,* equal to silver and gold, to be issued in order to call in the commonwealth's securities." The words that the writer has italicized are so startlingly clear as to render unnecessary all comment upon the villany of these precious proposals.

But the experience of the country with a depreciating paper currency finally taught a lesson which proved effective, so far as the federal gov-

[1] In New Hampshire there was a long and stormy agitation. Belknap, III. 460–477 ; Coll. of N. H. Hist. Soc., III. 117–122. For the uprising of the paper-money party in Massachusetts, see Barry, III. 218–260 ; Weeden, 843–847. Even in conservative Connecticut a paper-money party existed. Bronson, 168–169. In Maryland there was a bitter struggle between the two branches of the legislature. Scharf, II. 539 ; Pamph. on Const., 33. In Delaware a similar contest occurred. Libby, 61–62. In Virginia, the opposition of the great federalist statesmen crushed a determined movement in favor of paper money. Writings of Madison, I. 218, 332 ; Libby, 66–67.   [2] Quoted by Libby, 56.

ernment was concerned. In 1787, Madison could write [1] truthfully, "There has been no moment, since the peace, at which the federal assent would have been given to paper money," for the leading statesmen of the United States had become, almost without exception, stalwart opponents of a government paper currency.[2] In the constitutional convention there was an almost unanimous opposition to the proposal to allow either the states or the general government to issue bills of credit. By an overwhelming vote the states were prohibited from ever resorting to such an expedient.[3] Then, by a vote of nine states to two, the convention decided to strike out of the Constitution the clause that conferred such a power upon the national legislature.[4] A majority of the delegates that discussed the subject made it clear that they intended to take away from Congress the power to issue legal tender paper, and that they believed that this purpose had been accomplished.[5] The

---

[1] Elliot, V. 108.

[2] This is well shown by Bancroft, Plea for the Constitution. To take a single example, Washington, by 1785, had learned fully the evils of paper money. Writings of Washington, XI. 51. Cf. *Idem*, X. 489. See the denunciation of bills of credit in the Federalist, 295–296. [3] Elliot, I. 270–271. [4] *Idem*, I. 226, 245.

[5] See the debates in the convention. Elliot, V. 434–435. See also the opinion of Mercer. Sparks, Morris, III. 321–322. This much is fully established by Bancroft, in his Plea for the Constitution. Even Mr. Thayer, in defending the decision of the Supreme Court, admits that "in the debates of the convention, so far as we know anything about them, the majority of the speakers thought that they were prohibiting bills of credit and paper money." *Harv.*

Supreme Court, however, in our own time, has managed to find a constitutional warrant for impressing upon paper a legal tender character.[1] But the purpose of the framers of the Constitution was understood perfectly by the men who opposed ratification in 1788. The new plan of government was violently assailed on the ground that it forbade either Congress or the states to issue bills of credit.[2] Recent investigations have shown that this was one of the leading causes of the antagonism which the Constitution encountered. A detailed study of the votes taken in each state where it was proposed, in 1785 or 1786, to issue paper money, has proved that the inflationists and repudiators of that period were the very men who opposed ratification two years later.[3] Almost with-

Law Rev., I. 79. This was evidently the opinion of George Ticknor Curtis. Curtis, I. 524–527. Criticisms on this part of Mr. Bancroft's Plea are decidedly weak. *E.g.* James, 64–68.

[1] In 1870, the Court held that the law of 1862, making greenbacks a legal tender, was unconstitutional. Shortly afterwards, the personnel of the Court having changed, the law was upheld as an exercise of the very indefinite " war powers" of the Constitution. In 1884, a law of 1878, directing the reissue of greenbacks, was declared constitutional even in times of peace. 8 Wallace, 603 ; 12 Wallace, 457 ; 110 U. S. Reports, 421. Perhaps the ablest defence of the decisions is by Mr. Thayer, *Harv. Law Rev.*, I. Bancroft's Plea is the best-known attack upon the decisions. This Plea called out a reply by McMurtrie. Mr. Justice Miller has defended the decisions. Miller, 135–144. J. Randolph Tucker has criticised the position of the Court. Tucker, I. 508–516.

[2] See Luther Martin's " Letter." Elliot, I. 369–370, 376.

[3] This is shown conclusively by Libby. Cf. Hildreth, III. 466–467, 535, IV. 25, V. 415–416; Bates, Chaps. IV. and V.

out exception, the sparsely settled districts elected representatives who voted to emit a depreciating currency and then refused to adopt the new Constitution. On the other hand, the richer and more populous localities uniformly opposed the first policy and favored the second. The exceptions to this rule are all explained by particular circumstances of a local character; so that a map showing the geographical distribution of the vote upon the Constitution serves as a fair index of the population, wealth, and industry of the various sections of the thirteen original states. An examination of the letters that passed between the great leaders of the movement in favor of union shows that the antagonism of the paper-money party was both anticipated and actually encountered. Pickering wrote that, in New England, opposition would come "chiefly from the Shaysites and paper-money men."[1] Madison informed Washington that all men who favored paper money and tender laws contended against ratification.[2] Many similar citations might be presented if space would permit.[3] Among the leaders of the opposition, Symmes wrote to Osgood concerning the constitutional prohibition of bills of credit: "Here I suppose the principal weight of opposition will hang."[4] Luther Martin, in his letter to the Maryland legislature,

---

[1] Pickering, II. 358. [2] Elliot, V. 572.
[3] *Idem*, V. 577; *Hist. Mag.*, XVI. 271; Essays on Const., 176; Pamph. on Const., 243.
[4] Hist. Coll. Essex Inst., IV. 214.

made the most of arguments that were based upon the same grounds. In the *American Museum* may be found a set of satirical resolutions which purported to come from the enemies of the Constitution.[1] One of these reads as follows : " Resolved, that as this constitution most arbitrarily and inhumanly prohibits the emission of paper money, and other resources, by which the unfortunate debtor may throw off the discouraging burden of his obligations, it ought to be considered, as in fact it is, a system of tyranny and oppression, compelling citizens in many instances to do things extremely disagreeable, and contrary to their interest." The facts warrant the positive assertion that the last act of the inflationists of the eighteenth century was to antagonize most bitterly the only feasible plan for constructing a firm union of the thirteen feeble, selfish, jealous, and quarrelsome states.

[1] *Amer. Mus.*, III. 84–85. A somewhat similar piece of satire may be found in McMaster and Stone, 83.

CHAPTER VI

STATE BANKS OF ISSUE

IN 1792,[1] Congress established a national coinage system by providing for the concurrent circulation of standard gold and silver coins. The silver dollar was given pure contents of 371¼ grains of fine metal, and the gold eagle was to contain 247½ grains of pure gold.[2] This established a coinage ratio of 15 grains of silver for one grain of gold. Such a rating was not far from the actual market values of the two metals at the time when the law was passed, but silver soon cheapened and drove gold out of circulation; so that our first coinage act resulted practically in silver monometallism.[3]

[1] Various plans and proposals for a coinage system had been formulated during the Confederation. Some of these have been printed. See State Papers, Finance, I. 100–107; Rep. Mon. Conf., 417–453; Watson, 243–268. Cf. Sumner, Financier, II. 36–47.

[2] U. S. Stat., I. 248. For this and subsequent laws relating to money, see Rep't Mon. Com., Appendix; Dunbar. The history of the 371¼ grain silver dollar, recommended by Hamilton and adopted by Congress, has been correctly traced for the first time by Sumner, in *Amer. Hist. Rev.*, III. 607–619. On our coinage laws, see Bolles; Laughlin; Sumner, Currency; Upton ; Watson ; White ; and Linderman.

[3] Soetbeer, 130, gives 15.05 : 1 as the market ratio for 1791, and 15.68 : 1 as the ratio for 1800. From 1800 to 1810, the average ratio was 15.61 : 1. In 1819, the committee on coinage reported to the house of representatives that gold, being underrated, " can scarcely be considered as having formed a material part of our

79

Concerning this earliest legislation, Daniel Webster could declare, with entire accuracy, that "the
framers of the Constitution, and those who enacted
the early statutes on this subject, were *hard-money
men ;* they had felt, and therefore duly appreciated,
the evils of a paper medium ; they therefore sed-
ulously guarded the currency of the United States
from debasement. The legal currency of the
United States was gold and silver coin ; this was
a subject in regard to which Congress had run
into no folly." [1]

But if the national government had, for the time,
turned away from the paper-money policy, the
agitation for cheap currency did not die out in the
various states. An opportunity for such a movement was found in the development of banks of
issue.[2] The Bank of North America, established

money circulation for the last twenty-six years." State Papers,
Finance, III. 399. Benton states that gold disappeared "completely and totally" about twenty years after the adoption of an
erroneous ratio by the law of 1792. Benton, I. 442. Even American silver coins were displaced by light-weight Spanish money, so
that Jefferson ordered the suspension of the coinage of silver dollars after 1806. Watson, 73–74.

[1] Annals of Cong., 14th Cong., 1st Sess., 1091. In 1834, Benton argued strenuously that "the government of the United States
was intended to be a hard-money government." Benton, I. 436.

[2] An extended bibliography on banking in the United States
may be found in Sen. Ex. Doc., 38. To the books there mentioned
may be added: Macleod, Dict., 169–195; T. P. Kettell, in Eighty
Years, I. 198–211; White; Bryan; and Sumner, Banking. The
book last mentioned is the leading work upon the subject, and is so
comprehensive that the reader may be referred to it for information
on all the subjects discussed in this chapter.

in 1782, was the first institution in the United States that undertook to maintain a bank currency that should be at all times convertible into specie.[1] In 1784, banks were founded in Boston and New York; and before long a banking mania spread in all directions. In the Mississippi Valley, a bank was established in Kentucky as early as 1802; while, in 1813, Missouri was provided with a similar institution. In 1791, the first Bank of the United States was founded, and began to issue circulating notes that formed a uniform and convenient paper currency throughout the country, a function that was continued by its successor.[2]

But there were in the country only a few men who had any adequate comprehension of the true nature and the proper methods of banking. The common view seemed to be that a bank was a mysterious and magical means of creating wealth out of nothing; and it was supposed that, since a banker secures interest on his notes, the banking business offered a unique and beautiful opportunity to secure interest on one's debts. Banks were often formed for the sole purpose of issuing their paper; and the privilege of emitting such promissory notes, which were intended to circulate as currency, was claimed as a common law right.[3] It

[1] Lewis; Sumner, Financier, II. 21–35.

[2] On the banks of the United States, see Clarke and Hall; Bolles, II. 127–155, 317–358; Benton; Kinley; Sumner, Jackson; articles by Root and White, in *Sound Currency*, IV.; *J. P. E.*, V. 421–457.

[3] Cleaveland, XVII.

was with reason that Hugh Williamson complained, in 1812, that the constitutional prohibition of the issue of bills of credit by the states might be practically nullified " by a deluge of bank paper."[1] The people of the United States had embarked once more on the enterprise of substituting a cheaper medium, paper, for gold and silver, which they regarded as "dead stock," to use Hamilton's phrase;[2] and soon the issue of bank notes came to be regarded as the only method of providing the country with enough money to meet the needs of industry.[3]

In all parts of the country many of the earliest banks were conducted with extreme recklessness or utter dishonesty. In New England, the first crash came in 1809, and this was followed by the enactment of more stringent laws regulating the business. In 1814, 1837, and 1857, there occurred general suspensions of specie payments by most of the banks in the United States; while periods of suspension in particular localities were even more common. Only the New England banks withstood the first of these crashes, and a still smaller number maintained the convertibility of their notes during the crises of 1837 and 1857. During some parts of its existence, the second

[1] Williamson, II. 40–41.

[2] State Papers, Finance, I. 67. See Sumner's comments. Sumner, Banking, 24–25.

[3] Note the manner in which Gouge combated this view. Gouge, Part I. 45, 64–67, 117–123. See also quotations in Sumner, Banking, 25.

Bank of the United States exercised a restraining influence upon the issues of the state banks, since it could refuse to receive in payment of public dues the currency of any institution that did not maintain the convertibility of its notes.[1] Indeed, it was in part a demand for a national bank that should regulate the disordered paper medium of the country that induced Congress to grant the charter in 1816. But this wholesome restraint was often denounced as oppression and intimidation of the state banks, and it helped to produce in some localities a lasting hostility against the federal Bank.

At the present day, the abuses perpetrated by the state banks during the first half of the century may appear almost incredible. The capital of many institutions was only partially paid in, and stockholders frequently proceeded to borrow all that they had contributed.[2] Loans were made upon mortgage security, while it seemed impossible for the disastrous results that commonly followed such a policy to teach the obvious lesson that an institution that attempts to support a large amount of demand liabilities must invest its funds only in quick assets.[3] Notes were issued in such

[1] Clarke and Hall, 749–750; Gallatin, II. 461, III. 334, 336; Sumner, Banking, 72, 79, 109, 113, 166, 208.

[2] Gouge, 46–47 ; Raguet, 115–119, 145; Tucker, Money, 194, 365 ; Rep't Compt. Currency, 1876, XXXIII. ; Felch, 80.

[3] Hamilton, in 1790, had argued forcibly that land is "an unfit fund for a bank circulation." State Papers, Finance, I. 73. But in 1839, Condy Raguet expressed the belief that a bank should

small denominations as one shilling, or even five cents, in the expectation that it would never be worth any one's while to collect such infinitesimal currency and present it for redemption.[1] One notorious bank, which broke down in 1809, was found to have $580,000 of notes in circulation, and $86.46 in its specie reserve.[2] Banks were located in inaccessible places, "on some bottomless prairie road," or in the depths of forests, where it would prove as difficult as possible to find the "offices" at which the notes were payable.[3] When a Boston bank sent a batch of currency to New York for redemption, the collector of the port seized the bills upon the pretext of preventing a run on the New York banks.[4] A messenger sent to South

---

invest its *capital* in mortgages, since "the security of real estate" is safer than that of promissory notes. Raguet, 90. Mr. McCulloch tells us that the famous and conservative State Bank of Indiana, at the outset of its career, loaned very largely to men who were buying or improving lands. But the crisis of 1837 taught the managers that these loans were "sluggish and unreliable," so that, after that time, the loans were "mainly confined to bills of exchange" based upon produce shipped to Eastern or Southern markets. McCulloch, Men and Meas., 116.

[1] See especially Raguet, 135–140, on the circulation of bank notes of small denominations.

[2] Gouge, 45–50. This was not much worse than many other occurrences. In 1837, a Massachusetts bank failed, with $111,000 of notes outstanding, and $36.71 of cash on hand. Root, in *Sound Currency*, II. 258.

[3] Cooley, 268–269; Garnett, in *Sound Currency*, V. 142; Hadden, 186–187; Rep't Compt. Currency, 1876, XXXV.–XXXVI.; *Bank Mag.*, XIII. 235.

[4] Felt, 218.

Royalston to demand the payment of $10,000 in notes issued by the local bank, was arrested upon a frivolous charge in order to avoid such a request.[1] Nothing was more common than a state of public opinion which condemned every attempt to obtain specie from the banks. To ask one of these institutions to fulfil the promise printed on the face of its bills was a disgraceful act, which indicated a lack of public spirit, or was proof positive of a desire to start a "run."[2] In Ohio, Indiana, and Missouri, between 1855 and 1859, certain persons who presented notes for redemption were threatened with lynching or a coat of tar and feathers.[3] Some states established public institutions that were no better than the loan banks of colonial days. These were designed to do a banking business "upon the faith and credit" of the states, and to supply the people with paper money.[4] Thus, in 1820, the Bank of the Commonwealth of Kentucky was instituted. The legisla-

[1] Whitney, Suffolk Bank, 60.

[2] In Richmond a man who took legal measures to compel the payment of notes was subsequently sued for damages by the bank. Gouge, 84. Persons seeking the redemption of bills issued by the bank of Darien were obliged to swear, before a justice of the peace, to the ownership of each and every bill. *Idem*, 141. Raguet devotes a chapter to this subject. See also State Papers, Finance, III. 394–395 ; White, 365.

[3] *Bank Mag.*, X. 41, XII. 587, XIV. 323.

[4] Gouge, 131–133, 138 ; Conant, 330–337 ; Root, in *Sound Currency*, II. 221–252 ; Sumner, Banking, Index, "Banks of the States." In some cases state bonds were issued in order to raise capital, and repudiation allowed. Scott, 33–48.

ture appropriated $7000 in order to purchase
books, paper, and the plates for printing bills;
then $2,000,000 of paper was issued, and appor-
tioned among the counties to be loaned out on
mortgage security. This was practically an emission of state bills of credit, which was prohibited
by the Federal Constitution; but, in 1835, the Supreme Court, which had recently been "Jackson-
ized," found a way of arriving at the conclusion
that the act creating the bank was constitutional.[1]
Judge Story vigorously dissented from this opinion.

The consequence of the spread of this mania for
unsound banking was that from 1800 to 1860, an
inconvertible paper currency continued to vex the
United States. Bank notes were often at a discount of fifty or sixty per cent,[2] and the issues became so large as repeatedly to cause inflation.
Then a period of liquidation would ensue, and
prices would fall to extremely low levels.[3] In

[1] 8 Peters, 118; 11 Peters, 257. This case was first heard in
1834, and three judges out of five held that the notes were in
reality bills of credit. But, as two judges were absent, the case
was heard again a year later. Meanwhile Chief Justice Marshall
had died, and two other vacancies had occurred; so that now five
out of the seven judges were appointees of President Jackson.
Story stated in his dissenting opinion, at the final hearing, that
Marshall, at the first hearing, had decided that the notes of the
Bank of Kentucky were bills of credit. 11 Peters, 348. Cf. Sumner, Banking, 142–143.

[2] Some statistics of depreciation may be found in Gouge, 132–
133, 135, 166–168; Gallatin, III. 363; Sumner, Banking, Index,
"Depreciation."

[3] Gouge discusses intelligently these alternate periods of inflation

these periods of depression the favorite remedies suggested were more money or a higher protective tariff.[1] Men who had speculated on a rising market, and had been caught "long" when the reaction commenced, would cry out loudly for more currency in order that prices might be sustained until it should be possible to unload upon other people. Prodigality and dishonesty always attended every era of inflation; and when the false prosperity[2] thus created had collapsed, debtors began to clamor for legislative relief. In many states arbitrary stays of execution were granted, and unfair appraisement laws

---

and liquidation. Gouge, 110–126, 174–176. Raguet and Tucker also describe the process. Raguet, 142–148 ; Tucker, Money, 182–190. See also Gallatin, III. 365–488. Sumner makes his chapters follow this sequence of events : inflation, crisis, liquidation.

[1] In the hard times just prior to 1830, there was laid before the Senate a proposal for the issue of $50,000,000 of government paper. Such an addition to the currency, it was claimed, would make property "rise two thousand millions of dollars" and would restore prosperity. See Gallatin, III. 255. In the depression of 1840, the Pennsylvania "relief" system was authorized. This was intended to relieve the situation through the issue, by the banks, of $3,000,000 of notes *redeemable in state bonds*. See Gallatin, III. 409–412. The hard times succeeding the period of inflation that ended in 1818 had much to do with the agitation for higher duties on imports. See Clay's speech of 1824 and Webster's reply, in Taussig, Papers, 254–256, 324–326. Gouge appreciated this fact very well. Gouge, 125, 153. Cf. Taussig, Tariff Hist., 19–21, 68–69 ; Sumner, Protection, 39, 41.

[2] See the picture of the inflation period of 1816, in Gouge, 64–72. Matthew Carey called this the "golden age" of Philadelphia, and insisted that the prosperity was not artificial. Gouge, 71–72.

or replevin acts were passed.[1] In the period from 1820 to 1825, Kentucky succeeded in making things especially lively for the hated "money power."[2] Says Professor Sumner: "Under the replevin law, the judges instructed the jury to find 'scaling verdicts,' rating the judgment sum in specie according to the depreciation at the time of the contract. This sum could be collected after two years, unless the creditor indorsed the execution. If he did that, he obtained payment in three months in paper worth about fifty cents on the dollar, — that is, he obtained about one-fourth of his original claim." This, according to the governor of Kentucky, was "the paramount law of necessity." Before long, the state had two rival courts of appeals contending for "paramount" jurisdiction, while the legislature was rent by the efforts of the debtor party to secure the enactment of still more "paramount" laws. In 1820, a committee of the Pennsylvania legislature depicted the results of the issues of inconvertible currency in the following words: "In consequence of this most destructive measure the inclination of a large part of the people, created by past prosperity, to live by speculation and not by labor, was greatly increased; a spirit in all respects akin to gambling prevailed; a fictitious value was given to all descriptions of property; specie was driven from circulation, as if by com-

[1] Gouge, 131, 135 ; Sumner, Banking, Index, " Stay laws."
[2] Sumner, Banking, 121–137; Shaler, 173–185; Gouge, 131–132.

mon consent, and all efforts to restore society to its natural condition were treated with undisguised contempt."[1] Six years later the governor of Connecticut wrote: "It is amidst explosions of credit, principally occasioned by the conduct of Banks, that every class of industrious citizens, and all our enterprising young men, are exposed to repeated losses, against which no vigilance can guard, and no prudence exempt them."[2]

The growth of the banking mania was necessarily attended with a renewal of the old complaints and discussions concerning monetary affairs. In the Mississippi Valley the cry was heard that trade with the Eastern states drew off all the specie,[3] and this, too, in spite of the fact that large amounts of silver came into this region from New Orleans. The use of inconvertible bank notes would merely accelerate the export of specie; but the cheaper medium was often welcomed as a remedy for the alleged scarcity of hard money. When, in 1814, the general suspension of specie payments brought the country down to the basis of a depreciated paper currency, it was vigorously denied that the premium upon silver was proof of the depreciation of the inconvertible bank notes. In Philadelphia, Franklin had worthy successors who began to publish pamphlets refuting the "very fallacious and mischievous doctrines," that "the ability of a Bank to redeem, *i.e.* to pay specie, is the true criterion of excessive issues"; that "a

[1] Gouge, 120–121.　　[2] *Idem*, 161.　　[3] Butler, 295.

paper currency is depreciated when it ceases to be of equal value with gold and silver "; and that "the rise of specie, and a general increase of prices, are the certain indications of depreciation."[1] One Philadelphia pamphleteer declared: "The paper of the Bank of England preserves a value, as steady perhaps as any attainable, whilst the precious metals, like other commodities, fluctuate around this standard."[2] This scientist proposed the creation of a national bank which should issue circulating, legal tender notes redeemable in United States stocks. To perfect this scheme, he desired that the notes of state banks should be payable in those issued by the national bank. Matthew Carey pronounced this a "magnificent" idea, and "a sovereign remedy for all the financial difficulties of the country."[3] In 1819, the president and directors of the Bank of South Carolina submitted to the state legislature a franker plea for inconvertible paper money. The South Carolina address raises the query whether a sufficient metallic medium is not unobtainable, and whether it would not be better to dispense entirely with the use of gold and silver. Then it proceeds to recommend that the government should issue all money to the people, since government alone can adjust the amount of currency to the needs of trade. Finally it abuses the Bank of the United States for presenting for redemption state bank notes received in payment of the federal revenues.[4]

[1] Gouge, 70.　　[2] Bollman.　　[3] Gouge, 76.　　[4] *Idem*, 143.

The condition of the bank currency, however, was not equally bad in all sections of the country. As time wore on and the lessons of sad experience were learned, better methods of banking were developed in the older states. The New England banks led in this direction after the disaster of 1809. The city banks compelled those located in the country districts to maintain the convertibility of their notes, and wise legal restrictions gradually were perfected.[1] By 1860, Massachusetts had developed one of the best banking systems in the world. In New York, the safety fund and the bond security systems had been slowly perfected, and honest management was the rule; yet, in 1861, the *Bankers' Magazine* described some of the country banks as mushroom concerns.[2] Louisiana had passed a model banking law in 1842, under which

---

[1] Whitney, Suffolk Bank ; *Sound Currency*, II. 276–284. The most important restrictions were, briefly, as follows : (1) Banks must have a certain amount of paid-up capital, and must not impair this by loans on pledges of their own stock. (2) Small notes were prohibited. (3) The note issues should not exceed a certain amount, as twice the paid-up stock. (4) Noteholders were given a prior lien on assets of the banks. (5) Banks were forbidden to reissue the notes of other banks. (6) A certain minimum reserve was required. (7) Directors were made specially liable, and a double liability was imposed upon shareholders. (8) Public statements of accounts were required, and examiners were appointed to investigate the condition of the banks. (9) Dealing in shares of other banks or in merchandise was forbidden, and lending on mortgage security was sometimes prohibited. For an early discussion of methods of legal regulation see Tucker, Money, 191–232.

[2] *Bank Mag.*, XVI. 5.

her banks were, in 1860, the safest in the country in many respects.[1]   In other states individual banking institutions had become justly celebrated for the ability and honesty of their administration. The reader will at once call to mind the State Banks of Indiana and Ohio, the Bank of the State of South Carolina, and the banking house of George Smith and Alexander Mitchell in Wisconsin.[2]   But such distinguished exceptions merely serve to heighten the contrast presented by most of the banking institutions in the South and West. In the Upper Mississippi Valley the conditions remained particularly bad in 1860.   Attempts had been made to adopt the provisions of the banking codes of other states, but the laws thus framed had been badly administered.   North of Louisiana and Arkansas, there was practically no convertible bank money in the Mississippi Valley; and the notes of dead or doubtful banks were hawked about at from ten to ninety per cent discount.[3] In 1859, a bogus Ohio bank had started in business by investing $165 in a plate, and paying one quarter of a cent on a dollar for having its notes printed.   It had then established its credit firmly by giving $1900 to the publisher of a bank note

---

[1] Sumner, Banking, 387–391, 434–437.   Note what McCulloch says of the honorable action of the New Orleans banks in 1861. McCulloch, Men and Meas., 138–139.

[2] See *J. P. E.*, IV. 1–36 ; McCulloch, Men and Meas., 113–138 ; White, 374–394 ; *Sound Currency*, V. 114–120, 314–328 ; Sumner, Banking, 439–442 ; Rep't Compt. Currency, 1876, XXVI.–XXVIII.

[3] *Bank Mag.*, XII. 166, XIV. 152, 811–814, XVII. 396, 1002.

detector, who agreed to "quote the money right."[1] "*Quis custodiet ipsos custodes?*" This incident reminds us that note and counterfeit detectors were in universal use by all who would avoid loss from the receipt of bogus bank notes and the notes of bogus banks.[2] From the best data obtainable, it has been computed that, in 1860, the specie held by the banks of Illinois amounted to only 4.25 per cent of the circulation and deposits. In New York and Massachusetts, the specie reserves amounted, respectively, to 20.39 per cent and 21.63 per cent; while, in Louisiana, the percentage rose as high as 52.46.[3]

[1] *Bank Mag.*, XIV. 153.
[2] White, 397–404 ; Sumner, Banking, 455.
[3] *Bank Mag.*, XIV. 30.

CHAPTER VII

A RETURN TO GOVERNMENT PAPER MONEY

IN the last chapter it was shown that the coinage legislation of 1792 resulted in an undervaluation of gold, and the establishment of silver monometallism. As early as 1818, there began a movement in favor of such a change in the ratio of the two metals as would bring gold back into circulation.[1] In 1834 and 1837, the coinage laws of the United States were finally amended so as to accomplish this result. At that time the market ratio of silver to gold was about 15.8 : 1; but Congress adopted a rating of 16 : 1, with the evident intention of establishing in practice the single gold standard.[2] Unfortunately, the acts passed in 1834 and 1837 reduced the fine contents of the gold eagle from 247.5 grains first to 232 grains and then to 232.2 grains. Just before this change, the

[1] See documents reprinted in Rep't Mon. Conf., 502–697. Gouge, Part I. 109, proposed to strike gold coins on whose face the pure contents should be stamped. These would not need to be made a legal tender, and could be used in all large payments. Benton, chaps. 105 and 108, is an important reference on this subject. Gallatin advocated a change of the mint ratio to 15.6 : 1. Gallatin, III. 309. See also Raguet, 204–250.

[2] U. S. Stat., IV. 696, V. 136. See Laughlin, 52–91; Soetbeer, 131. In 1840, the market ratio was 15.62 : 1.

gold dollar had been worth a few cents more than the silver dollar, which was the actual standard of value. But this reduction in the weight of the eagle produced a gold dollar that was about two cents less valuable than the silver dollar.[1] Thus Congress robbed creditors of two per cent of the value of existing debts, and established a precedent that was fraught with danger for the future. It was predicted that this action would enable gold to replace silver as the actual medium of exchange;[2] and this result was gradually brought about, especially after the great gold discoveries of 1849 caused a marked decline in the value of the yellow metal. By 1853, the silver dollar was worth $1.04 in gold, and had become an obsolete coin;[3]

---

[1] At the ratio of 15.73 : 1, which Soetbeer gives for the year 1834, the gold dollar of 23.2 grains established by the act of that year would have been worth slightly more than ninety-eight per cent of the 371.25 grain silver dollar. In subsequent years the ratio sometimes rose to 15.8 or 15.9 to 1, and this change in the value of the gold dollar made it worth about ninety-nine per cent of the value of the old silver dollar. Cf. the tables given by Linderman, 161–162.

[2] The committee that reported in 1834 made such a prophecy. II. Rep., 278, p. 56. Raguet, 210–212, 247, predicted the same ultimate result.

[3] This displacement of silver was a very gradual process prior to 1850. In 1839, Raguet, 208–209, said that little progress had been made in this direction. McCulloch says that the specie currency of the West was composed almost exclusively of silver until the discovery of gold in California. McCulloch, Men and Meas., 119. In 1850, the ratio of the two metals in Europe was 15.7 : 1, about the same as it had been in 1834. But by 1853, it had changed to 15.33 : 1. Soetbeer, 131. In this year even our fractional silver disappeared from circulation, and Congress had

while the product of the Californian mines supplied the country with an abundant gold circulation. In 1861, it was estimated that the currency of the United States consisted of about $250,000,000 of specie and $202,000,000 of bank notes.

Soon after the opening of the Civil War,[1] the government negotiated a loan of $150,000,000 from the banks in the leading Eastern cities. Congress wisely gave Secretary Chase permission to keep this money in solvent banks, and to draw upon these funds by check as fast as should be necessary. But the Secretary foolishly refused to follow such a course, and withdrew from the banks a large portion of their reserves, — an action which was soon followed by a general suspension of specie payments by the banks throughout the country.[2] At the opening of 1862, the credit of the United States was not sufficiently high to enable the government to dispose of its six per cent bonds at their par value; and the authorities at Washington objected to selling the public securities for what they would bring in the market. Under these circumstances, Congress finally de-

to establish a debased subsidiary coinage. U. S. Stat., X. 160. At this time it was explicitly recognized in the debates in Congress that the United States had practically but a single standard of value, and that gold. Cong. Globe, XXVI. 629, Appendix, 192.

[1] On this period of our finances, see Bolles, III.; von Hock; Taussig, in Shaler's United States, II. 537–544.

[2] *J. P. E.*, VII. 289–326; Sumner, Banking, 458–461; Rep't Mon. Com., 402–404; White, 149–152. Even Spaulding, 1–4, criticises this action of the Secretary.

cided, against the emphatic protests of many of its ablest members, to issue $150,000,000 of notes that were declared to be legal tender in all payments, except for customs duties and interest on the national debt.[1] Other issues were subsequently authorized, so that finally $450,000,000 of irredeemable paper was placed in circulation. In 1864, the limit of the permanent issues was placed at $400,000,000; and the favorable turn of both military and financial operations enabled the government to adhere to its promise.[2]

As is well known, the greenbacks depreciated, and the country was again involved in all the evils of a fluctuating paper medium. The bills were injected into a currency that already contained more than $200,000,000 of bank notes that had ceased to be redeemable in specie,[3] while the situation was made worse by the issue of interest-bearing, legal tender paper.[4] Before the end of 1862,

[1] U. S. Stat., XII. 345. Mr. Spaulding, who claimed to be the father of the greenbacks, discussed their history in his Legal Tender Paper. He was well criticised by Walker and Adams, in *N. A. R.*, April, 1870. On the greenbacks, see Newcomb; Bowen, 347-367; Sumner, Currency, 189-227; Walker, 369-375; Knox, 80-147; White, 148-165, 191-197; Noyes, 1-72; Rep't Mon. Com., 389-490.

[2] U. S. Stat., XII. 532, 710, 822, XIII. 219.

[3] Of the issues of the state banks in 1861, probably $150,000,000 was in the North. After the suspension of specie payments these issues increased to $183,000,000 in 1862, and $238,000,000 the following year. After 1863, the notes of the national banks began to replace these issues. Rep. Sec. Treas., 1897, CXXXI.–CXXXVIII.

[4] In 1861 and 1862, Congress authorized the issue of $60,000,000

gold was selling for $1.34 in currency; and, during the year 1864, the greenbacks showed an average depreciation of more than fifty per cent.[1] The government did not avoid the necessity of selling its bonds for what they would command in the open market, and was obliged to create a nominal debt of $2,565,000,000, for which it received not more than $1,695,000,000 in gold. When all elements are taken into consideration, it seems certain that, before the close of the war, the " paper-money plan of finance " had cost the United States an un-

of demand notes not bearing interest, but receivable for public dues and finally made a legal tender. U. S. Stat., XII. 259, 313, 338. These were exchanged for greenbacks. For their history, see Breckenridge, in *Sound Currency*, V.; Tenth Census, VII. 372. In 1863, interest-bearing notes, running for not more than three years and a legal tender for debts, were issued to the amount of $211,000,000. U. S. Stat., XII. 710; Tenth Census, VII. 377–378. In 1863 and 1864, "compound interest notes" were issued to the amount of $266,594,000. These were a legal tender, and $177,045,000 of the issue replaced the notes mentioned above. U. S. Stat., XII. 710, XIII. 218; Tenth Census, VII. 378. These notes entered into circulation to a greater or less extent, and were periodically hoarded as the time for interest payments approached.

[1] From the suspension of specie payments by the banks to the time of the issue of greenbacks, the premium on gold was only two or three per cent. By July, the average value of $100 of greenbacks had fallen to $86.60, and the following January it was only $68.90. During the year 1863, the average gold value of the greenbacks was $68.90, the value of the paper remaining nearly stationary. Then in 1864, it sank to an average value of $49.20. The highest price ever paid in currency for one dollar in gold was $2.85. Tables of depreciation may be found in Knox, 97; Muhleman, 29 ; Rep. Mon. Com., 562.

necessary expense of more than $500,000,000.[1] In
other respects the experiment with the greenbacks
proved equally costly. Wages did not rise immediately in proportion to the increase of prices, so
that the laboring classes suffered a considerable
loss in their real incomes.[2] Business was given
an unhealthy, speculative impulse, which necessitated a severe period of liquidation in 1873. A
dishonest medium of exchange was productive of
the most notorious extravagance and corruption,
which gave to the decade following the close of
the war a character that was perhaps more un-
savory than that of any epoch since the adoption
of the Constitution. James Fisk and Jay Gould, the
Crédit Mobilier scandals and the Belmont impeach-
ment trial, were the natural products of this period
of reckless inflation.

In 1866, Secretary McCulloch was authorized to
retire a certain amount of the greenbacks each
month ; but this necessary and wholesome policy
of contraction was opposed by all who had invested
while prices were still rising, and desired an opportunity to unload their investments upon other people. Accordingly, when the greenbacks had been
reduced to $356,000,000, Congress prohibited the
further retirement of the notes.[3] Meanwhile, the

---

[1] Adams, 131 ; Rep. Mon. Com., 445–461 ; *J. P. E.*, V. 117–156.
[2] Rep. Mon. Com., 470–479.
[3] U. S. Stat., XIV. 32, XV. 34. On contraction, see McCulloch,
Men and Meas., 210–213 ; Noyes, 7–16. According to the law of
1862, the greenbacks had been convertible into six per cent bonds,
but this provision was repealed in 1863. U. S. Stat., XII. 711.

proposal was made to redeem with the paper money a portion of the bonded debt of the United States. When the 5-20 bonds were authorized in 1862, the pledge was made that interest should be paid in coin, but nothing had been said concerning the principal. This oversight was corrected in the issues of bonds authorized in 1863 ;[1] but the claim was made that the obligations created under the act of 1862 were lawfully redeemable in greenbacks, since the government had promised to pay only the interest in specie. The Democratic platform of 1868 advocated the payment of the principal of the 5-20 bonds in depreciated paper,[2] but this plank was practically repudiated by the candidate of that party. The defeat of the Democrats was fol-

[1] U. S. Stat., XII. 345–346. The law of 1862 did not specify in what money the bonds should be repaid, since no greenbacks had been issued at the time when it was enacted, and there seemed to be no occasion for a specific declaration. Another section of the law provided for the issue of greenbacks and specified that they should not be a legal tender for the interest on the debt. The bonds issued in 1863 were specifically made payable in coin. U. S. Stat., XII. 710.

[2] Ann. Cyc., 1868, p. 747. President Johnson recommended that the interest on the bonds should be applied to the payment of the principal until that should be extinguished. Many Republicans believed that the 5-20 bonds of 1862 should be paid in greenbacks ; even John Sherman advocated such action in 1868. Cong. Globe, 40th Cong., 2d Sess., V., Appendix, 181. Cf. speech of Thaddeus Stevens. *Idem*, 4178. In 1868, the Republican convention of Indiana wanted to have these bonds " honestly " paid in greenbacks, except where coin was specified ; and desired to have this done in such a manner as to make the money in circulation equal to the wants of the country, but without "*too great an inflation of the currency.*" Ann. Cyc., 1868, 378.

lowed by a resolution of Congress pledging the country to redeem all its bonded debt in coin, and promising to adopt the same policy with respect to the greenbacks.[1] But many people still insisted that " the bondholders should be paid in the same currency that had been given to the soldiers," as if two wrongs could make a right; while, in some quarters, threats were heard that the debt would be repudiated if Congress refused to redeem it with depreciated paper.[2]

All the conditions that prevailed in 1868 contributed to the growth of a strong sentiment in favor of the retention of the greenbacks as a permanent feature of our monetary system. The creation of the national banking system during the war had resulted in a prohibitory tax of ten per cent upon the notes of state banks.[3] Since the continuation of " wildcat " bank issues was no longer possible, it was evident that the withdrawal of the greenbacks, and the restoration of the gold standard, would leave the country, for the first time in its history, without any form of cheap currency. It was not strange, therefore, that in many sections there should be manifested a violent opposition to parting with the only form of irredeemable paper that remained available. Besides this, as has been noted, many persons had made extensive investments during the period of inflated prices, and

[1] U. S. Stat., XVI. 1.
[2] See Democratic platform in Ohio in 1869. Howard, 91.
[3] U. S. Stat., XIII. 484.

would naturally oppose the restoration of the currency to a specie basis. These were the causes that led to the passage of the act of 1868 prohibiting the further retirement of the greenbacks.

As a matter of course, some people began to deny that there had been any real inflation of the currency on account of the issue of the greenbacks. In December, 1862, when the premium on gold ranged sometimes as high as thirty-four per cent, Secretary Chase, in his Annual Report, expressed a doubt whether this was due to an excessive issue of paper. In the following January, it was often contended in Congress, that the paper currency had not depreciated; that King Gold had been "degraded to a commodity of traffic, like corn and wine and pork," so that its value was subject to "all the fluctuations of supply and demand"; and that the greenback commanded the same quantity of commodities that it formerly did, so that the premium on gold did not indicate a depreciation of the paper.[1] A year later, a writer in the *North American Review* contended that it was "the duty and the prerogative of a government to supply a currency to the people," and that the greenbacks were "the best currency that ever a nation had," "such a currency as was never dreamed of in the philosophy of the framers of the Constitution."[2]

[1] Cong. Globe, 37th Cong., 3d Sess., 383, 386, 391, 409.
[2] *N. A. R.*, XCIX. 210, 227. Hon. W. D. Kelley stated in 1876 that this article was by his "late townsman and friend," Sydney George Fisher. Cong. Globe, 44th Cong., 1st Sess., 1173.

Then Henry C. Carey expressed the belief that it was the wicked free-traders who attributed the high price of gold to the greenbacks, which had in reality "fallen on the country as the dew falls." He considered paper money "democratic in its tendencies" and wanted $200,000,000 more of it, for he denied that any "plethora of money" existed. The changes in prices that had occurred since 1862 were such as must have taken place "had the idea of a legal tender note had no existence." He desired the retention of "a national system of circulation based entirely on the credit of the government with the people and not liable to interference from abroad."[1] Some years later, the echoing voice of Henry Carey Baird was raised[2] in favor of a national paper currency interchangeable with government bonds. Mr. Benjamin Butler desired an "American system of finance," based upon a dollar, "of some convenient and cheap material," which should have "a certain fixed and stable value," and should no more be redeemable than a yardstick or a quart measure. This "American" currency, which should be the counterpart of the "American System" of protection, was to be issued only by the government, and should be convertible into interest-bearing bonds. Mr. Butler despised gold and silver, which were "the money alike of the barbarian and the despot."[3]

[1] Carey, Currency, 25, 29 ; Carey, McCulloch, 1, 13, 19, 46.
[2] Baird, 11.
[3] Butler's Book, 953–954. This contains speeches in Congress.

In 1875, Congressman Kelley, of Pennsylvania, declared the "Bullion Report" to be an antiquated production of David Ricardo, a "bond and bullion monger." For his own part, Mr. Kelley was ready to "go for what old Ben Franklin says," and to follow the guidance of Horace Greeley, who had demonstrated the beauty of the "interconvertible bond system."[1] Finally, Peter Cooper persistently urged the necessity of adopting a "strictly national currency," "always interconvertible with Government bonds at a low rate of interest," "which cannot be taken from the hands of the people by the ever-shifting balances of commodities between nations."[2] Such utterances are fairly typical of the inflationist arguments that were current in the years following the war; and it may be interesting to note that the quotations from Mr. Cooper end with the argument, advanced by Cotton Mather nearly two centuries earlier, that paper money is "an abiding Cash."

In 1870, the Supreme Court finally succeeded in reversing its earlier decision and declaring the issue of legal tender notes to be constitutional. In the opinion delivered by Justice Strong, the act of 1834, which reduced the value of the dollar by two per cent, served to give point to one of the arguments advanced in behalf of the greenback, which had given the country a paper currency of

---

[1] Quoted by Leavitt, 193.   Cf. Kelley's argument for an "inexportable currency."   Kelley, 392–396.

[2] Cooper, 10.

fifty per cent less value than the medium used in 1861. The opinion was also expressed that it is incorrect to speak of a "standard of value," since "value is an ideal thing."[1] Then, in the panic of 1873, the Secretary of the Treasury, without express authority of law, reissued a considerable quantity of greenbacks that had been retired and were supposed to be retained in the Treasury.[2] This was followed, in 1874, by the passage of the "Inflation Bill," which provided for the issue of $14,000,000 of the paper; but this measure was vetoed by President Grant.[3] With all this encouragement, the greenback rapidly became an important political issue.

In 1872, the National Labor Reform Party demanded an irredeemable paper currency, issued by the government "directly to the people." In the following year, William Allen, a noted "Greenbacker," was elected governor of Ohio upon a platform which apprehended danger to the debtor's interests from the resumption of specie payments, but did not demand a permanent paper currency. In 1874, the Democracy in this state called for a "sound currency," but wanted "an increase of the circulating medium," which should be secured by substituting government paper for the notes issued by national banks. The next year the platform denounced "the forced resump-

[1] 12 Wallace, 548, 553.
[2] Muhleman, 28 ; Rep. Mon. Com., 425.
[3] Rep. Mon. Com., 424–425 ; Noyes, 19–20.

tion of specie payments," and demanded that the
" volume of currency be made and kept equal to
the wants of trade"; and, after a close and excit-
ing contest, Rutherford B. Hayes, the Republican
candidate, was elected governor by a majority of
only 5000 votes.[1] This development of a movement in Ohio for a permanent paper currency is
typical of what occurred in several other states.
As a result, a National Greenback Party was organ-
ized for the presidential contest of 1876; and Peter
Cooper was nominated for the presidency upon a
platform that demanded national paper money, convertible into interest-bearing bonds.[2] In the fall
elections, 81,737 votes were cast for Cooper; and it
is interesting to notice that 66,000 of these came
from the states of the upper Mississippi Valley,
and 7187 from Pennsylvania. This, however, was
but the beginning of the movement; and the votes
cast in 1876 for the National Party by no means
represented the strength of the " greenback idea."

Two years later, in the Congressional elections,
the agitation for an irredeemable paper currency
reached its climax.[3] In several states a fusion was
effected between the National and the Democratic
parties, while in a great many others the Democratic platforms contained a more or less qualified

[1] For these various platforms, see Ann. Cyc., 1872, 773; 1873,
610–611 ; 1874, 667 ; 1875, 607.

[2] On the history of this party, see Andrews, Hist., I. 274–275,
286, 290–291 ; Leavitt ; Ann. Cyc., 1876–1884.

[3] See *Atl. Month.*, XLII. 521–530 ; Nat., XXI. 208–209, XXVII.
64, 221–222.

indorsement of the proposals of the inflationists.[1]
It is impossible to determine with any accuracy
the real strength of the movement in this year, on
account of the complication of issues that arose
when the Democratic organizations in many states
became infected with Greenback principles.[2] Andrews has placed the aggregate Greenback vote of
1878 at 1,000,365, while a Greenback writer states
it at 1,400,000.[3] In 1880, however, the issues were
once more clearly drawn, and the National Greenback party polled 307,740 votes.[4] Of these,
195,066 came from the upper Mississippi Valley;
60,019 came from the South; 35,778 came from
New York, Pennsylvania, New Jersey, and Delaware; 11,803 came from New England; and about
5000 came from the Pacific coast. This is probably the fairest test obtainable of the geographical
distribution of the inflationist votes, although the
elections of 1878 furnish a better test of the aggregate strength when the movement reached its
height. The results of our computations are sufficient to demonstrate that the real stronghold of
this Greenback movement was found in the newer
and more thinly populated regions of the West and

---

[1] Ann. Cyc., 1878.

[2] To assume that the total Democratic vote in those states where
the platform inclined in any degree toward a paper currency represents accurately the strength of the inflationists, would be wholly
unjustifiable. Thus, in Massachusetts, the large vote cast for
Butler was the result of his peculiar personal following.

[3] Andrews, Hist., I. 291 ; Leavitt, 224 ; Ann. Cyc., 1878, 808.

[4] Ann. Cyc., 1880, 702.

South, which, prior to 1860, had been supplied with a bank currency that was often nothing more than a form of irredeemable paper money. More will be said in the following chapter of the causes that produced this sectional distribution of the vote of the National Greenback Party.

After suffering disaster in the elections of 1874, the Republican Party passed the "Specie-Resumption Act" early in the following year before the control of Congress passed out of its hands.[1] Under this measure, skilful management of the Treasury Department and a favorable revival in trade enabled the government to resume specie payments in 1879. Congress seems to have exhausted its powers of unwisdom in efforts to obstruct the administration; but it finally became evident that the policy of resumption was certain to prove successful. Then the inflationists became alarmed at the prospect, and enacted the law of May 31, 1878.[2] This act prohibited the further cancellation of the greenbacks, which had been reduced to $346,681,000, and provided that, when redemption in specie should begin, the notes should not be withdrawn, but must be paid out again and kept in circulation. Thus the paper currency has remained with us, a permanent burden upon the Treasury and a constant menace to the business interests of the country.

---

[1] U. S. Stat., XVIII. 296 ; Tenth Census, VII. 389 ; Muhleman, 28–29 ; Noyes, 19–47 ; Rep. Mon. Com., 426–433.

[2] U. S. Stat., XX. 87 ; Muhleman, 28.

After 1880, interest in the agitation for a national paper currency died out for a time, only to be revived by the People's Party a decade later, in a movement that was most clearly conducted by the agricultural classes of the South and West, although a union was formed with the labor element in the cities of the East.[1] In 1892, Mr. Weaver was nominated for the presidency upon a platform that called for a national currency, "safe, sound, and flexible," to be issued by the government, and to have a volume of $50 per capita. This money was to be issued in payment for public improvements, and was also to be loaned to citizens at two per cent interest.[2] The exact vote cast by the People's Party in 1892 and 1894 is not easily determined, but a careful estimate places it at 879,469 votes in the former year and 1,434,253 in the latter.[3] Of these ballots, Maryland and the states north and east of her cast but 33,881 in 1892 and 53,717 in 1894.

[1] McVey ; *Q. J. E.*, X. 270–285.
[2] Ann. Cyc., 1892, 753–755.
[3] But see Ann. Cyc., 1892, 755, where Weaver's vote is placed at 1,122,045.

CHAPTER VIII

GOLD AND SILVER

THE agitation for the free coinage of the silver dollar forms the last chapter of the history of cheap money in the United States. In 1870, with a view to the resumption of specie payments, Congress began to consider the question of revising the coinage laws of the country. The silver dollar was then worth more than one dollar and two cents in gold,[1] and had been out of circulation for more than a generation. After deliberating upon the subject during five consecutive sessions, and securing expert advice, Congress passed the "Act of 1873."[2] This law, in accordance with a plan formulated three years before, dropped the obsolete silver dollar from the list of authorized coins.[3] Its deliberate intention, as stated repeatedly in Congress,[4] was to establish legally the single gold standard, upon which the currency of the country

[1] Stat. Abst., 1898, 56.
[2] U. S. Stat., XVII. 424; Laughlin, 98; Rep't Compt. Currency, 1876, 170.
[3] See report on the act, in Sen. Misc. Docs., 132; statement in Knox, 150; Rep't Dir. Mint, 1896, 461–573.
[4] Cong. Globe, 42d Cong., 2d Sess., 2305, 2306, 2308, 2310, 2316. Cf. speech by Senator Stewart, Cong. Globe, 43d Cong., 1st Sess., 1392, 1678.

had actually been based prior to the issue of the greenbacks in 1862. The measure aroused no opposition at the time because the inflationists felt no interest in a silver dollar that was worth more than gold, and were then concerned for the maintenance of a depreciated paper medium. But, in 1875, the "Resumption Act" was passed, while the value of silver fell, so that the silver dollar became cheaper than the gold. In 1876, when the time for the resumption of specie payments was approaching and the silver dollar was worth only ninety cents, it was discovered that a *crime* had been committed in 1873.[1] From that time to the present, the "remonetization" of silver has offered the best practicable method of securing a cheap medium of exchange.

In 1876, "Pig-iron Kelley," "Silver Dick Bland," and a number of other statesmen introduced in Congress bills that provided for the free coinage of the old silver dollar, and gave that coin unlimited legal tender power.[2] The following year, a free silver bill passed the House of Representatives, with the support of such modern "sound money men" as John G. Carlisle and William McKinley.[3] This measure was altered in the Senate so that it required the government to purchase a limited quantity of silver bullion each

---

[1] See Cong. Rec., VII. 205, 584, 1263, 1265, 1271. For a plausible statement of this charge, see Coin, 15–20. For milder criticism of the action of Congress, see Walker, Bimetallism, 184, 185.

[2] Cong. Rec., IV. 4704, 5186.   [3] *Idem*, VI. 241.

month, and coin it into silver dollars; and, in 1878, the amended act was finally passed over the courageous veto of President Hayes, who appreciated the folly of temporizing with the policy of the inflationists.[1]

The causes of the strong movement which secured the enactment of the "Bland-Allison Act," have been carefully analyzed by Professor Laughlin, in his "Bimetallism in the United States."[2] The inevitable reaction from the speculative activity and high prices of the era of paper-money inflation had resulted in a process of liquidation that involved the panic of 1873. The consequent period of depression was attended by most unpleasant consequences for all persons who had borrowed money on a rising market; and distress caused in this manner was especially prevalent in the West, where land speculation had been most active, and a large amount of mortgage indebtedness had been incurred. In the years following 1873, all the conditions were ripe for an inflationist movement, since debtors were clamorous for relief and there was an abundance of demagogues and invertebrate statesmen ready to lead such an agitation. This movement, moreover, was certain to assume a sectional character, because much Eastern capital had sought investment in the West, and the debtor party was most numerous in the

---

[1] U. S. Stat., XX. 25. On the history of this law, see Taussig, Silv. Sit., 8–49; Laughlin, 179–214; Noyes, 73–126.

[2] Laughlin, 186 *et seq.*

newer and poorer states. For this reason, the vote in the House of Representatives upon the original free coinage bill "was non-partisan and almost wholly sectional." "From districts west or south of Pennsylvania, only six votes were cast against the bill, two of these votes being cast by Democrats; from Pennsylvania and the districts east or north of it, the bill received only nine supporting votes, and three of the nine votes were Republican."[1]

An examination of the debates in Congress[2] discloses the fact that the arguments of the free silver men were generally pleas for currency expansion as a means of relief to oppressed debtors;[3] and threats were made that, if the measure failed to pass, the "Resumption Act" would be repealed, national banks would be destroyed, and the United States would begin to "issue all the money to be in circulation in the country." Mr. Bland was ready, in certain dire contingencies, to issue "paper money enough to stuff down the bondholders until they are sick," a sentiment that met with the applause of the House of Representatives. The "Crime of 1873" played its part in the discussions; members declared that no discrimination should be made against a great American product such as silver; one speaker invoked "the roar of maddened labor" sounding "like a trumpet-blast of

[1] Noyes, 40. Cf. *Harper's Weekly*, Nov. 24, 1877.
[2] Blaine, II. 605–608, summarizes the debate in the Senate.
[3] Cong. Rec., VII. 601, 602, 957, 958, 1244, 1264, 1265, 1279.

prophecy " ; and gold was denounced as "the money
of monarchs," the "idol of the miser and the
thief," the "most cowardly and treacherous of all
metals."[1]

Under the operation of this law, 378,160,000
silver dollars were coined at our mints;[2] but the
"friends of silver" were not satisfied. In 1890,
therefore, the "Sherman Act" was pushed through
Congress, as the price for which Western support
was secured for the tariff act of that year.[3] This
was most distinctly an inflationist measure, designed to increase the government's purchases of
silver to 4,500,000 ounces per month;[4] and the
arguments advanced in its favor were the same

---

[1] For these references, *in order*, see Cong. Rec., VII. 602, 1278;
1251; 584, 890, 1263, 1265, 1271; 926, 1251, 1271; 589; 1052.

[2] Muhleman, 21.

[3] U. S. Stat., XXVI. 289. Senator Sherman's statement that
the bill was passed to prevent the adoption of a free coinage law is
clearly erroneous. Sherman, II. 1061 *et seq.* Cf. *Amer. Hist. Rev.*,
I. 556. Mr. McKinley distinctly stated in the House of Representatives that the "Sherman Act" was the most favorable measure
for the silver cause that was obtainable, for, "we know we cannot
have free coinage now." Cong. Rec., XXI. 5812, 5813. There
seems to be evidence that President Harrison would have vetoed a
free coinage bill, and no such measure could have been passed over
his veto. Senator Teller gave what is probably the inside history
of the "Sherman Act," in his speech of April 29, 1896; and his
statement that Western members extorted silver legislation as the
price of their votes in favor of the tariff of 1890 passed unchallenged.
Cong. Rec., XXVIII. 4561, 4562.

[4] On the working of this act, see Taussig, Silv. Sit., 50–83; Noyes,
139–206; Muhleman, 31–33; White, 204–212; Rep. Mon. Com.,
138–145.

that had done service in 1878. Thus Representative McKinley, in closing the debate upon the law of 1890, argued,[1] that it was necessary "that the country should have an increase of its circulating medium"; that "the silver product of the United States" should be used for this purpose; that this would be "just to the silver producers of this country"; and that such action would create a demand for silver that would "so increase the value of that product" as to restore it to a parity with gold at the ratio of 16 to 1. The closing words of his speech were as follows: "For one, Mr. Speaker, I will not vote against this bill and thus deprive my people, my country, and the laborers, and the producers, and the industries of my country, of thirty millions annually of additional circulating medium." But this concession to the inflationist sentiment served merely to add fuel to the fires of the silver agitation. After three years of disastrous experience under its operation, the "Sherman Act" had to be repealed; and this action brought the free silver sentiment of the country to a climax, and precipitated the campaign of 1896.

It is unnecessary to review the events that attended the last presidential election, since they must be familiar to all the readers of this essay; but it will be desirable to study the geographical distribution of the silver and the gold parties. It will be remembered that, in 1877, the free silver

[1] Cong. Rec., XXI. 5812, 5813.

movement swept everything before it in all but six
of the Congressional districts west and south of
Pennsylvania; while the "Bland Act" received
only nine votes in the Keystone State and in all
districts north and east of it. By 1896, however,
the upper Mississippi Valley had undergone a
complete change in sentiment, and cast its votes
in favor of the maintenance of the existing gold
standard. The area controlled by the silver party
was pushed southward as far as Virginia, Tennessee, and Missouri; and westward as far as Kansas,
Nebraska, and South Dakota. Even within these
boundary lines, the states of North Dakota, California, and Oregon were lost to the cause of silver.

This survey of the recent inflationist movement
may be completed by a detailed examination of the
votes cast in 1896.[1] In making the analysis of the
results of that election, the following method has
been employed. The strength of the National
Democratic Party has been added to the votes
cast for the Republican candidate, and these figures have been taken as the correct measure of the
sentiment in favor of maintaining the existing conditions. Then the votes of the Democratic, the
National Prohibition, and the Socialist Labor parties have been combined, in order to determine the
true strength of the forces that favored inflation;
because the platforms of these parties advocated
either the free coinage of silver or a paper cur-

[1] The statistics of the vote cast in 1896 may be found in the
World Almanac.

rency issued directly by the government. The Prohibition Party has been omitted from the computation, for the reason that its platform ignored the question upon which the election turned. After this, the writer determined the percentage which the anti-inflation vote bears to the total vote of the five parties selected for consideration. In presenting the results, it will be convenient to divide the states into three groups according to their average density of population in the last census year.[1] The first group includes the eleven states of the greatest average density of population, and it will be seen that all of these were carried by the gold party, usually by an emphatic majority : —

STATES	AVERAGE DENSITY	PER CENT OF GOLD VOTE
Rhode Island .	. . . 318.44	. . . . . 71.9
Massachusetts	. . . 278.48	. . . . . 72.9
New Jersey	. . . . 193.82	. . . . . 62.3
Connecticut	. . . . 154.03	. . . . . 66.4
New York.	. . . . 126.06	. . . . . 59.5
Pennsylvania .	. . . 116.88	. . . . . 62.9
Maryland .	. . . . 105.72	. . . . . 56.9
Ohio	. . . . . . 90.10	. . . . . 52.3
Delaware	. . . . . 85.97	. . . . . 56.8
Illinois .	. . . . . 68.33	. . . . . 56.8
Indiana.	. . . . . 61.05	. . . . . 51.3

The second group includes eighteen states of a medium density of population, and these show a

[1] These statistics may be found in Eleventh Census, Population, I., p. XXXV. Another table containing the results of some slight corrections may be found in Willcox, 395. In this computation Willcox's figures have been used.

fairly even division of sentiment, eight casting a majority vote in favor of the gold standard, and ten showing a majority in favor of silver or paper:

STATES	AVERAGE DENSITY	PER CENT OF GOLD VOTE
Kentucky	46.47	50.5
Tennessee	42.34	47.5
New Hampshire	41.81	73.5
Virginia	41.27	47.0
Missouri	38.98	45.7
South Carolina	38.16	14.6
Michigan	36.46	55.6
Vermont	36.39	83.1
Iowa	34.47	56.6
North Carolina	33.30	47.1
Georgia	31.15	39.9
Wisconsin	31.10	61.9
West Virginia	30.95	53.0
Alabama	29.36	31.9
Mississippi	27.83	8.8
Louisiana	24.63	23.6
Maine	22.11	70.3
Arkansas	21.27	25.2

The third group comprises sixteen states with the least density of population, and it will be noticed that only four of these cast a majority vote in favor of the gold standard: —

STATES	AVERAGE DENSITY	PER CENT OF GOLD VOTE
Kansas	17.48	48.2
Minnesota	16.54	58.3
Nebraska	13.83	47.3
Texas	8.52	31.7
California	7.78	52.1

States	Average Density	Per Cent of Gold Vote
Florida	7.22	26.7
Washington	5.34	44.0
South Dakota	4.54	49.8
Colorado	3.99	13.9
Oregon	3.36	51.6
North Dakota	2.72	56.0
Utah	2.56	17.3
Idaho	1.05	21.4
Montana	.98	19.7
Wyoming	.64	48.5
Nevada	.43	18.7

It is evident, therefore, that the inflationist movement at the present day, as in all previous times, finds its strength in the sparsely settled regions where the scarcity of capital is most keenly experienced.

Since this essay is dealing only with certain underlying and fundamental facts in the monetary history of the United States, it is unnecessary to enter into a discussion of all the forces that have contributed to produce the agitation for the free coinage of silver.[1] It suffices for the present purpose to demonstrate that the silver movement is primarily a continuation of the old struggle which the debtor classes in the sparsely populated districts have waged persistently in behalf of a cheap form of currency. In this respect, the similarity between the silver agitation and the greenback movement is perfect, whether one considers many

[1] On this subject see Walker, Bimetallism, 217–219; *J. P. E.*, I. 163–178; *Q. J. E.*, X. 269–295.

of the arguments advanced or the sections in which popular support has been found. But it should be added, in order to avoid misapprehension, that other causes contributed to produce the persistent strength of the sentiment in favor of the free coinage of silver. The continued fall of prices for more than twenty years caused undoubted injustice to many debtors, and furnished telling facts in support of inflationist arguments. Many fair-minded men found it hard to choose between the evils of a single silver standard and the hardships of the existing situation. A second cause may be found in the political influence of the owners of silver mines, who have taken an active part in spreading the propaganda of the silver party, and have furnished a large part of the needful sinews of war. Then, since 1889, seven sparsely settled states have been admitted to the Union, and have added fourteen votes to the strength of the free silver element in the Senate. In 1896, these states cast twenty of their electoral votes for Mr. Bryan, and only three for Mr. McKinley.

If this essay has portrayed and interpreted correctly the monetary history of the United States, one important conclusion may be drawn concerning the probable future of the agitation for a cheap form of currency. If the scarcity of capital in sparsely settled areas has been hitherto the primary cause for the persistent demand for barter currencies, paper money, and a depreciating metallic medium of exchange, such a movement must gradually subside with the growth of numbers, wealth, and diversified industries in the regions that now form the seat of the silver party. Only a few generations have passed since this agitation was effectually quieted in the Northern Atlantic states. Within the last twenty years, the valley of the upper Mississippi has been won from its adherence to the old propaganda. The area that will henceforth feel the lack of ready capital, and desire some cheap form of money, cannot be greatly increased by the admission of new states. Each passing decade will tend to remove the causes that now contribute to the strength of the silver movement in the extreme South and West. An improvement of banking facilities in these regions would contribute materially to the accomplishment of this result. In periods of great industrial depression, especially in times of distress and discontent among the agricultural classes, the familiar nostrums will still be proposed, and the demand for "more money" may be renewed for a long time to come. But, in the absence of some great industrial cataclysm, there will be a continual narrowing of the field within which the agitation for a cheap currency can hope to secure any large measure of popular support.

Part II

THE PAPER CURRENCY OF NORTH CAROLINA

CHAPTER I

EARLY ISSUES (1712–1748)

THE early settlers in North Carolina, like those in other colonies, were driven by their poverty to resort to the use of a barter currency. In 1709, Rev. William Gordon wrote: "In this as in all other parts of the province, there is no money; every one buys and pays with their commodities, of which corn, pork, pitch, and tar are the chief." The prices of these articles were fixed by law, but at figures that a person could seldom secure for them "after considerable expense and risk." The result was that three shillings of this barter money were reckoned as no better than one shilling sterling.[1] The lords proprietors naturally enough objected to receiving such a medium in payment of quit rents, and instructed the receiver general to demand sterling money upon all occasions. In 1713, the receiver represented to the council of the province that he could not comply strictly with this requirement, and was advised to accept "any Good and Merchantable Commoditys of this country at ye rated price."[2] The council further expressed the opinion that rice well-dressed and cleaned, when

[1] This letter is reprinted in Hawks, II. 309.
[2] Col. Recs. N. C., II. 34–35.

accepted at the rate of 17s. 6d. per cwt. "is ye true value of Sterl. money."

An enactment of 1715 made seventeen leading commodities a tender for debts.[1] These staple articles were not receivable, however, unless in good condition; and special contracts were excepted from the operation of the law.[2] A few years later three other commodities were added to the list, and the ratings of wheat and corn were raised; while it was provided that five of the most bulky articles must be delivered at some convenient landing upon a navigable stream.[3] Governor Burrington claimed that when this last enactment was made, rice was valued at a rate that led to a depreciation of the commodity standard.[4] In 1731, he said, concerning the practical working of the act of 1715, that, however accurate the original rating of the goods may have been, it soon became incorrect and unequal; so that, for instance, while deer skins had remained at about the value fixed by the law, pitch and tar had fallen to one-quarter of the legal valuation.[5] The result was that "People generally take advantage to pay in the worst Commodity which often occasions unfairness in Trade and Dealings." Burrington expressed the belief that the law was especially liable "to perplex

---

[1] Records, III. 185, IV. 292, 920–921; Basset, 60. On the incomplete and fragmentary nature of the early records of the colony, see Records, I., pp. III.–V.

[2] *Idem*, IV, 292. Cf. Williamson, I. 163; Hawks, II. 163–164.

[3] Records, IV. 293.   [4] *Idem*, III. 615.

[5] *Idem*, III. 185. Cf. p. 615.

strangers tradeing," and to encourage frauds in such cases.

In 1750, Governor Johnston stated that payment of the provincial taxes in produce had continued "with very little Alteration" of these earlier laws, and that this had resulted in "great Damage to the Revenue," since it was "a stated rule, that of so many Commodities the worst sort only were paid." [1] The people of the colony, however, clung persistently to the practice, despite the governor's complaints.[2] Even the quit rents had to be collected in this barter currency,[3] since the only alternative would probably have been a complete non-payment of these unpopular dues, which were always in arrears at the best.

North Carolina for various reasons long remained an extremely poor colony, and was slower in developing an extensive commerce than many of her neighbors.[4] For this reason specie would

[1] Records, IV. 920–921. Cf. the opinion of Governor Burrington, III. 185.

[2] Johnston called it "an odious sham method of supporting the Charges of Government." Records, IV. 923.

[3] Johnston wrote in 1740 that the colonists insisted "on paying their Rents in the worst and most bulky kind of their produce," and they insisted on paying these "hopefull Commodities" either at their houses or at forty-two different landings. Yet he thought it was impossible to abolish the practice entirely. Records, IV. 415. In 1738, the Board of Trade inquired into the matter particularly, and found that the practice had been forced upon the collectors. Records, IV. 294.

[4] See Basset, 14, 15. Hawks, II. 252–289, gives an account of the trade of the province.

have been scarce even without the influence of the barter and paper currencies that were introduced. Yet coins and plate are sometimes mentioned in the early laws. In 1715, an act was passed "ascertaining the currency of Dollars," and Governor Burrington states that this was intended "to bring Dollars into the Country";[1] but, he adds, "it never had the effect." This enactment probably rated "the Lion dollar" at three bushels of Indian corn.[2] Since a law of the same year rated corn at 1*s.* 8*d.* per bushel,[3] this was equivalent to a rating of 5*s.* for the lion dollar, which was worth but 3*s.* 7.7*d.* sterling.[4] This was a little more than the one-third advance over sterling allowed by the royal proclamation of 1704 and the act of 1707. Hawks states that another provincial law of this period provides for the distribution of silver plate forming part of estates belonging to orphans.[5] In 1724, Governor Burrington was instructed to enforce the statute of 1707 relating to the valuation of foreign coins;[6] but in 1729, after the paper currency had fallen to one-fifth of the value of sterling, silver

[1] Records, III. 18.

[2] I assume that this is the law mentioned by Hawks, II. 164. Mr. Hawks evidently examined the manuscript copies of the laws of 1715.

[3] Records, IV. 292.

[4] Sir Isaac Newton assayed the lion dollar of Holland at 14 dwts. 2.7 g. fine contents, and valued it at 43.7*d.* sterling. See Postlethwayt, I. 523; Chalmers, 67.

[5] Hawks, II. 174.

[6] This statement is made on the authority of Martin, I. 295.

was rated at 25s. per ounce,[1] which was nearly five times the sterling rating of 5s. 2d. per ounce. At the same time gold was rated at £1 per dwt., which would give a ratio of 16:1 between the white and the yellow metals.

North Carolina resorted to paper money for the first time in 1712 in order to "defray the Charges of an Indian War then kindled."[2] Taxes had been levied for this purpose, but £4000 of bills were issued in order to anticipate the work of collection.[3] The notes bore interest, and were to be redeemed at stated times out of the receipts from the taxes.[4] They seem also to have been made a legal tender for all payments in which the rated commodities were receivable.[5] But the Indians remained troublesome, and the war continued; so that an issue of £8000 was made in 1713,[6] probably upon the same terms as that of the previous year.[7] From a report made in 1740[8] we learn

---

[1] Hawks, II. 286.

[2] Records, I. 838, III. 145, IV. 576.

[3] *Idem*, III. 484.   [4] *Idem*, III. 145, 484.

[5] The Records state merely that this first issue was made "Current in all payments." III. 145. But the issue of 1713 was made "passable for all debts for rated commodities of the country." II. 50. This was probably the case with the first issue.

[6] Records, II. 50, IV. 576. The historians have erroneously stated that this was the first emission. Williamson, I. 205; Martin, I. 264; Hawks, II. 280. On these early issues see also Records, II. pp. IV.–V.

[7] Records, II. 50; Martin, II. 264-265; Williamson, I. 205.

[8] Records, IV. 576. Williamson says that these bills depreciated. History, I. 205.

that this emission "depreciated the value of the whole" about forty per cent, a fact that is not surprising since the population of the colony at this time was less than 10,000[1] and the total amount of paper in circulation was £12,000, equal to $40,000.[2]

In 1715,[3] a new issue of £24,000 was ordered.[4] One-half of this sum was to be used for retiring the £12,000 then in circulation, and the remainder was applied to the payment of public debts. Holders of the old bills were required to bring them in for exchange before March 25, 1716, after which date the notes should "be of no value." Two years' interest was to be paid on the old bills thus exchanged. The new issue was made legal tender "for any of the rated Commodities of the

---

[1] In 1717, Colonel Pollock estimated the number of "tithables" at 2000, which would give 9000 or 10,000 as the total population, black and white. Records, II., p. V. All estimates of this character are mere approximations to the truth, but are the best that are possible.

[2] I assume that the proclamation rates prevailed in North Carolina at this time. This accords with the rating of the lion dollar at 5s. in 1715. At proclamation rates the colonial pound was $3.33.

[3] There may be some uncertainty as to the date of this enactment. The report of 1740 places it at 1714, and says the bills were continued by an act of 1715. Records, IV. 576. The editor of the Records makes the date 1714. See II., p. V. On the other hand, Governor Burrington in 1733 gives 1715 as the date. Records, III. 485. Hawks, who examined the manuscript records, gives the same date. History, II. 280. The text of the act itself seems to point to the year 1715. See Records, III. 178–179.

[4] This act is preserved. Records, III. 177–179. Extracts are given by Hawks. History, II. 280–281.

Country or other Money allowing fifty per cent between the same and sterling." Probably the intention of the law was to make the paper equal to the barter currency of the colony, which was below sterling and was called "Proclamation money,"[1] since £150 colonial was reckoned by the men who framed this law as equal to £100 sterling.[2] This may be taken as the base from which to compute the depreciation of the paper. To this tender law was added a forcing clause which provided that any one who refused the paper at fifty per cent advance over sterling, should forfeit one-half the value of the sum refused; while a later section enacted that any member of the assembly who should thereafter make any motion judged to be "derogatory and prejudicial to the Publick Credit of the said Bills," should be denounced as an enemy to the country and fined twenty pounds. Martin justly observes that a proposal to issue more bills was not considered to be a remark of this character.[3] Finally, the law of 1715 enacted that any person convicted of counterfeiting the

---

[1] See Records, III. 615, where Governor Burrington refers to the rated commodities as "Proclamation money."

[2] The standard of value in North Carolina was the barter shilling or pound, before paper was issued. We have seen that in New England the barter money was worth only two-thirds as much as specie. Bronson, 21. Then £150 colonial would equal £100 sterling. This may well have been the rate of exchange for the best commodities in North Carolina. Commonly the barter currency was at a greater discount. Hawks, II. 309.

[3] History, I. 293.

bills should be punished "as guilty of Felony without the benefit of Clergie." The new bills bore no interest, and no time was set for their redemption.[1] The legislature, however, in the same year levied a tax on polls and land, which was intended to bring in £2000 annually "till the Publick Debts are answered and paid." At the same time a pledge was made that the tax should not be lowered or repealed, and that no more bills should be emitted, until all of the outstanding paper should be retired.[2]

These earliest acts for issuing paper money illustrate perfectly the usual course of legislation upon the subject. The first emission was small, and it bore interest and was redeemable at stated periods. It was justified, furthermore, as an emergency measure. But the needs of the government did not decrease, and the legislature made a new emission twice as large as the first. This caused a depreciation of forty per cent. The next steps were to cure the inflation by issuing twice as much money as was already in circulation, to make the new bills redeemable at no definite time, and to pay no interest upon the notes emitted. Then, under the pretext of supporting the credit of the bills, a forcing law was passed to compel creditors to receive the paper, which was already depreciated. Finally, a tax was levied which would, if collected, make it possible to retire the notes in

[1] Cf. Records, III. 485.
[2] Idem, III. 189, 485. Cf. Martin, I. 275.

ten years; and the legislature pledged the public faith to issue no more paper, and to keep the tax in operation as long as it might be needed. We shall see how these promises were kept, and what such a pledge of the public faith was worth.

But doubling the amount of the currency did not improve its condition, for in 1717 Colonel Eden reported it to be "at a vast discount,"[1] while four years later it was reported at 150 per cent advance over sterling.[2]   Accordingly, as a further support to the credit of the paper, the assembly petitioned the proprietors of the province to receive the bills in payment of the rent for lands; but this request was refused, although the proprietors expressed a willingness to receive the rated commodities of the country instead of specie,[3] for these articles could be transported to England. Colonel Pollock thought that the bills would become "very current in a short time" if they could be used in these payments.[4]   For a time the tax levied in 1715 seems to have been collected, and some of the paper seems to have been retired, in

[1] Records, II. 270. The report of 1740 says that the bills issued in 1715 depreciated eight per cent " from the value of their first emission." *Idem*, IV. 576. This can hardly be correct in the face of the other evidence.

[2] *Idem*, II. 417. This meant that £100 sterling was equal to £250 colonial.

[3] *Idem*, II. 243-244, 250; Williamson, I. 205-206. It is possible that some payments may have been made in paper after all. See Remarks of Burrington, III. 145.

[4] Records, II. 296.

accordance[1] with the pledge made at that time. But, as Governor Burrington wrote,[2] "that Faith was afterwards broke in upon." The tax had called for 15*s.* per poll and 2*s.* 6*d.* for every hundred acres of land.[3] In 1722, the legislature committed "the first public breach of the Funds laid for sinking the bills," and reduced this tax to 5*s.* per poll.[4]

By this time it was estimated that about £12,000 of the bills of 1715 were yet outstanding;[5] while, if the annual tax of £2000 had been faithfully collected and applied to the proper purpose, the notes in circulation could not have exceeded £10,000. A new emission of £12,000 was now (1722) voted in order to exchange the old bills, which were said to be torn and defaced.[6] These new notes were to be a legal tender at fifty per cent advance on sterling in all contracts where payment in specie was not expressly required, and holders of the old money were given a few months in which to effect an exchange of old for new bills.[7] Counterfeiting was

[1] Records, III. 485, IV. 576. In 1717 Pollock said that the bills then outstanding amounted to no more then £16,000. *Idem*, II. 296. But this seems to be too small a figure, because the tax levied in 1715 to sink the £24,000 then issued amounted to only £2000 annually, if collected.

[2] *Idem*, III. 145.

[3] *Idem*, III. 189.

[4] *Idem*, III. 190, 485. Hawks describes this law. History, II. 282.

[5] Records, II. 485, IV. 576; Hawks, II. 282.

[6] Records, III. 190, 485, IV. 576.

[7] These facts are taken from Hawks, II. 282. Cf. Martin, I. 293.

again made a capital offence. The consequence
of this legislation was that from 1722 to 1729 the
bills of credit circulated "at the proportion of five
for one sterling,"[1] a result which probably was not
regretted by the men who made the paper legal
tender at a rating of 1.5 to 1. It appears, moreover, that no more bills were cancelled after 1722;[2]
but that the assembly, when bills were drawn in
through payments of the poll tax of five shillings,
"usually ordered them to be pay'd — out again,"
for contingent expenses.[3] Thus the public faith
was continually broken, in a manner not uncom-
mon in the colonies.

For the reasons just stated there were in circulation, in the year 1729, fully[4] £12,000 of bills
issued prior to 1716 and reemitted in 1722. The
assembly had succeeded in preventing a contraction of the redundant currency, although Governor
Burrington is said to have received instructions in
1724 to have the paper redeemed and cancelled.[5]
Not content with this, the inflationists took advantage of the prospective transfer of the province
from the proprietors to the Crown to secure a

[1] Records, IV. 576.

[2] Idem, III. 190.

[3] Idem, III. 485–486.

[4] In 1729, the assembly estimated that £2000 of the currency
had been lost, and that only £10,000 was in circulation. Idem,
III. 190, IV. 576. But the £2000 finally proved to be in the
hands of citizens. Idem, IV. 101–102.

[5] This is Martin's statement. History, I. 295. I have been
unable to find Burrington's instructions of an earlier date than 1730.
See Records, III. 66.

large addition to the bills of credit. The last proprietary governor, foreseeing that he would soon
have to leave his position, is said[1] to have been
induced, "by a shameful collusion" with the legislature, to consent to an issue of £40,000.[2] Of
this sum, £10,000 was to be exchanged for the
old bills emitted in 1722 and still in circulation, all
of which must be brought in within a certain time.
The remainder, amounting to £30,000, was to be
loaned to the inhabitants upon the security of mortgages on unincumbered lands of double the value
of each loan. The bills were apportioned among
the precincts according to the number of tithables
in each, and placed in the hands of the precinct
treasurers. One-fifteenth of the principal of each
loan was to be repaid annually, with interest at a
little more than six per cent. Twenty shillings of
the new currency were to be rated at 15 dwts. of
silver. This was four times the rating of silver in
Virginia,[3] which the legislature took for a basis,
and is an admission of a depreciation of four to
one proclamation money, or more than five to one
sterling.[4] Existing obligations were to be settled

---

[1] This is Williamson's statement. History, II. 38.

[2] Records, III. 145, 175, IV. 178, 419, 576. Cf. Martin, I. 301;
Williamson, II. 37–39. Hawks gives a long account of this law,
but gives 1727 as the date. History, II. 282–287.

[3] An act of 1727 in Virginia had rated silver at 4*d.* per dwt.
Hening, Stat., IV. 218.

[4] Since silver was worth 5*s.* 2*d.* per oz. according to the sterling
standard, this would make exchange about £517 North Carolina
currency to £100 sterling. Cf. Records, IV. 419.

according to the usage at the time when they were incurred, but future contracts were to be in terms of these bills. If the new currency should depreciate, the legislature was annually to ascertain and declare the value of twenty shillings of bills in terms of silver. The notes were declared a legal tender at the specified ratings, and fourteen of the rated commodities were given new values in terms of this new currency, while silver was rated at 25s. per ounce.[1]

Thus was established a loan bank system such as had been introduced in several other colonies, and it was computed that the interest and principal would amount to £45,000 at the end of fifteen years. This would redeem all the bills emitted in 1729, and leave a surplus of £5000 available for the current expenses of the government, which thus expected to derive direct pecuniary benefit from the scheme.[2] Since the population of North Carolina must have been, in 1729, considerably less than 36,000,[3] and the trade of the province was not large, a further depreciation of the paper ensued. By 1731, exchange was[4] at £700 or £800 provincial currency for £100 sterling, and the gov-

---

[1] These figures are given by Hawks, II. 286. The rating of 25s. per ounce for silver is inconsistent with the rating of 20s. of the bills at 15 dwts. of silver.

[2] See Records, IV. 178–179 ; Hawks, II. 285. For a copy of one of these bills see Hawks, II. 280.

[3] In 1732, the population was estimated at 30,000 whites and 6000 blacks. Records, II., p. XVII.

[4] *Idem*, III. 146.

ernor could call the paper "worse than any of the commoditys."[1]   The royal officials in the colony suffered from this advance in exchange on London, since their salaries had been fixed before the bills had been emitted.[2]   When the assembly voted a salary of £100 in paper for the chief justice of the province, the governor asked for an increase, stating that £800 in currency would be worth but £100 sterling.   The assembly replied that exchange was, in their opinion, only £500 for £100, and that the salary would suffice.[3]   Williamson has spoken very forcibly concerning this enactment of 1729.   He says:[4]   "Although every man in the colony saw that too much paper was in circulation, for it passed below the nominal value, excuses were formed, once and again, for making more."   "Of all the varieties of fraud that have been practised by men, who call themselves honest, and wish to preserve a decent appearance, none has been more frequent, in legislative bodies, than the attempt to pass money for more than its proper value.   There are men who conceive, that crimes lose their stain, when the offenders are numerous ; that in the character of legislators, they cannot be rogues, ' *defendit numerus.*'   There are men, who would be ashamed to acquire five

[1] Records, III. 185.

[2] *Idem*, III, 271, 309.

[3] *Idem*, III. 283.   Burrington wrote the Lords of Trade that he had offered to take silver at 8 for 1, but only one man had been willing to pay the governor's fees at that rate.   *Idem*, III. 208.

[4] History, II. 38, 39, 40.

shillings by stealing, picking a pocket, or robbing on the highway; but they would freely, and without blushing, assist in passing a law to defraud their creditor out of half his just demand. There are instances of men being banished from Carolina for stealing a hog, not worth five dollars; while the men who banished them, would contend for paying a debt of seven pounds with the value of twenty shillings."

Since the act of 1729 was passed just after the surrender of the province to the Crown, and had been approved by the proprietary governor, the assembly managed to get the new bills into circulation at once; and thus secured the best of the argument when the validity of the law was called in question by the royal governor.[1]   In 1730, Burrington, who had come out as governor, received instructions to approve no more bills for issuing paper money unless they contained a clause suspending their operation until the royal assent had been secured; and his successor was given similar directions.[2]   As happened elsewhere, frauds were committed in the valuation of lands, and bills were loaned upon inadequate security.[3]   Then, too, when the precinct treasurers in 1734 were ordered to render accounts and produce the money paid in for interest and annual instalments of the principal, they turned in only one-tenth of the amount

[1] Records, III. 146, 175, 486, IV. 179.
[2] *Idem*, III. 95, 498.
[3] *Idem*, III. 145.

actually due.[1] Of the £12,000 of old notes issued
prior to 1729, £9555 were exchanged for new
bills by 1731, and were subsequently burnt.[2] The
£2000 of old bills that were assumed to be lost in
1729 turned up in the hands of the receiver of the
powder duties six years later, and were exchanged
for new currency.[3]

When the assembly of North Carolina met in
January, 1735, the governor called its attention to
the bad state of the currency, caused by the counterfeiters who seemed to be industriously at work.[4]
The assembly readily agreed to remedy this evil at
once,[5] and proceeded to prepare an act for exchanging the old bills for new. If the annual
instalments of one-fifteenth of the £30,000 loaned
in 1729 had been punctually paid with interest, at
least £16,000 of the £40,000 emitted would have
been returned by the end of 1734. Such payments, however, had not been made in many cases;
and the receivers had turned in only one-tenth of
the money then due.[6] But under the law as it
stood, the annual instalments of the principal
were due, and should be retired from circulation.
Accordingly the assembly seized upon the gov-

[1] Records, IV. 179.

[2] *Idem*, III. 324, 546, 583.

[3] *Idem*, IV. 101–102.

[4] *Idem*, IV. 78. The severe penalties of the early laws had
been continued by the act of 1729. Hawks, II. 286. In 1726, an
indictment was found against a counterfeiter. Records, II. 669.

[5] *Idem*, IV. 82.

[6] *Idem*, IV. 179.

ernor's proposal to remedy the evils of counterfeiting, as an excuse for preventing the withdrawal
of any of the bills then in circulation. The pretext
for this action was that large arrears of quit rents
were due, and could not be paid without the currency.[1] An act was passed,[2] therefore, providing
that all the money due and to fall due on the principal of the loan of 1729 should be let out again at
six per cent interest for the space of ten years, at
which time the original fifteen years would expire
and the entire sum loaned would become due.
This law provided, also, that, in order to remedy
counterfeiting, all the notes outstanding should
be brought in and exchanged for new bills. The
notes of this issue were not made a legal ·tender
at any fixed rate,[3] and it was probably intended
to have valuations of the currency fixed from time
to time. Governor Johnston wrote to the Board
of Trade[4] that this enactment "was intended purely
for the benefit of the Inhabitants of the Province
that they might be certain of at least a Currency
of £40,000 for Ten years to come." By means of
it the assembly made impossible the gradual retirement of the paper, and so shaped matters that
at the end of ten years the whole sum of £40,000
would be legally subject to retirement. Since

[1] Records, IV. 179, 576–577.
[2] *Idem*, IV. 179–180, 419. In a report made in 1740 the date
is erroneously given as 1734. *Idem*, IV. 576–577. Martin makes
the same error. History, II. 18.
[3] Records, IV. 419. Cf. p. XXII.
[4] *Idem*, IV. 179.

there was absolutely no prospect that any subsequent legislature would consent to the immediate retirement of the entire currency, it seems probable that the law of 1735 was intended to make certain the permanence of the paper money.

But while the assembly was at work on this subject, it did not stop with providing for the continued circulation of the amount of currency already outstanding. The commissioners appointed to stamp the bills were authorized[1] to manufacture £2500 more "to defray the Charges" of the operation. Then ways and means had to be devised for paying various debts amounting to £14,150. Since the governor considered it "absolutely necessary these debts should be paid off as soon as possible," he consented to an emission of £10,000 in bills of credit, which were to be sunk by a poll tax which should continue in operation for five years.[2] Thus the currency of the province was increased to £52,500; whereas, if the law of 1729 had been enforced in good faith, the issues outstanding would have been reduced to less than £24,000 by 1735. By this time the population of the province was about 50,000, whites and blacks;[3] and the

---

[1] Records, IV. 179–180.

[2] *Idem*, IV. 108, 179–180, 419. The report of 1740 says that £1250 were emitted. IV. 577. This is clearly a clerical error, and £12,500 is meant. This is the sum of the two emissions mentioned in this paragraph.

[3] In 1735, the whites alone were estimated at 40,000. *Idem*, II., p. XVII. Mr. Saunders estimates the total population at 50,000 in 1734. *Idem*, IV., p. XX.

circulating medium, therefore, amounted to about $3.50 *per capita*.[1] This was a large sum for such a poor colony, but not a larger relative amount than was outstanding in 1729. Exchange on London was at six hundred per cent advance over sterling in 1736,[2] which would make £700 colonial equal to £100 sterling.

Meanwhile the governor and assembly had become involved in a dispute concerning the payment of the quit rents.[3] Governor Johnston insisted that, if rated commodities were tendered in these payments, they should be delivered at four convenient places; whereas the people insisted that the articles could be tendered on the land where the rents accrued, and thus endeavored to throw the heavy costs of transportation on to the government. But, more than this, Johnston announced[4] that he would receive payment in sterling money or in bills of credit *at ratings fixed by his council.* The assembly protested vigorously, but without effect; and then tried unsuccessfully to pass a law providing that the value of the bills of credit should be determined yearly by the governor and delegates from each branch of the legislature.[5] The governor then endeavored to secure the

[1] This is computed upon the basis of proclamation rating, which gives $3.33 to the pound.

[2] Records, IV. 225. This is the estimate of the provincial council, and may be less than the actual rate of depreciation.

[3] This dispute was an old one. See Records, III. 541, 548-549.

[4] On this subject see Records, IV., pp. XIV-XVIII.

[5] *Idem*, IV. 175-185.

passage of orders in council authorizing him to settle the rates at which paper money or rated commodities should be received.[1] The dispute continued until 1739, when an act was passed providing that the governor, council, and delegates from the assembly should "regulate the value" of the bills annually.[2] In March, 1739, the depreciation was fixed, in accordance with this law, at £1000 colonial currency for £100 sterling.[3] Since the delegates of the assembly participated in this action, it is probable that a depreciation of ten to one was too patent to be denied.[4]

There is a statement to the effect that in 1738 the members of the legislature applied to the payment of their own salaries interest money received from the bills emitted in 1735, although these funds had

[1] Records, IV. 205. In 1737, the assembly ordered that collectors of the quit rents should be arrested for compelling people to pay in the manner desired by the governor. *Idem*, IV. 272. Cf. Williamson, II. 41–43. The governor dissolved the assembly.

[2] Records, IV. 416, 419.

[3] *Idem*, IV. 416, 419, 577. Governor Johnston said that the bills had previously been accepted at seven for one, and that the valuation of 1739 would increase the revenue. *Idem*, IV. 416. This law of 1739 was disallowed by the Crown, and the entire controversy was reopened in 1741. This continued for eight years before another quit rent act could be passed. *Idem*, IV., pp. XVII–XVIII.

[4] Williamson, II. 38–39, gives some statistics of depreciation. He states the depreciation at $3\frac{1}{2}$ for 1 in 1730 and $7\frac{1}{2}$ for 1 in 1739. The reader must notice, however, that this relates to the exchange between paper and proclamation, or barter, currency. This was only two-thirds the value of sterling; and with this allowance, Williamson's figures are nearly like those given here.

been pledged for sinking the bills.[1] However this may be, it is certain that a violation of all good faith was committed in 1739. In February of that year the commissioners appointed for exchanging the bills of 1729 for those issued in 1735 reported that, out of the £40,000 of old notes, £37,849 had been replaced by bills of the last emission.[2] This left a balance of new bills which the legislature ordered to be issued "in order to discharge the Publick debts of this Province."[3] It turned out that these "Publick debts" were the wages of the legislators themselves; and the lower house, in asking the concurrence of the upper chamber in this action, admitted[4] that the balance in question "ought to be applyd (by Acts of Assembly) to other purposes," so that the proposal might "be deemed a violation of the Publick faith." The council without delay passed this resolution, which is actually termed in the minutes of the assembly "a message" "in relation to the payment of the wages of the Members of Assembly out of other funds than are or ought to be appropriated for said use."[5] Thus it appears that a legislature of manufacturers of paper money could not only violate the public faith for personal ends, but could do this openly and deliberately with a brazen effrontery that would make a highwayman blush.

In 1739, Dr. William Douglass wrote, concerning the currency of the colony, the following

---

[1] Records, III. 185.   [2] *Idem*, IV. 367, 370–371, 398–399.
[3] *Idem*, IV. 399.   [4] *Idem*, IV. 409.   [5] *Idem*, IV. 413.

words :[1] " North Carolina, an inconsiderable Colony scarce capable of any Fund for Paper Emissions; have notwithstanding 40,000*l.* upon *Loan,* and 12,500*l.* upon Funds of *Taxes.* At present Exchange is settled by their legislature at 10 *North Carolina for I Sterling.*" It will be seen that this statement is correct, except that the amount "upon Loan " was £30,000.[2]

In 1740, Great Britain having become involved in war with Spain,[3] North Carolina was called upon to take part in an expedition against Florida.[4] The assembly promptly resolved " that a certain Quantity of New Bills will be the most speedy way to defray the Expenses of transporting the Troops to be raised in this colony," but the governor refused assent,[5] since his instructions forbade him to approve of a law for issuing bills of credit unless it contained " a suspending Clause " providing that it should not go into effect until " his Majesty's pleasure should be known." Accordingly a tax was levied[6] and made payable in rated commodities or in bills of credit at the ratio of £7.5 in paper for £1 in proclamation money.[7]

[1] Douglass, Discourse, 316–317.

[2] This error was natural since the entire amount emitted in 1729 and reëmitted in 1735 was £40,000, of which £30,000 was loaned. Cf. Records, IV. 178–179.

[3] Winsor, V. 381–385; Hildreth, II. 376–377.

[4] Records, IV. 552, 553.   [5] *Idem,* IV. 557.

[6] *Idem,* IV. 558, 574.

[7] The Records contain only one allusion to this provision, and that mentions a rate of 7 for 1. But the bill was amended several

It was estimated that this levy would bring in a sum equivalent to £1200 sterling.[1] The colony was now to receive a striking demonstration of the disadvantages of its barter and paper currencies. When an effort was made to secure transportation for the four hundred men raised in North Carolina, "no owners of Vessels cared to take their Paper Currency and Commodities in Payment."[2] The governor then found that bills of exchange on London could not be negotiated in the province, so that he was obliged to draw upon the commissioners of the royal navy in order to raise passage money for the troops.[3]

In 1740, Governor Johnston had written that the £52,500[4] then outstanding was equivalent to no more than £5000 sterling, that it would be retired in 1745 in accordance with the existing law, and that he hoped "after that we shall never more be

times after that. Martin and Williamson state that the rate was 7.5 for 1, and I have accepted this statement. Martin, II. 34; Williamson, II. 55–56. Proclamation money was, of course, the pound or shilling of North Carolina's barter currency. Since this was worth only two-thirds as much as sterling, a rating of £7.5 paper for £1 barter, or proclamation, currency was the same as £11.25 paper for £1 sterling.

[1] Records, IV. 421.

[2] *Idem.*

[3] *Idem.*

[4] This statement omits the balance of something more than £2000 which the assembly had paid out for its own wages in 1739 instead of using for the redemption of old bills. The balance was stated by the commissioners as £3300 ; but this cannot be correct, as they had redeemed £37,879 out of £40,000 of the former issues. *Idem,* IV. 398–399.

plagued with any Paper money."[1] But the legislature was of a different mind. In 1744, when
under the existing law the whole batch of paper
had but one more year to remain in circulation, the
governor called the matter to the attention of the
assembly.[2] The lower house proposed to "sink
the Bills of Currency" by replacing them with a
new issue.[3] The contemplated emission was to
be for £16,000, "equal in value to Proclamation
money."[4] Since the £52,500 of bills then in
circulation were worth no more than £5000 sterling, or £7000 to £7500 proclamation money, it is
evident that the legislature hoped to inflate the
currency still more by the expedient of manufacturing bills of a new tenor. But the upper house
objected to one clause of the measure that provided
for the payment of the wages of the members of
the legislature out of the new bills.[5] It was also
thought that the new emission was to be made
current for too long a period, and that the taxes
laid for redeeming it were not sufficient. The
council proposed to limit to five years the time that
the notes should run, and to make the tax two shillings per poll.[6] Thereupon the lower house sent
up to the council a message, probably of remonstrance, with an alteration in the style of address

[1] Records, IV. 416. [3] *Idem*, IV. 714, 717.
[2] *Idem*, IV. 720. [4] *Idem*, IV. 717, 726.
[5] The bill provided " for the payment of the wages of the Council and Assembly out of the funds on each Branch of the Bill."
Idem, IV. 717. [6] *Idem*, IV. 727.

which the upper chamber deemed an "affront and indignity."[1] The council accordingly refused to "receive any Message from the House of Burgesses" until proper satisfaction should be given for this injury to its dignity, and the governor at once dissolved the assembly.[2]

Eight months later a new session was called, and the governor again urged that the public debt should be provided for.[3] A land tax was proposed by a committee of ways and means,[4] but the lower house decided to prepare "a Bill for emitting a new Currency."[5] This contained the objectionable clause providing for the wages of the legislature; and the council rejected it,[6] saying this could not be done, "unless both Houses will consent to joyn in proclaiming that they are still resolved to persist in that little regard too often shewn to public faith heretofore." A deadlock then ensued over this measure, and the legislature was again dissolved.[7] Shortly after these performances James Moir writes that the assembly is "pretty well versed in the American Lotteries of cancelling any kind of obligations by the easy Method of over rating a Commodity or by causing Paper Bills of credit to be issued out where there is no Fund to support them."[8] He adds that a majority of the members at the last session

[1] Records, IV. 719.
[2] Idem, IV. 719, 732.
[3] Idem, IV. 734.
[4] Idem, IV. 738.
[5] Idem, IV. 739.
[6] Idem, IV. 746, 747.
[7] Idem, IV. 752.
[8] Idem, IV. 755.

were in favor of repudiating the paper altogether, and that this fact was making the currency about as valuable as "a little waste Paper." In April, 1745, the governor called another session of the legislature. He told the members that they ought to give their attention to public affairs instead of confining all their "cares and endeavors" to getting into their own pockets "the money which was appropriated to sink the Public Bills and preserving the public faith." [1] In this affair, he said, they had been so "Wretchedly anxious" that they had inserted in the bill their own names "with the particular sums affixed to them"; and he considered this conduct so indecent that he was "not sufficient master of words to bestow the proper epithets upon it." After some altercation between the two houses, the legislature at last passed a bill levying a tax, with the proceeds of which the outstanding bills should be redeemed.[2] Williamson has very justly remarked that the policy of the assembly at this time "exhibits little more than repeated and disgusting proofs of a desire to discharge debts by fictitious payments." [3]

But the tax levied in 1745 did not accomplish its purpose, and the condition of the currency was not improved. In 1748, exchange on London was £1000 colonial for £100 sterling.[4] Governor

---

[1] Records, IV. 772.
[2] *Idem*, IV. 773, 775, 779, 782, 788, 791.
[3] History, II. 66.
[4] Douglass, Summary, I. 494.

Johnston gives us to understand that one reason for the failure of the law of 1745 was the breaking down of the old system of paying taxes in commodities.[1] In any event, the treasury of the colony remained empty, and the most necessary public services were neglected. Then began "a loud and clamorous Demand for a large and speedy Emission of a Publick Currency,"[2] which was probably due to the fact that the old depreciated bills had fallen into such bad repute as to be almost useless "but to such as are in Debt."[3] It was claimed that more money was necessary in order to pay off arrears of quit rents, as well as to provide for public expenses. In 1747, some small expeditions sent out from St. Augustine by the Spanish committed depredations along the coast,[4] and this resulted in a demand for paper money with which to erect forts.[5] Finally the governor yielded to the pressure that was brought to bear upon him, and, in violation of his instructions, consented to the emission of more bills of credit without waiting for approval of the act from the English authorities.[6]

The law of 1748[7] was designed to make provi-

[1] Records, IV. 921–923.

[2] Idem, IV. 922.   [3] Idem, IV. 755.

[4] Idem, IV. 922.   [5] Idem, IV. 866.

[6] Idem, IV. 900, 915. On p. xxii of this volume the editor places the date of this issue at 1747. This is clearly wrong, as the Records show the date to be 1748.

[7] The entire text of this act may be found in Iredell's Laws of North Carolina, 115–118.

sion for the outstanding currency, to furnish means
for erecting forts, and to pay off certain debts of
the province. All bills of credit then current were
to be exchanged in one year for new bills, at a rate
of 7½s. old currency for 1s. proclamation, or new
money. Then £6000 was set aside for constructing four forts, and the rest of the bills were appropriated for paying "the several Persons to whom
the Public is Debtor." We know that the governor had become at this time " the most considerable " of the public creditors,[1] and it is reasonable
to suppose that the other persons included in the list
were the members of the assembly, who could not
have failed to urge their claims for whatever wages
might have been due to them. If we assume that
all of the £52,500 of bills of credit emitted in 1735
were still outstanding,[2] it would have required no
more than £7000 of new bills to exchange all of
the old at the rate of 7½ for 1. Thus not more
than £13,000 could have been needed to provide
for the old currency and to construct the forts.
But the law of 1748 authorized the issue of
£21,350, so that the claims of the governor and
assembly must have been estimated at very liberal
figures. The new bills were made a legal tender
at proclamation rates, "that is to say, At four
shillings Proclamation Money for three Shillings

---

[1] Records, IV. 922.

[2] We have no means of determining how many old bills were
outstanding in 1748, but it is certain that the number retired could
not have been large. Cf. Records, IV. 921.

sterling,"[1] and severe penalties were to be imposed upon persons who should counterfeit them. The tax law enacted in 1745 was repealed, and a new tax was levied, payable in gold, silver, or paper. This act seems to have discontinued the old practice of receiving barter currency for taxes,[2] a fact which was urged by the governor as one excuse for his approval of it.

We have no means of knowing how completely the money loaned by the colony to its citizens had been repaid; but the law of 1748 recites that "there are divers considerable Sums of Loan Money due and unpaid," and directs the county treasurers to take measures for collecting such arrears. Since it is doubtful if these arrears could have been collected any better than the quit rents were, these debts due to the colony by borrowers became a charge against the public treasury when the bills originally loaned were exchanged for those issued in 1748. And this was the result of a scheme for defraying the charges of government out of the interest of bills issued in 1729 and 1735. The law of 1748 brought to the English authorities loud complaints from the attorney general of the colony and others.[3] It was alleged, with how much truth we cannot determine, that the construction of forts

[1] This was the correct ratio of the sterling and proclamation rates, and exchange would be £133 proclamation to £100 sterling. In the law of 1715, exchange had been placed at fifty per cent advance over sterling.

[2] Records, IV. 923.

[3] *Idem*, IV. 927–928, 932, 940.

was a mere pretence for issuing bills,[1] for "it was made a job," and "two or three persons who were in the Governors interest took the bills, and employing a few Negroes to throw up a little ground which they called a Fort, charged the Province to the amount thereof." The governor himself evidently feared that he would lose his official head on account of his violation of instructions, and accordingly wrote the English authorities a long and rather lame explanation of his action.[2]

Thus the old currency was replaced by an issue of new bills, and debts contracted in the early decades of the century were still unpaid. North Carolina's issues had expanded from £4000 in 1712 to £24,000 in 1715. Then the currency was contracted to about £12,000 in 1722, by the redemption of bills out of the proceeds of taxes. At that time the redemption of the bills ceased, and the currency remained stationary until 1729, when it was increased to £40,000. In 1735, the paper money was increased to £52,500, and soon after this it had depreciated to one-tenth of the value of sterling, whereas it was issued at a nominal rating of two-thirds of sterling money. Finally, contrary to the law of 1735, limiting the currency of the money to a period of ten years, the bills of credit remained outstanding until 1748, when they were replaced by an emission of a new tenor. Thus North Carolina had actually redeemed none

[1] Records, IV. 932, 940.
[2] *Idem*, IV. 919–923.

of the notes issued since 1712, with the exception of £12,000 cancelled between 1715 and 1722, while about eighty-six per cent of the original nominal value of the money had been repudiated by the law of 1748.

CHAPTER II

THE LAST COLONIAL ISSUES (1749-1774)

THE old currency of North Carolina, known as
" Old Proc.," [1] was superseded by the issue of 1748,
which was thenceforth known as " Proc.," [2] since it
was declared to be equal to three-fourths the value
of sterling. The £21,350 of the bills of the new
emission had, therefore, a legal value of £16,012
sterling,[3] or $71,093. Under the tax law of 1748,
only £703 of the bills had been drawn in and
destroyed [4] up to September, 1750. This left
£20,646 of proclamation money, or $68,751, in cir-
culation. Since the population of the colony had
increased to nearly 90,000 by this time,[5] this amount
of money would not seem to be excessive. But it
is to be remembered that barter currency was still
in use in private payments; while, as will be shown
presently, a new form of paper medium was soon
introduced. Moreover, the colony had in the past
shown such a shameful disregard of all good faith

[1] Martin, II. 51.
[2] Williamson, II. 114, 115 ; McRee, I. 114-116.
[3] This is £4 proclamation for £3 sterling, as declared in the
law of 1748.
[4] Records, IV. 1073.
[5] In 1752, the population was 90,000. *Idem*, IV., p. XX.

that its "promises to pay" must necessarily have been regarded with suspicion. Therefore, the bills of the new emission soon depreciated.[1]

The inconveniences of the old barter currency had become so great that in 1748, as we have seen, the tax levied for sinking the bills issued at that time was made payable only in gold, silver, or paper. In 1754 and 1764, the legislature adopted more radical measures of reform, and, in doing so, originated a new kind of paper currency.[2] Laws passed in these years provided that the old "rated commodities" should no longer be a legal tender for debts. In the future the commodities might be brought to the warehouses established in accordance with the statutes, and should there be inspected by public inspectors, branded, and deposited for further shipment or for safe keeping. When this had been done, the person depositing the goods might receive from the inspector an amount of notes equal to the value of the commodities at official ratings. These notes were made a legal tender for public taxes and for private debts with some restrictions as to time. Thus North Carolina instituted a system of currency that resembled

---

[1] In November, 1748, James Moir wrote that he had offered the new bills at ten per cent discount for cash, and could "get nothing for them." Records, IV. 878. Yet, in September, 1750, a report of the legislature said that the bills had until then "supported the value they were emitted at." *Idem*, IV. 1073. This statement of the official report was intended for the English authorities, and is probably incorrect. See, finally, Williamson, II. 114.

[2] Records, VII., p. XVIII.

very closely the "tobacco notes" which were so extensively employed in Virginia [1] after 1730. But there was one great drawback with this new substitute for money. The warehouses, where alone the notes could be secured upon the deposit of commodities, were necessarily situated in the vicinity of navigable streams. The result was that the frontier counties, where the complaint of scarcity of money was greatest, could not share in whatever benefits may have arisen from the use of inspectors' notes; and this finally became a subject for complaint.[2] In the tidewater districts, however, these notes formed a very important, if, indeed, not the principal, part of the circulating medium.

In 1754, the final struggle with the French for the control of the Mississippi Valley began, and North Carolina was called upon by Governor Dinwiddie, of Virginia, to aid in the expulsion of the enemy from the Ohio region.[3] In this manner new debts were incurred, and pretexts were found for emitting more bills of credit. The first of these new issues was in 1754,[4] when £40,000 was placed in circulation. That this was really an act intended to inflate the currency is quite certain. Governor Rice had died shortly before Dinwiddie's call for troops arrived, and Matthew Rowan was tempo-

---

[1] See Ripley, Financial History of Virginia, 145–153.
[2] Records, VII., p. XIX. Cf. Basset, Regulators, 154.
[3] Records, V., pp. X–XI. See also Records, 178.
[4] Iredell, Laws, 157–163; Records, VI. 1308.

rarily the chief magistrate of the colony. Williamson says[1] that Rowan "stooped to a bribe for
assisting dishonest men to defraud their creditors,"
and "assented to a bill for increasing a currency
that was already greatly depreciated." Martin
states[2] that the inflationists insisted that more
paper was needed, since the outstanding currency
would gradually be contracted by the operation of
the taxes levied for the purpose of sinking it. The
lower house, therefore, refused to provide for the
projected expedition unless Rowan would consent
to the issue of another batch of paper, and desired
to establish a loan office for the purpose of emitting
£80,000 on loan. In any event, the law of 1754
shows, upon its very face, the intention of the men
who framed it. This act authorized the issue of
£40,000, but of this sum only £12,000 was applied
to the expedition in question. The sum of £4000
was to be expended upon forts, and £1000 was to
be applied to purchasing arms. The remaining
£23,000 was expended for different purposes. The
law appropriated £4200 "towards paying the
public Debts of this Province," and we may hazard
a conjecture that these debts represented among
other things the salaries of the members of the
assembly, for we have encountered a similar item
in previous inflation bills. The rest of the money
was devoted to various "charitable and pious uses
of liberal education and public worship," such as
a school, parish church buildings, and the like;

[1] History, II. 81. [2] *Idem*, II. 66–67.

all of which goes to show that almost anything could serve as an excuse for inflation.[1] Williamson assures us that the "projected public school had no patrons, whence it followed, that the money, said to be given for the increase of learning, was converted to other uses."[2] Finally the act levied a poll tax and imposed duties on imported liquors, for the purpose of sinking the bills.

The province learned once more that it is difficult to support expeditions in distant regions by means of a paper currency. The troops sent to Virginia had to be supplied by direct shipments of pork from North Carolina, and at a greatly increased expense. Sometimes produce was shipped to the West Indies, and sold there for bills of exchange on New York, which were used for the support of troops sent to that province. Since the commodities had to be disposed of at a forced sale in "a dull market," the cost of the war was considerably increased.[3]

Governor Dobbs, who came out to the province shortly after this law had been enacted, received positive instructions to assent to no bills for emit-

[1] Upon the act of 1754 Mr. Rivers solemnly remarks : " Rowan's short term of service was distinguished by liberal contributions for building churches and purchasing glebe lands for the support of ministers of the gospel." Winsor, IV. 303–304.

[2] History, II. 83. Letters from Governor Dobbs show us that first £8000, then £9000 more, and finally the whole of the money appropriated for churches and schools, was expended by the assembly for military purposes. *Idem*, V. 333, 439–440, 573.

[3] *Idem*, V., pp. XI–XII.

ting paper unless these should contain the familiar suspending clause.[1] He proceeded to project schemes for establishing a copper coinage, and creating a loan office by means of which the colony would be enabled to sink the outstanding bills.[2] He seemed, moreover, to have the "balance of trade" disease in a very violent form.[3] But, as nothing came of his proposed measures, we may conclude that the English authorities did not approve of them, for they could not have failed to secure support in North Carolina. The bills of credit issued in 1754 were not at first accepted by the people in the northern counties on account of questions that had been raised respecting the regularity of the proceedings of the legislature.[4] In 1755, we learn that the currency had depreciated "ninety per cent below Proclamation money, at which it was originally issued."[5] Yet money was said to be very scarce in the southern part of the province. The paper currency, we learn from the same authority, would "neither purchase indigo, cash, (if such can occasionally be had,) nor bills of exchange." Indigo was said to be "the best money to be had" in the province. In the same year Governor Dobbs expressed[6] some apprehension about the currency, since the assembly was not "inclinable" to maintain the credit of the bills in circulation. But in 1756, he wrote that the bills

[1] Records, V. I, 116.
[2] *Idem*, V. 324-326, 333.
[3] *Idem*, V. 392.
[4] *Idem*, V. 573, 595.
[5] *Idem*, V. 451.
[6] *Idem*, V. 440.

were then circulating freely in the northern counties, so that the issue was not excessive.[1]

In 1756, military expenditures were again necessitated, and a new form of obligations was issued. The outlays occasioned by the war were met by the emission of £3600 of treasury notes.[2] These were not made a legal tender, but they bore interest for one year and were to be redeemed out of the proceeds of taxes levied for that purpose. The use of such treasury notes had been introduced into New England shortly after 1750, and thereafter many colonies employed this method of anticipating the collection of taxes. In 1757 and 1758, the province made further issues of £25,806, which raised the total amount emitted during the three years to £29,406.[3] Finally, in 1759, £5500 of these notes that had been drawn back into the treasury by means of the taxes levied to redeem them were reissued without interest, and were secured by a new tax. A report made in 1764 states that, upon all the notes, interest was paid to the amount of £1370. By the year just mentioned, bills had been redeemed and cancelled to the amount of £23,807; so that, of the £30,776 representing the total principal and interest, only

[1] Records, V. 573.

[2] *Idem*, VI. 1309. On the treasury notes, cf. Records, V., p. XLV. Williamson says that this form of obligations was issued because the governor refused to consent to further emissions of bills of credit. History, II. 114.

[3] The details of all these issues may be found in a report made in 1764. Records, VI. 1309–1311.

£6968 remained in circulation.[1] This was in itself a legitimate and unobjectionable method of borrowing, and the notes were redeemed with fair punctuality. But, as they were thrown into a currency that was already depreciated, they may have tended to increase the confusion.[2]

Meanwhile the colony was blessed with still another form of circulating medium. In 1757, it appeared that James Murray, a member of the council, had been issuing upon his own account a decidedly novel kind of promissory paper. Murray was in collusion with Rutherford, the receiver general of the quit rents, and he proceeded to issue bills which bore on their face a promise that the receiver general would accept them in payment of the rents. At first these notes were made receivable in only four counties, then they were declared a tender for quit rents in all parts of the province. Whenever the bills were brought back to Murray, he refused to accept them except for debts due to him or in payment for commodities rated at exorbitant prices. Governor Dobbs finally interfered with this peculiar enterprise of Murray and Rutherford.[3]

[1] These are the figures of the report of 1764. This states that the £5500 reissued in 1759 " neither adds or diminishes the Country Bills." Records, VI. 1310.

[2] Williamson states that these notes depreciated despite the fact that they bore interest. History, II. 114. I have been unable to find other evidence upon this point, but with the bills of credit at forty or fifty per cent discount, these treasury notes must have depreciated.

[3] An account of this transaction may be found in Records, V. 941-944, 951.

The bills of credit of 1748 and 1754 failed to rise to proclamation value, at which they were emitted. In 1756, a Spanish dollar,[1] worth 6*s.* at proclamation rates, could not be had for less than 8*s.* in paper, which showed that exchange was at £177 colonial for £100 sterling. Three years later the governor stated that exchange had advanced to 190,[2] and the same rates are reported for 1760.[3] In 1759, a number of London merchants trading to North Carolina complained to the home government that they had suffered losses from the depreciation of the bills issued in 1748 and 1754,[4] and Governor Dobbs received instructions[5] to have the laws of those years amended in such a way as to make the paper a legal tender only at its actual value in specie. The legislature, however, asserted[6] that it could find no merchants or English creditors who had suffered such losses, and therefore believed the complainants to be " Persons of no Weight." Accordingly the desired amendment was not passed. In this same year the legislature attempted to issue some more bills, but was restrained by the veto of the governor.[7] At this time the outstanding issues of bills of credit were estimated at £50,000,[8] or $166,000, while the population of the colony was something more than 100,000.[9] This would make it appear that about £11,000 of the £61,350 issued

---

[1] Records, V. 558.   [2] *Idem*, VI. 4, 17.   [3] *Idem*, VI. 305.
[4] *Idem*, VI. 17.   [5] *Idem*, VI. 71.   [6] *Idem*, VI. 218.
     [7] *Idem*, VI. 149–151. Cf. Martin, II. 103.
     [8] Records, V. 951.   [9] *Idem*, V., p. XXXIX.

by the laws of 1748 and 1754 had been redeemed. But we find that bills drawn back into the treasury were often paid out again for current expenses,[1] so that the notes in circulation must have fluctuated in amount from time to time.

In 1760, renewed military outlays seemed peculiarly urgent, and Governor Dobbs ventured to depart from his instructions and to advise the legislature [2] to issue more paper currency for the purpose of feeding and clothing the troops of the province. The lower house tried to issue the bills without providing a tax to sink them,[3] but failed to carry its point. The measure finally adopted provided for the emission of £12,000 in bills of credit [4] for paying military expenses, contingent outlays, and bounties for killing Indians. The bills were made legal tender at proclamation rates, and a poll tax was laid for the purpose of providing for their redemption. In 1761,[5] the governor consented to another issue of bills of credit, this time to the amount of £20,000, upon the same conditions as in the previous year. As a result, the outstanding legal tender bills were increased to about £80,000,[6] and exchange on London rose to £200 colonial for £100 sterling.[7]

---

[1] Records, V. 951.   [2] *Idem*, VI. 234.   [3] *Idem*, VI. 246.

[4] Iredell, Laws, 192; Records, VI. 1309. Cf. Martin, II. 130.

[5] Iredell, Laws, 198; Records, VI. 1309. Martin incorrectly puts the amount of this issue at £12,000. II. 147.

[6] Records, VI. 615.

[7] *Idem*, VI. 612, 615. A silver dollar came to be worth more than 9*s*. in paper.

It is necessary to refer briefly to an interesting episode in colonial politics which was being enacted at about this time. For its outlays in the war with France, North Carolina received from Parliament[1] a grant of money that amounted to £7789. Both the governor and assembly desired to get exclusive control of these funds. The latter proposed at one time to use the Parliamentary grant in redeeming a part of the outstanding paper, which certainly seems a singular thing for a colonial assembly to wish to do. The explanation of this action may perhaps be found in a statement made by the governor[2] to the effect that a junto of assemblymen had united with the treasurer in a scheme to buy up the paper at the current rate of exchange, £200 colonial for £100 sterling, and then redeem it in specie at a rate of £133 colonial for £100 sterling. The governor devised a plan of his own for redeeming the paper, but this was rejected by the Board of Trade on the ground that it was liable to the same kind of objections as the plan advocated in the assembly.[3]

The whole amount of bills of credit issued under the laws of 1748, 1754, 1760, and 1761 was £93,350. In 1764, a statement of the condition of the currency was prepared for the legislature. This document[4]

[1] See Records, VI., pp. XI, XII.

[2] *Idem*, VI. 305.

[3] *Idem*, VI., p. XII. I cannot find that any part of this sum was used for redeeming the paper. It was probably applied to current expenses.

[4] *Idem*, VI. 1308-1311. Cf. Williamson, II. 255-257.

informs us that, up to November, 1764, there had been withdrawn and cancelled the sum of £25,286; so that £68,064 of the bills of credit remained in circulation. Of the £30,776 representing the principal and interest of the treasury notes emitted between 1756 and 1759, the sum of £23,807 had been retired; so that £6968 was still outstanding. From these data it appears that the province had, in 1764, a paper circulation of £68,064 bills of credit and £6968 in treasury notes, a total of £75,032. For sinking these bills taxes had been levied, and a simple enforcement of the law would retire all the paper within a few years. Since the population of the colony was now about 200,000,[1] the £75,032 of currency ($250,000) should not have been a heavy burden. The fact that the apparently moderate amount of paper in circulation remained depreciated may seem somewhat singular. But it is to be remembered that the trade of the province was not large,[2] that in the frontier

---

[1] Estimates of population in 1765 vary. Mr. Saunders estimates it at 125,000 in one place and 220,000 in another. Records, V., p. XXXIX ; *Idem*, VIII., p. XLV. Since the number of taxable inhabitants was 45,912 in 1765, the entire population may have been in the vicinity of 200,000. See Records, VII. 145, 289, 539.

[2] It is difficult if not impossible to present any data concerning the value of the imports and exports of the province. Statistics for North and South Carolina in 1769 may be found in Macpherson, III. 571-572. But it is impossible to determine accurately North Carolina's share of the total exports and imports of the two provinces. It may have been something less than £200,000 sterling in 1769. But the figures would not represent the trade of the colony adequately even if they could be secured, because, on

districts exchanges were effected chiefly by barter, and that in the tidewater regions inspectors' notes circulated to a very large extent. Consequently the $250,000 of province paper, amounting perhaps to $1.25 per capita, was a relatively large sum. Moreover, the credit of the province had been so greatly injured by the antics of the inflationists in the past, that any kind of a public obligation must inevitably have been held in suspicion. No one could foresee what amount of paper might be emitted in the future, and no one could feel certain as to the fate of the currency then in circulation.

In 1764, Parliament passed the act [1] which prohibited any colony from issuing bills of credit and making them a legal tender for debts. This law did not interfere with the issue of treasury notes, such as had been emitted in 1756; and in 1773, Parliament made an express declaration to that effect.[2] In 1764, Governor Dobbs advised the assembly to call in the bills then circulating, which were said to be much worn and counterfeited, and to replace them with new ones.[3] The assembly, however, decided that such action would involve needless expense, and that bills already paid in, if in good condition, could be exchanged

account of the lack of good harbors, much of North Carolina's foreign commerce was conducted through the ports of Virginia and South Carolina. See Smyth, II. 98–99.

[1] Stat. at Large, 4 George III. c. 34.

[2] Stat. at Large, 13 George III. c. 57.

[3] Records, VI. 1090.

for any torn or defaced money that might be in circulation.[1] Complaints of a scarcity of currency still continued, and, in spite of the Parliamentary prohibition, various petitions came to the legislature asking for more paper money.[2] Governor Tryon, who assumed the reins of government in 1765, seems to have sought to gain the favor of the assembly by promising to use his influence with the English authorities to obtain their approval of the issue of more currency. By means of these promises, he secured from the assembly various enactments that he desired, but his attempts to gain the assent of the home government to renewed issues of paper failed completely.[3] In the "back counties" the scarcity of even the paper money aggravated the causes of discontent that led to the uprising of the Regulators between 1765 and 1771.[4] These facts show that a currency large enough to depreciate did not still the complaints of a lack of money.

In 1767, exchange fluctuated from £175 to £182 colonial for £100 sterling,[5] and foreign bills were

[1] Records, VI. 1154 a.

[2] *Idem*, VII. 386, VIII. 77. In 1766, the assembly complained. *Idem*, VII. 417. In 1768, the assembly drew up a petition upon the subject. *Idem*, VII. 619.

[3] See accounts of these transactions in Records, VII., pp. XII–XIII, VIII. pp. XI–XIV. See Tryon's announcement of the refusal of a petition for paper money in 1769. Records, VIII. 17, 87. Cf. Martin, II. 245.

[4] Basset, Regulators, 150–155.

[5] We have two statements for this year. Records, VII. 491, 493. Wright, LXI., edition of 1767, says that exchange in North

not easy to obtain in the province.[1] By 1768, the gradual withdrawal of the old bills of credit and treasury notes issued prior to 1761 had reduced the outstanding paper to £60,107, which was about £15,000 less than had been in circulation in 1764.[2] This was not an inconsiderable contraction of the currency for a period of four years, during which the number of taxables in the province increased from 34,000[3] to 51,000,[4] which indicates a large growth of population. This contraction, however, did not bring the bills back to their legal value of £133 colonial for £100 sterling, a fact which may have been due to an increased issue of inspectors' notes, or to the disturbances caused by the troubles with the Regulators. In 1769, Governor Tryon placed the amount of outstanding "proclamation bills" at £58,535,[5] a statement which corresponds nearly, but not exactly, to the figures above presented.

Late in 1768, it became necessary to defray the

Carolina had been at 145 shortly before 1767. This must be an error, since we have trustworthy evidence from North Carolina of a higher rate.

[1] See letters of McCulloh to Iredell, in McRee, I. 42–43.

[2] See a report made in January, 1768. Records, VII. 215. Here the total amounts redeemed up to date are stated at £37,162 of bills of credit and £26,857 of treasury notes. Subtracting these sums from the total amounts issued (viz. £93,350 of bills of credit and £30,776 of treasury notes), we have left in circulation £56,188 of bills of credit and £3919 of treasury notes.

[3] *Idem*, VI. 1040.

[4] *Idem*, VII. 539.

[5] *Idem*, VIII. 12, 212.

expenses of raising a body of troops which had been called out by the governor in order to suppress an uprising of the Regulators, and the assembly seized upon this as a good opportunity to secure the issue of more currency.[1] The cost of raising the troops was only £4844,[2] but the assembly straightway passed a bill for the emission of £30,000 in notes [3] which were to be used for a variety of purposes, including of course the payment of the wages of the members of the legislature. But the governor and council refused to consent to this measure. In the end a bill was passed providing for the issue of £20,000 of debentures, which were to be redeemed out of the proceeds of a poll tax of two shillings.[4] The notes were not, however, to be a legal tender; [5] and the English authorities finally approved of the act as an emergency measure.[6] Although these debentures found their way into circulation, the assembly proceeded in 1770 to pass a valuation act,[7] which prohibited sheriffs from selling property taken in executions unless it realized two-thirds of the valuation set upon it by a board of appraisers. This was defended, of course, upon the ground of the scarcity of money.[8] In the spring of 1771,

[1] On this incident see Basset, Regulators, 185.
[2] Records, VII. 887–888.
[3] *Idem*, VII. 915–916.
[4] *Idem*, VII. 917, VIII. 5, 6, 9. Cf. Martin, II. 249.
[5] Records, VIII. 9.   [6] *Idem*, VIII. 266–267.
[7] Acts of N. C., 485–486; Martin, II. 271.
[8] See Records, IX., p. XV.

another body of troops had to be raised in order to suppress the Regulators; and, in order to meet the expenses incurred in this manner, one of the treasurers issued notes to the amount of £6000,[1] which were a further addition to the currency of the province. These treasurer's notes proved to be especially objectionable, since they bore but a single signature and were readily counterfeited.[2]

In July, 1770, £58,535 of the old " proclamation money " was outstanding, besides the £20,000 of certificates, or debentures, issued in 1769; and all this currency was said to be in brisk circulation.[3] In August, 1771, Josiah Martin, Governor Tryon's successor, reached the colony.[4] He found himself confronted with a large amount of unpaid claims caused by Tryon's expedition against the Regulators, while the outstanding paper currency was becoming discredited by the activity of the counterfeiters,[5] who had placed a large quantity of spurious bills in circulation. He urged the home authorities to consent to an emission of new currency, which should be used for replacing the old bills and for defraying the debts recently incurred by his predecessor;[6] and was told that this could be permitted provided the notes were not made a legal tender.[7] The assembly complained of the

---

[1] Records, VIII., p. XXIX. Cf. Williamson, II. 275.
[2] Records, IX. 18. [3] *Idem*, VIII. 212.
[4] *Idem*, IX., p. III. [5] *Idem*, IX. 18.
[6] *Idem*, IX. 19. [7] *Idem*, IX. 65.

difficulty of paying the debts of the province without resorting to the issue of paper,[1] and drew up a petition to the Crown, praying that permission might be given to make the currency a tender for debts.[2] If this could be allowed, the assembly pledged itself to "frame this Law, so as to prevent *British* creditors from suffering, should such currency depreciate in value." In this quotation the italics are the author's, and the reader will hardly fail to be struck by the implied willingness of the legislature to rob *domestic* creditors. A bill was then passed providing for the issue of £120,000 in debenture notes,[3] but this was vetoed by Governor Martin.[4] The governor wrote to Earl Hillsborough[5] that a majority of the delegates "from the Southern district in which the people are almost universally necessitous and in debt,[6] and whose policy it has been to overflow the province with paper money," advocated this large emission of new currency. He stated also that the "minority from the Northern districts as warmly opposed this system." In the end Martin consented to the issue of £60,000 of "stamped debenture notes," equal to proclamation money.[7]

[1] Records, IX. 142.　　[2] *Idem*, IX. 213.　Cf. VII. 619.
[3] *Idem*, IX. 197.　　[4] *Idem*, IX. 222.　　[5] *Idem*, IX. 76.
[6] This southern district was thinly settled and in much less comfortable circumstances than the northern and eastern counties. In 1755, Abercrombie reported that money was especially scarce in "the Southward parts of the Province." *Idem*, V. 451.
[7] The text of this act may be found in Acts of North Carolina, 496–497. See also Records, IX. 76.

The notes were not made a legal tender, and an annual tax of two shillings per poll for ten years was levied upon the province [1] in order to provide for their redemption. By means of these bills Governor Martin planned to retire the notes issued during Tryon's administration, and he hoped that such action would prevent the new currency from depreciating.[2] His course in this matter was approved by the English authorities.[3] Martin tells us [4] that the currency thus authorized was placed in circulation much sooner than he had expected, on account of "the alacrity with which the base and false substitute of specie is manufactured here." He adds that the new bills had affected exchange far less than he had apprehended.[5]

At this point it is necessary to refer to the few available facts concerning the coin currency of North Carolina. The law that provided for the issue of bills of credit in 1748 [6] declared the paper to be a legal tender as proclamation money,

[1] Thus one-tenth of the bills was to be sunk each year. In order for a poll tax of two shillings to supply the means for doing this, the number of taxables must have been 60,000. This would indicate a population of about 250,000. See Records, IX., p. XV.

[2] *Idem*, IX. 77. [3] *Idem*, IX. 275, 278.
[4] *Idem*, IX. 260. [5] *Idem*.

[6] Prior to 1748 the laws were not uniform. The bills issued in 1715 were made a tender at £150 colonial for £100 sterling, the same as the barter currency. Proclamation rates were £133 to £100 sterling. Records, III. 178. Then the act of 1729 declared 20s. of the new paper equal to 15 dwts. of silver. Hawks, II. 284. This made silver worth 26.6s. per ounce, while the proclamation

or as sterling money at proclamation rates.[1] But, as we have seen, the currency did not retain its nominal value, and depreciated as soon as issued. At the rate fixed in 1748, £133 of the paper ought to have equalled £100 sterling; but exchange rose in a few years to £190 and even £200.[2] By 1767 it seems to have fluctuated about £180 colonial for £100 sterling.[3] We know that, as early as 1756, a Spanish dollar exchanged for 8s. of the paper,[4] whereas the proclamation value of this coin was only 6s. When exchange finally settled down to £180, or perhaps less, a dollar came to be rated, "by long usage," at 8s.;[5] for with the paper currency worth £177 [6] colonial for £100 sterling, this valuation of the dollar would just keep it in circulation.[7] This seems to furnish an explanation of the fact that in North Carolina the Spanish dollar came to be rated at 8s. In 1767, a bill giving a legal rating to gold and silver coins was introduced in the legislature,[8] but it does not seem to have become a law. The

rating was about 6s. 10½d. The rate indicated the depreciation of the paper.

[1] Iredell, Laws, 117. Cf. Williamson, II. 39.

[2] Records, V. 451, VI. 4, 17, 305, 612, 615.

[3] *Idem*, VII. 491, 493.

[4] *Idem*, V. 588.

[5] Note Williamson, II. 115.

[6] Thus in 1767 exchange is quoted at from £175 to £182. Records, VII. 493.

[7] Such an overvaluation of the dollar would make 20s. of silver of the same nominal value as 20s. of paper. See tables in Wright, 4.

[8] Records, VII. 593.

next year a law was passed "to encourage the Importation of British Copper Halfpence, and for making them a Tender for the Payment of small Debts," but this was disallowed by the Crown.[1]

Various acts passed by the assembly give the reader the impression that gold and silver circulated in the province to some extent at least. In 1729, gold and silver were included among the rated commodities.[2] Seven years later, a law providing for the collection of quit rents made gold and silver payable at proclamation rates.[3] The same thing was done in tax laws enacted in 1745 and 1748.[4] After the bills of the new tenor came to circulate at a relatively stable exchange of £175 to £182, the assembly, as we have seen, tried to enact a law[5] making gold and silver legal tender at fixed ratings. Such measures would hardly have been enacted if there had been no specie in the province. In 1766, when Governor Tryon mentions the subject of the scarcity of specie,[6] he does not say that there is none in the colony. Governor Glenn of South Carolina wrote to Governor Dobbs in 1755[7] that, since that province had retired a considerable part of its paper, "gold and silver begin to take up their abode with us, two-thirds of all Payments being now made in those Metals." Specie must have circulated to some extent in

---

[1] Acts of N. C., 449.
[2] Hawks, II. 286.
[3] Records, IV. 185.
[4] *Idem*, IV. 781; Iredell, Laws, 117.
[5] Records, VII. 593.
[6] *Idem*, VI. 144, 201.
[7] *Idem*, V. 378–379.

North Carolina after the paper currency came to have a relatively stable value. In 1770, Wynne wrote concerning both Carolinas:[1] " A very inconsiderable quantity of English money circulates in either province; the current cash consisting almost wholly of Spanish dollars and pistoles."

It will be recalled that, in 1760 and 1761, the province made two emissions of bills of credit, amounting in the aggregate to £32,000. For sinking each issue a poll tax was levied,[2] and it was pledged that these taxes should continue in operation until both of the emissions should be redeemed. In 1768, after efforts to secure new issues of paper had failed,[3] the assembly voted to repeal these taxes, alleging that enough money had been collected to suffice for the purposes for which the taxes were laid.[4] Governor Tryon, however, vetoed this act,[5] the real purpose of which was to lighten taxation and prevent the reduction of the number of bills then in circulation. The fact is that the tax system of the colony was both wrong in

[1] Wynne, II. 301.

[2] Iredell, Laws, 192, 198.

[3] Basset gives an account of this transaction. Regulators, 152, 153.

[4] Records, VII. 922, 923. This was not correct. The total amount of bills of credit of the emissions of 1748, 1754, 1760, and 1761 that was cancelled between 1761 and 1768 was less than £24,000. Idem, VIII. 215. Many of these bills were, doubtless, of the emissions of 1748 and 1754.

[5] Idem, VII. 986. In 1771, Governor Martin stated that these taxes were suspended by resolves of 1768. Idem, IX. 231. Compare an act passed in 1770. Iredell, Laws, 254.

principle and administered with a laxity that is appalling. Nearly all the taxes levied in North Carolina took the form of uniform assessments upon polls, in the list of which adult white males and adult colored males and females were included.[1] At the time of which we are writing, the principal auxiliary form of taxation was a light duty upon imported spirits. Such a crude system of raising revenue necessarily produced the grossest inequalities, and these were made worse by bad administration. The taxes legally in force in 1761, and pledged to the redemption of the outstanding paper, ought to have brought in about £8000 annually.[2] But the sheriffs were exceedingly lax in making collections, and were both negligent and dishonest in turning money over to the treasurers of the province; while the duty on liquors was largely evaded by reason of the extensive scale upon which smuggling was practised. In some years the sheriffs turned in not more than one-third of the amounts levied,[3] and, in 1770, it was found that in every county of the colony there was at least one defaulting sheriff. In the year last mentioned, the aggregate indebtedness of all the sheriffs was £64,000.[4] Thus there was good reason for the belief in 1768 that the burden of taxa-

[1] On this subject see Basset, 72 ; Williamson, I. 122 ; Records, VII., p. XI, X., p. XXV. In 1713 and 1715 a tax had been laid upon land, but this was not permanent. Records, III. 189, 485.

[2] Records, V., pp. XLV, XLVI.

[3] *Idem*, VII., p. XVII.

[4] *Idem*, VII., p. XVII, IX. 68. See Wheeler, 311.

tion should be lightened, but the proper remedy would have been to hold the sheriffs to a strict accountability. This would have lightened taxation without a violation of the public faith.

In 1771, the assembly turned its attention to the taxes levied in 1748 and 1754 for the redemption of the bills of credit emitted in those years. The clerk of the committee of accounts submitted a report which purported to show that, of £61,350 of bills of these two emissions, £53,104 had been burned ; while there was in the hands of the treasurers a sum of money amounting to £12,585, which would more than suffice to redeem the rest of these issues.[1] Accordingly the assembly voted to repeal the taxes levied in 1748 and 1754, on the ground that they had accomplished the purpose for which they had been imposed.[2] Then Governor Martin vetoed the bill, and denounced it as a fraudulent measure. The assembly, however, anticipating this action, prepared a resolution that would have had the effect of discontinuing the collection of the taxes ; but the governor, learning of this proposed action, dissolved the legislature before the obnoxious resolution could be entered upon the records.[3] After this, the speaker of the lower house informed the provincial treasurers of the contents of the resolution, and these officials omitted

[1] Records, IX. 166.
[2] *Idem*, IX. 167. See accounts of this affair in Records, IX., pp. XVI, XVII ; Sikes, 11-14.
[3] Records, IX. 232, 233.

these taxes from the lists[1] sent out to the sheriffs for collection. Thereupon, the governor issued a proclamation requiring[2] the sheriffs to make the collections as usual, and threatening to have them sued for any amounts that they should fail to collect.

Although the assembly's statement of the case seems to be fair and plausible, the governor was probably right in his criticisms upon its action. The £53,104 of bills said to have been cancelled were probably not exclusively bills of the two emissions of 1748 and 1754. The governor said[3] that, in the accounts of the bills that had been cancelled, no pains were taken to distinguish between bills of the four emissions of 1748, 1754, 1760, and 1761. This is certainly the case in the report submitted in 1770,[4] and was probably true of the report of 1771. The facts then would seem to be that bills amounting to £93,350 had been emitted in 1748, 1754, 1760, and 1761; and that £53,104 had been redeemed by 1771, while £12,585 more were said to be in the treasury but not yet destroyed. This left a considerable quantity of the old legal tender paper still in circulation,[5] and bills of the emissions of 1748 and 1754 were undoubt-

---

[1] Records, IX. 233, 234.

[2] *Idem*, IX. 229, 234.

[3] *Idem*, IX. 231.

[4] *Idem*, VIII. 215.

[5] The governor said that £42,800 in legal tender paper was still outstanding. *Idem*, IX. 231. This is about the difference between the £93,350 representing the four emissions and the £53,104 said to be burned.

edly outstanding when the legislature proposed to repeal the taxes levied for redeeming the two issues just mentioned. But there is still another point to be considered. The governor stated that in 1768 the poll tax levied for sinking the bills issued in 1760 and 1761 had been illegally suspended by a resolution of the assembly.[1] If it is true that the assembly circumvented Tryon's veto of the bill suspending the taxes of 1760 and 1761 and succeeded in abolishing those taxes, then its action in 1771 was quite as "fraudulent" as Martin represented it to be ; for the repeal of the taxes levied in 1748 and 1754 would have taken away the only remaining funds available for redeeming the bills of credit.

In 1771, it appears that about £40,000 of the old legal tender notes were still in circulation,[2] and during that year the £60,000 of debenture notes authorized by Governor Martin were added to the currency of the province.[3] This made a total of about £100,000 of notes,[4] while the population

[1] This incident is discussed by Martin, II. 291, 292; Williamson, II. 164–166 ; Jones, 74–75, 101.

[2] This is the difference between the £93,350 emitted in 1748, 1754, 1760, and 1761, and the £53,104 said to be burnt in 1771.

[3] These debenture notes replaced all the notes issued in Tryon's administration.

[4] I assume that practically all the £30,776 of treasury notes issued between 1756 and 1759 had been redeemed. Of this sum, £26,857 was reported burnt in 1770. Records, VIII. 215. The £100,000 in circulation in 1771 was equivalent to $333,000, at its nominal value. With exchange at 177, it would be equivalent actually to $250,000.

of North Carolina was about 250,000.[1] No more
paper money was issued during the colonial period,
but in 1774 we find the assembly petitioning for
permission to emit bills of credit and make them a
legal tender.[2] Inspectors' notes probably continued
to be extensively employed as currency, and a
law was passed in 1770 making special regulations
concerning the receipt of indigo notes for taxes.[3]
The £60,000 of debenture notes issued in 1771
do not seem to have affected exchange materially,[4]
and the condition of the currency remained about
the same until the opening of the Revolution. In
July, 1772, Iredell stated that exchange was at
£160 colonial for £100 sterling,[5] which indicates,
perhaps, some appreciation of the currency.[6] In

[1] Records, IX., p. XV.   [3] Acts of N. C., 461–462.
[2] Martin, II. 325.   [4] Records, IX. 260.

[5] McRee, I. 115. Smyth states that in 1774 exchange was at
£133. Smyth, II. 99. But this was certainly a mistake, and was
probably due to an oversight of the fact that "proclamation
money" in North Carolina meant a rating of the dollar at eight
shillings instead of six.

[6] With the rating of a dollar at 8s., the nominal par would be
£177. But at this time the pound sterling was in reality a certain
quantity of gold, because that metal had been overvalued by English law, and silver was being displaced. Therefore Spanish silver
coins when shipped to England would have a value that changed
whenever the ratio of gold to silver varied. The legal rating of
silver was 5s. 2d. per ounce, which made the dollar worth 4s. 6d.
But silver was sometimes more valuable than this, so that the
dollar became worth 4s. 8d. When this happened, the actual par
of exchange would fall from £177 to £171, with the dollar rated
at 8s. See Wright, 4. Besides this, it must be remembered that
the English gold coins were in very bad condition, having been

1775, at least £40,000 of the debenture notes issued in 1771 must have remained outstanding;[1] and, in addition to this, a considerable quantity of the bills of credit was still in circulation.[2]

subject to great loss from abrasion and clipping. The mint price of gold was 77.87s. per ounce ; but gold bullion in the market often sold for as much as 80s., because that sum of money was paid in light-weight gold coins. See Smith, W. of N., I. 43–44 ; McCulloch, 318. In 1773, it was decided that the gold coins weighed on the average from 2.5 to 5 per cent less than they should have done ; and £3,418,000 of selected coins showed a loss of nine per cent. 34 Journals of House of Commons, 734–735. Such a condition of England's gold coins might lower exchange in North Carolina several per cent below 171. Finally, the cost of shipping and insuring specie was much more than at the present day. In 1760, the cost of freight and insurance was over four per cent in Massachusetts. Acts of Mass., IV. 541. If exchange happened to be in favor of North Carolina in 1772, the rate would be lowered by an additional amount. Perhaps, in this manner, we can account for Iredell's statement.

[1] The tax levied to redeem them was supposed to bring in £6000 annually for ten years. See Acts of N. C., 496–497. The tax would have redeemed not more than £24,000 by 1775, if thoroughly and punctually collected. Probably it brought in considerably less than that sum.

[2] We know that some of these legal tender bills were in circulation as late as 1778. McRee, I. 389, 406.

CHAPTER III

THE LAST ISSUES (1775–1788)

NORTH CAROLINA was badly prepared to enter the struggle for independence. Her credit had been impaired by previous violations of the public faith; and she had a considerable quantity of paper in circulation, so that the margin of safety for future issues was a narrow one. In April, 1775, the final message [1] of the last royal governor called the attention of the legislature to the fact that the treasury was empty, while large demands of various creditors were unsatisfied and the dues of public officers were unpaid. The assembly contemplated [2] "with great concern" the "exhausted state of the public funds," and said that this unfortunate condition was not due to its own misconduct. Owing to a dispute between the governor and the legislature, no list of taxables had been drawn up since 1772, and consequently no taxes had been collected for more than two years. [3] But more than this, the province had no system of taxation, except a primitive poll tax and a few imposts on commerce. Even these were badly administered,

[1] Records, IX. 1195; Jones, 166.
[2] Records, IX. 1204; Jones, 169.
[8] Records, IX. 1204.

184

as is shown by the fact that the tax collectors in 1770 were indebted to the province for £64,000.[1] The manner in which county officials sometimes attended to their duties is shown in a letter written about 1772, in which the writer states that, in his county, "no County tax is laid, no list of taxables is returned, no Sheriff qualified," so that "all is confusion, anarchy, and uproar."[2] Under such conditions, a debt of £60,000 was considered almost beyond the resources of the province in 1771,[3] when North Carolina had a population of about 250,000; and an annual tax of £6000, levied in order to sink this indebtedness,[4] was probably regarded as a heavy burden. Under the most favorable circumstances, the development of an adequate system of taxation would have been difficult in such a sparsely settled colony;[5] but the long-continued use of paper money, for the payment of both ordinary and extraordinary outlays, greatly impeded this process. Why should the people submit to taxation, if the payment of one debt by creating another is to be considered a proper method of meeting public obligations?

When a provincial congress met in August, 1775, a committee of ways and means reported[6] that the

[1] Records, VII., p. XVII.
[2] McRee, I. 75.
[3] See Records, IX., pp. XII–XIV.
[4] Acts of N. C., 496.
[5] These facts are well stated by Williamson, in the *American Museum*, II. 122, 123, 127.
[6] Records, X. 183–184; Jones, 222–223.

colony was in debt to various creditors; that no money "on the Contingent fund" was in the hands of the southern treasurer; and that no information could be secured concerning the condition of the treasury of the northern district. The committee recommended that measures should be adopted to recover the "diverse large sums of money due from sundry sheriffs,"[1] and that the money collected since 1771, under the tax laws of 1748 and 1754, should be returned to the taxpayers. In order to provide the funds needed for the defence of the province, the congress then voted[2] to emit $125,000 in bills of credit. These were to be a legal tender at the rate of eight shillings for a dollar; persons who should "speak disrespectfully" of the bills or offer a premium for specie were to be treated as enemies of their country; and finally a poll tax of two shillings, running for a period of nine years, was levied for the purpose of sinking the currency. This tax, however, was not to be collected until 1777. Thus the war was to be carried on for 1775 and 1776, if it should last so long, without resorting to the unpleasant expedient of paying taxes.

In April and May, 1776, more money had to be raised, and the congress issued[3] £500,000 more of

[1] Acts were subsequently passed for this purpose. See Iredell, Laws, 334, 386.

[2] Records, X. 194–196; Jones, 223. Martin incorrectly places the amount of bills at $150,000. History, II. 365.

[3] £100,000 was authorized in April and £400,000 in May. Records, X. 532 573. See Martin, II. 386; Jones, 254, 257.

its paper, or $1,250,000. These bills were emitted upon the same terms as the issue of 1775, and were to be redeemed by a poll tax which should go into operation in 1780. Jones states that these bills were badly engraved on a poor quality of paper, and that they were extensively counterfeited. In 1777, a tax of one shilling on every £100 of property was established for the purpose of meeting county expenses,[1] but no such provision was made for the needs of the state. In 1778, more funds were required, and the legislature authorized the emission of £850,000 of paper, or $2,125,000.[2] Some of these bills were to be used for replacing former issues, which were much counterfeited; and the rest were to be applied to defraying military expenses. Mr. McRee says that no adequate fund was provided for sinking this last emission, and that the legislature was unwilling to hazard its popularity by levying sufficient taxes to place the credit of the state upon a proper basis.[3]

In 1779, however, the legislature applied to other purposes that portion of the bills issued in the previous year which was to have been exchanged for the emissions of 1775 and 1776.[4] By this enactment the redemption of the two early issues was postponed until 1780, and later laws

---

[1] Iredell, Laws, 348–349. This tax was modified in 1779. *Idem*, 378. Iredell wrote that the action of the assembly in 1777 left "a faint glimmering of hope." McRee, Life of Iredell, I. 359.

[2] Iredell, Laws, 360–361.

[3] Life of Iredell, I. 404.   [4] Iredell, Laws, 369.

provided for a further postponement for four
years.[1] Meanwhile the depreciation of the paper
was increasing at an alarming rate. The official
tables established in 1783 recognized no depreciation before March, 1777, but these figures are
notoriously incorrect. The continental paper
began to decline in value as early as the middle of
1776, and this process could not have been much
longer delayed in North Carolina. By January,
1778, a depreciation of $3\frac{1}{2}$ for 1 is recognized by
the official tables.[2] In this year, Iredell urged the
grand jury at Edenton to proceed against all persons guilty of offering a premium for specie.[3] He
stated that it was a common practice to " make a
difference " between paper issued by the colonial
government and that issued by the state, or between continental paper and the bills emitted by
North Carolina. By January, 1779, six dollars in
paper were worth only one in specie ; and a year
later the rate of depreciation had increased to
32 for 1.

Meanwhile the evils of counterfeiting had become
so great, in spite of the severe penalties prescribed
by the laws,[4] that the legislature appointed in each
county inspectors of the currency.[5] Persons who
should be offered any of the bills were authorized
to bring them before these officers, who were to
stamp all counterfeits. When the assembly was
convened in April, 1780, the state currency had

[1] Iredell, Laws, 401–414.   [2] Idem, 452.   [3] McRee, I. 389.
[4] Iredell, Laws, 389–390.   [5] Idem, 400.

depreciated[1] to one-fiftieth of its nominal value, if not less; while the continental money had been practically repudiated by the action of Congress on the eighteenth of the preceding month. Up to this time taxation had been practically suspended in the state, except for the small sums that may have been raised for county purposes. This assembly levied a tax for the year 1780;[2] but it also emitted bills of credit to the amount of £1,240,000, or $3,100,000, and made this money a legal tender at its nominal value.[3] This law contained one section which authorized the governor to emit "such further Sum or Sums" as might be needed during the recess of the assembly.[4] But the paper money had become so nearly worthless that the war could no longer be carried on through such an agency, and in September[5] it was necessary to call for a specific tax payable in provisions. This was afterwards described by Governor Johnston as the "most oppressive and least productive tax ever known in the State."[6] Yet, in 1781, "a money and specific Provision Tax" was imposed.[7]

By the opening of 1781, one dollar of the paper issued by North Carolina was worth less than one-

[1] Iredell, Laws, 452.

[2] *Idem*, 397.

[3] *Idem*, 397–398.

[4] Of the laws passed at this session Iredell wrote, "They are certainly the vilest collection of trash ever formed by a legislative body." McRee, I. 446.   [6] Elliot, IV. 79.

[5] Iredell, Laws, 405.   [7] Iredell, Laws, 417.

half of one per cent of its nominal value.[1] Yet
the legislature proceeded to authorize the issue of
$26,250,000 of notes in order to raise and equip
four battalions of continental troops.[2] These notes,
or certificates, were payable in 1782, and bore
interest at six per cent. It has been impossible
to determine whether they were made a legal
tender,[3] but they must have found their way into
circulation, as such certificates usually did. In
February of this year, the salaries of judges were
fixed at £20,000 annually;[4] and by December,
$725 in paper was worth but $1 in specie.[5] In
the early months of the year the currency was so
nearly worthless that the legislature provided that
all future purchases on the part of the state should
be made at specie rates,[6] and paid for by issuing
certificates that should be redeemed in gold or
silver. But this was little better than a mere
impressment of supplies, and added to the paper
of the state a new form of indebtedness. At the
same time provision was made for adjusting tem-
porarily old claims against the state by appointing
district auditors to examine the demands of creditors and to issue certificates for the amounts due.[7]

[1] Iredell, Laws, 452. [2] *Idem*, 409–410.

[3] Iredell does not print all the sections of the law.

[4] McRee, I. 488. In 1780, Iredell paid £160 per day for board
and lodgings. *Idem*, I. 472.

[5] Iredell, Laws, 452. [6] *Idem*, 412.

[7] *Idem*, 410. The law fixed the prices that should be allowed
for each article furnished to the state. These prices were such as
prevailed in the period of inflation, as 32*s*. per pound for beef. The

THE LAST ISSUES (1775–1788)

As the paper currency approached a condition of utter worthlessness, it circulated with increasing difficulty, and finally collapsed. At the same time specie began to return to circulation. This process, of course, was attended with considerable inconvenience; and, for a time, it seems to have been necessary to resort to barter.[1] In May, 1780, Iredell received $19 in silver.[2] By 1781 and 1782 specie became plentiful, and remained so until it was once more replaced by paper.[3] In 1783, the legislature repealed all acts making the old currency a legal tender, and established an official scale of depreciation for use in the settlement of debts contracted during the period of inflation.[4] At the same time valuations were established for foreign gold and silver coins, the dollar being rated at eight shillings. This valuation of the dollar was a mere confirmation of the rate at which it had previously been received.[5]

certificates, therefore, were placed on the level of the depreciated currency; and, accordingly, they were made receivable for taxes at the rate of 200 for 1. *Idem*, 417.

[1] Thus in 1780 Iredell's sister is found trying to barter sugar for chickens. McRee, I. 517.

[2] Iredell, Laws, 451.

[3] In 1787, Williamson wrote that money had been "very plenty" three years before. *American Museum*, II. 107. In 1788, speakers in the state convention commented on the abundance of specie after the close of the paper-money period of the war, and said it remained plentiful until paper was issued again. Elliot, IV. 90, 189.   [4] Iredell, Laws, 452–453.

[5] Thus in 1779 an act relating to confiscated debts, which were contracted in specie, placed exchange at 175, which shows the

By 1780, North Carolina began to levy taxes for state purposes,[1] as we have seen. The exigencies of the times had compelled the legislature to supplement the assessment of polls by a tax on property;[2] and, in 1782, a law was passed providing for the assessment and collection of poll and property taxes.[3] Real estate was the principal item of property taxed,[4] and the assessments were commonly called land and poll taxes.[5] In 1785 and 1786, other imposts were added to the revenue system of the state.[6] The taxes introduced in 1780 did not prove effective at the start, and North Carolina was able to give but little financial support to the federal government. Prior to December, 1779, the state seems to have paid nothing on her quotas of the requisitions of Congress. Then, between that month and June, 1780, North Carolina paid $2,380,000 in depreciated paper, for which she received a credit of $73,304 in specie,[7] an amount that was perhaps fifty per cent more than the bills were actually worth.[8] In 1780, Congress asked the

dollar to be rated at 8*s.* In 1782, Morris reported a rating of 8*s.* Sparks, Diplomatic Correspondence, XII. 91.

[1] See Iredell, Laws, 397, 405, 417.

[2] See laws passed in 1777 and 1779. *Idem*, 348, 378.

[3] *Idem*, 429–430.

[4] See State Papers, Finance, I. 435–436.

[5] See Letters to Washington, IV. 69; *American Museum*, II. 122.   [6] Iredell, Laws, 519, 586.

[7] State Papers, Finance, I. 62.

[8] This sum was rated according to the tables of depreciation established by Congress, a scale which understated the extent of the deterioration of the paper. Cf. Bullock, 132–133.

state to furnish $1,000,000 per month for twelve months in order to sink its quota of the continental bills. Upon this requisition[1] North Carolina paid nothing until 1789, when she turned in $5,061,061 in paper, for which a credit of $126,671[2] in specie was allowed. From 1781 to 1788, Congress called upon the state for $463,906 in specie and $674,739 in indents. Of these sums North Carolina paid only $48,626 in specie.[3] This is a poorer showing than was made by any other state except Georgia.

The Revolution left North Carolina with a large debt consisting of depreciated paper[4] and certificates of many kinds issued at various times to the public creditors.[5] By 1783, the paper currency had disappeared from circulation, and the state was upon a specie basis after seventy years' experience with a fluctuating medium of exchange. Then began a renewed agitation for an issue of bills of credit. In May, 1783, the legislature voted to issue £100,000, or $250,000,[6] ostensibly in order to pay continental soldiers and officers of North Carolina;[7] but one clause of the act provided for

[1] See Bullock, 158; Williamson, II. 281–282.

[2] State Papers, Finance, I. 59. This paper was valued at 40 for 1, which was several times as much as it was worth. The continental paper was funded in 1790 at 100 for 1, and had been as low as 500 or 1000 for 1.

[3] *Idem*, I. 54–57.

[4] Writings of Madison, I. 513.

[5] Williamson has described this part of the debt. *American Museum*, II. 126.   [6] Iredell, Laws, 443.

[7] Note title of act, and compare McRee, II. 63.

the payment of members of the assembly out of the new bills. The paper was made a legal tender in all payments, and a tax was levied for its redemption. Moreover, the property recently confiscated by the state was pledged as security for this new emission. A contemporary writer characterized the assembly that passed this act as a "set of unprincipled men, who sacrifice everything to their popularity and private views."[1] A few months later the inhabitants of Edenton entreated the legislature to make no further issues, and to redeem the last emission as quickly as possible.[2] Instead of doing this, the legislature soon broke its solemn promises, and the money[3] derived from the confiscated estates was "converted to another use."

The bills emitted in 1783 soon depreciated, and then arose a clamor for another issue of paper.[4] Accordingly, in 1786, an emission of £100,000 was authorized.[5] The new bills were declared a legal tender in all payments, and a tax was levied for their redemption. It was promised, furthermore, that when the tax brought bills into the treasury, the money should not be placed in circulation again. Some of the new bills were used for state expenses, and a debt was thus incurred for expenditures on the "civil list," which should have been defrayed out of the taxes of the year. Then a cer-

---

[1] McRee, II. 46.
[2] Idem, II. 63.
[3] American Museum, II. 110.
[4] Idem.
[5] Iredell, Laws, 550–553.

tain amount, not to exceed £36,000, was appropriated for the purchase of tobacco on the account of the state.[1] This was intended as a means of providing for the state's quota of the interest due for that year on the foreign debt of the United States. The tobacco was to be sold for the highest price obtainable, and the proceeds were to be placed at the disposal of the Board of Treasury of the United States. The law provided at first that the commissioners appointed to purchase the tobacco should not pay more than 50*s*. per cwt.[2] Madison writes that the agent "was authorized to give nearly the double of the current price; and as the paper was a tender, debtors ran to him with their Tobacco, and the creditors paid the expence of the farce."[3] Maclaine states that, in March, 1786, no one was purchasing tobacco in Wilmington except the commissioners, and that "the merchants will not take it at the public price."[4] This seems to confirm Madison's statement that the state made the purchases at excessively high prices. Probably on account of the disadvantageous rates paid by the commissioners, a law was passed late in 1786[5] requiring that "the said Commissioners shall not on any Pretence give more than the current Cost Price of the Day." But this did not save the state from a loss upon the transaction.

[1] See also explanatory act passed in 1786. Iredell, Laws, 590–591.

[2] *Idem*, 552.

[3] Writings of Madison, I. 244.

[4] McRee, II. 139.

[5] Iredell, Laws, 591.

Williamson stated [1] in 1787 that the tobacco had
been purchased "for two prices." In 1788, in the
North Carolina convention, Hill asserted [2] that the
state had "purchased tobacco at an extravagant
price, and sold it at a considerable loss," receiving
"about a dollar in the pound." This would mean
a loss of sixty per cent. At the same time and
place Johnston said: [3] "We are swindlers; we
gave three pounds per hundred weight for tobacco,
and sold it for three dollars per hundred weight,
after having paid very considerable expenses
for transporting and keeping it." He said that
a merchant who "purchases dear and sells cheap"
is certainly a swindler. Since these statements
passed uncontradicted, we may safely conclude
that North Carolina lost more than fifty per
cent upon this speculation in tobacco. More than
this, the paper quickly depreciated. In August,
1786, Madison reported a depreciation of twenty-
five or thirty per cent. [4] The following year Williamson wrote that twelve or thirteen shillings of
paper were worth only one dollar in specie, [5] which
indicates a depreciation of more than fifty per
cent. [6] In 1788, two dollars in paper were worth
only one dollar in specie. [7] Williamson states [8] that

---

[1] *American Museum*, II. 110.   [2] Elliot, IV. 84.

[3] *Idem*, IV. 89.   [4] Writings of Madison, I. 244.

[5] *American Museum*, II. 113.

[6] In this same year Hamilton reported a depreciation of 2 for 1.
Hamilton, II. 37.

[7] Elliot, IV. 183.   [8] *American Museum*, II. 113.

a guardian bought up paper "at twelve or thirteen shillings for a dollar," and used it in paying to an orphan the principal of an estate of $2000.

While North Carolina had furnished the federal government almost no financial support, the people of the state generally exhibited considerable fear and dislike of the idea of taxation by any federal authority.[1] It was not surprising, therefore, that the Federal Constitution encountered bitter opposition in the state. Paper money was another issue involved in the contest. North Carolina's delegates in the federal convention had voted to prohibit the states from emitting bills of credit,[2] and had favored the proposition to take this dangerous power away from Congress.[3] The leaders of the federalist party in the state had wearied of the paper-money policy adopted after the close of the Revolution,[4] while some of the anti-federalists had favored the measures of inflation.[5] Outside of the state the delay of North Carolina in ratifying the Constitution was attributed to the desire "of preserving paper money and tender laws."[6] The fear was expressed[7] that the provision of the Constitution prohibiting the

[1] McRee, II. 178, 181, 217, 286, 329.
[2] Elliot, I. 271.   [3] *Idem*, I. 245.
[4] See opinions of Iredell, Maclaine, Davie, and Johnston. Elliot, IV. 89, 156, 157, 173, 183, 184 ; McRee, II. 60, 63, 246, 247, 267.
[5] See McRee, II. 246-247, 267. In the state convention one speaker objected specifically to the prohibition of paper money. Elliot, IV. 169.
[6] McRee, II. 241.   [7] Elliot, IV. 182-185.

issue of bills of credit by the states would interfere with the paper currency already in circulation, and it was proposed[1] to amend the plan of government in such a way as to make such interference impossible. In the votes upon ratification it appears that the counties adjoining Albemarle and Pamlico sounds were the real support of the federal cause; and it will be noticed that this region was the oldest and most populous part of the state, representing distinctly the commercial interests of North Carolina.[2] Five out of the six towns represented in the convention of 1788 favored ratification,[3] and it was from one of these that a protest against paper money had come in 1783.[4] On the other hand, the opposition to the Constitution centred in the thinly populated districts of the interior and of the southern parts of the state.[5] We have already noticed that, in 1771, the delegates from this southern district had been most anxious to flood the province with paper money; and it seems certain that, in 1788, the desire for such a currency was greatest in the

[1] Elliot, IV. 247.
[2] Libby, 38.
[3] *Idem*, 41. Cf. *American Museum*, III. 71-74.
[4] McRee, II. 63.
[5] See Libby's map of the distribution of North Carolina's vote. With this compare the map of the Eleventh Census showing the density of population in 1790. Eleventh Census, Report on Population, I., p. XIX. This shows that the southern and western counties had a population of from two to six persons per square mile.

sparsely settled regions of the south and west. It is evident, therefore, that there was a close connection between the inflationist movements in 1785 and the opposition to the Constitution in 1788.

Although so large a part of the debt contracted during the Revolution had been wiped out by the depreciation of the paper,[1] to the great loss or utter ruin of the holders of the bills, North Carolina had a large debt in 1787. This consisted of certificates issued to creditors, the almost worthless bills of credit emitted during the war, and the currency created in 1783 and 1785. The convention called to consider the constitution in 1788 recommended[2] that the legislature should "take effectual measures for the redemption of the paper currency"; and the town of Wilmington, at least, instructed its representative to favor such a policy.[3] A few months later it was proposed to adopt a scale of depreciation for the paper emitted in 1783 and 1785, and some members desired to issue £70,000 more;[4] but no such measures were adopted. In 1789, the paper had begun to appreciate, and complaints of a great scarcity of money were renewed.[5] During the following year the assembly was "again running riot" over the action of Congress in voting to assume the debts of the states.[6] Taxes had been levied in 1788 and

---

[1] See McRee, II. 63; Annals of Congress, 4th Cong., 2d Sess., 1800.

[2] Elliot, IV. 252.

[3] McRee, II. 243.

[4] *Idem*, II. 246, 267.

[5] *Idem*, II. 276.

[6] *Idem*, II. 301.

1789 for calling in the continental and state paper and the certificates issued to public creditors,[1] so that a certain amount of these obligations had been paid in at the treasury.[2] Maclaine reports that, in 1790, some persons proposed to subscribe these funds in the hands of the comptroller and treasurer as a part of the debt of the state.[3] The assembly did actually draw upon these securities in the treasury for £12,000 to defray contingent charges for the current year.[4] Under the funding act of 1790, the United States authorized the assumption of $2,400,000 of North Carolina's indebtedness, and the national government actually assumed $1,793,803 [5] of this amount.

But a large part of the bills of credit issued in 1783 and 1785 remained in circulation. In 1796, Walcott reported[6] that the "debt of the State consists principally of paper bills of credit, of which about one hundred and fifty thousand pounds are estimated to be in the treasury and in circulation." A year later the debt of North Carolina was reported to be $430,000,[7] which represents probably the approximate amount of currency then outstanding. In 1804, the state chartered the Bank of Cape Fear and the New-bern Bank, and required that the capital of each

---

[1] Iredell, Laws, 630, 666.
[2] McRee, II. 304.
[3] *Idem*, II. 301.
[4] *Idem*, II. 304.
[5] Tenth Census, VII. 327 ; U. S. Stat., I. 142.
[6] State Papers, Finance, I. 434.
[7] Annals of Congress, 4th Cong., 2d Sess., 1802.

institution should be subscribed in specie. The managers of these banks [1] "contrived to get possession of nearly all the paper money which had been issued on the faith of the State, which being at the time a legal tender, enabled them to evade demands for specie, which they did, by thrusting this ragged paper at those who presented their notes for specie." This makes it seem probable that in 1804 there was some difference between the value of paper and that of gold or silver. The bills of credit were still in circulation in 1810, when the State Bank of North Carolina was chartered. The law establishing this institution provided [2] that the capital stock should be $1,600,000, and that one-fourth of this amount should be paid "in the paper currency emitted by this State." After the bank should be ready to commence business, the notes were to be no longer a tender for debts due to or from the bank. Finally, the dividends on the $250,000 of stock owned by the state were to be applied to the redemption of the paper subscribed to the bank's capital. But this law did not fully accomplish the purpose of retiring the paper money, [3] for the subscriptions to the stock of the bank proved smaller than was desired, in spite of the fact that addi-

[1] Gouge, 144.
[2] Laws of North Carolina, 1171–1180. This law was entitled "An act to redeem the paper currency now in circulation, and to establish a bank," etc. Cf. Gouge, 145.
[3] On this bank see Sumner, Banking, 46–47, 85, 176–177.

tional inducements were offered by a subsequent act of the legislature.[1] In 1814, the charters of the Banks of Cape Fear and Newbern were extended upon condition that, in case the State Bank should be voluntarily dissolved before December 18, 1816, these institutions should redeem the bills of credit with their own bank notes at the rate of one dollar for ten shillings.[2] This showed, of course, a depreciation of twenty per cent in the value of the old currency, which was issued at the rate of one dollar for eight shillings. In 1814, 1816, and 1823, the state treasurer was authorized to issue $262,000 of treasury notes in order to pay for subscriptions to bank stock.[3] The dividends received from these investments were used in retiring the notes, but in 1836 it was stated[4] that $50,887 were still outstanding.

In 1837, John C. Calhoun made the following statement[5] concerning the history of the bills of credit issued in 1783 and 1785: " North Carolina, just after the Revolution, issued a large amount of paper, which was made receivable in dues to her. It was also made a legal tender, but which, of course, was not obligatory after the adoption of the Federal Constitution. A large amount, say between four and five hundred thousand dollars, remained in circulation after that period, and continued to circulate for more than twenty years at

[1] Laws of North Carolina, 1199. [2] *Idem*, 1301–1302.
[3] *Idem*, 1301, 1346; Sumner, Banking, 177.
[4] *Idem*, 177. [5] Calhoun, III. 86.

par with gold and silver during the whole time, with no other advantage than being received in the revenue of the State, which was much less than $100,000 per annum. I speak on the information of citizens of that State on whom I can rely." If Calhoun had consulted the law passed by the legislature of North Carolina in 1814, he would have learned that ten shillings of bills of credit were worth at that time only eight shillings in specie. In 1787, as we have seen, the depreciation was very much greater.

We have now followed the history of paper money in North Carolina through three periods, of which the first begins in 1712 and the last ends about a century later. The first period ended with an act of utter bankruptcy, the paper currency having sunk from £150 colonial in 1715 to £1000 colonial in 1748 for every £100 sterling. The experience of the province during the second period, which ended in 1774, was much less disastrous. Yet the bills of credit issued in 1748 and subsequent years depreciated from £133 to £200 colonial for £100 sterling. That worse results were not reaped during these years was due solely to the restraining influence of the governors, who were bound by explicit instructions and by the act of 1764; for the assembly desired repeatedly to emit large sums of new paper. In respect of the repeated violations of public faith, the second period was hardly better than the first. Moreover, the province entered upon the contest for independence, burdened with a paper currency and unprovided with an adequate system of taxation. The third period saw the rise and fall of the continental paper currency and the issue of $34,100,000 by the state; all of which became practically worthless in 1781, entailing a second bankruptcy. Then £200,000 more paper was issued in 1783 and 1785, only to depreciate to one-half its nominal value and to involve the state in a losing speculation in tobacco. What the subsequent policy of North Carolina might have been if the Federal Constitution had not prohibited the issue of bills of credit by the states, can be only a matter of conjecture. Perhaps the War of 1812 would have furnished a pretext for another reckless inflation of the currency. In any event, the state was unwilling to levy taxes to redeem the paper that was outstanding in 1789.

Part III

THE PAPER CURRENCY OF NEW HAMPSHIRE

CHAPTER I

COLONIAL ISSUES (1709–1739)

DURING Queen Anne's War, New Hampshire became involved in debt, and began to issue bills of credit in order that "the government may stand fair with her Majesty's good subjects, and the soldjers may be encouraged in the defense of the Province."[1] The first issue of £3000 was made in 1709,[2] and the bills then emitted were declared to be receivable for taxes at five per cent advance;[3] so that they practically bore interest. Taxes seem to have been established to redeem the bills within a period of five years.

During the following year, it became necessary to raise additional funds,[4] and a second issue of £2500 was authorized.[5] In 1711, the legislature voted[6] to reissue £2000 of bills that had been brought into the treasury in payment of taxes, and emitted £2000 of new currency.[7] At about

---

[1] Papers of New Hampshire, III. 420.

[2] *Idem*, III. 410–411. The house of representatives declared that it would prefer to borrow from Massachusetts the money needed.

[3] *Idem*, III. 430.

[4] See Letters of governor. *Idem*, III. 440, 449.

[5] *Idem*, III. 460.

[6] *Idem*, III. 474, 475, 477, 503, 505.

[7] *Idem*, III. 503, 505.

the same time it was decided to discontinue the five per cent advance allowed on money paid into the treasury, since it was thought that the bills circulated readily enough without such a concession.[1] It now became necessary to pass an act for suppressing counterfeiting.[2] In 1712, in order to pay various claims against the province, it was decided to reissue the £1000 that would be received from the payment of taxes for that year, and to make a new emission of £500.[3] This brought the total issues up to £8000 ($26,660);[4] and, since the £3000 of bills reissued must have represented practically all of the money received from the taxes levied to sink the currency, it is probable that the whole amount of the original emissions was in circulation. In May of this year the legislature authorized the treasurer of the province to receive torn or defaced bills in exchange for currency that was in good condition.[5]

In April, 1713, the war was ended by the Treaty of Utrecht, and no more paper money was manufactured during that year. But, in 1714, £1200 was emitted "for the payment of the province Debts."[6] In this year it was found[7]

[1] Papers, III. 473–474.

[2] Idem, III. 477. The text of this act may be found in Acts of N. H., 34. It made the penalty for counterfeiting the same as for forgery. [8] Papers, III. 533–534.

[4] I assume that the dollar was rated at six shillings.

[5] Papers, III. 514.

[6] Idem, III. 565. These bills were to be redeemed in five years.

[7] Idem, III. 563.

that the taxes were being paid partly in bills
issued by Massachusetts, Rhode Island, and Connecticut; and accordingly the legislature voted to
lend the entire £1500 of taxes collected during the
past year to persons who would agree to repay
the loan in New Hampshire currency.[1] Thus in
the second year of peace the province managed
to increase its issues by £1200, and to prevent
the retirement of £1500 of bills that should have
been withdrawn from circulation.

The bills issued by each New England province
came to circulate freely in all of the others,[2] so
that Douglass could speak of the "promiscuous
Currency in the four Governments."[3] In 1712,
we find that New Hampshire deposited a certain
quantity of her bills in Boston in order that they
might be exchanged for worn and defaced money.[4]
The result was that practically a single currency,
subject to a uniform rate of depreciation, circulated
in New England until 1749.[5] Thus, in 1741, a writer

[1] Papers. The money appears to have remained in the hands of
the borrowers for a long time. In 1715, it was reported that the
loan had been made and good security taken. *Idem*, III. 605. In
1716, £230 more was loaned in the same manner. *Idem*, III. 643.
In 1722, it was reported that the £1500 loan and the £230 loan
were represented by bonds that were in safe keeping. *Idem*, IV.
341. In 1732, the borrowers of this £1730 loan were required to
pay arrears of interest and renew their bonds. *Idem*, IV. 655.

[2] Bronson, 52–53; Douglass, Discourse, 309; Papers, V. 565.

[3] Douglass, Discourse, 311.

[4] Felt, 64.

[5] This is evident from a comparison of tables of depreciation in
the four colonies. See Felt, 83, 135; Diary of Hutchinson, I. 53;

in Boston stated that " public bills of four Provinces " were circulating in Massachusetts at 29s.
for an ounce of silver.[1] In 1739, the secretary of
the province of New Hampshire wrote to the
home authorities as follows:[2] "The rate of
Silver and Exchange between this Currency and
Sterling has always been the same as at Boston,
which is the Grand Mart of New England, and in
that respect governs the whole country." The
New England money began to depreciate in 1713
or 1714; and, by the latter year, 9s. in New
Hampshire paper was required to purchase one
ounce of silver, whereas 8s. would have sufficed
at the time the first bills were issued.[3] With a
view perhaps to preventing further depreciation,
the legislature now decided that the paper should
once more be received at the treasury at five per
cent advance.[4]

In 1715, it was found that £1500 of province
bills had been drawn into the treasury; and the
legislature voted to reissue £500 of this money,
while it was decided to have the remainder burnt.[5]
This was the first time that the law had been
obeyed by destroying the paper received from the
taxes levied to sink the bills. By this means the

Douglass, Summary, I. 494; Wright, LXV.; Belknap, III. 225;
Coll. N. H. Hist. Soc., V. 258; Bronson, 52; Potter and Rider, 55;
Weeden, 473–474, 484.

[1] Felt, 107.   [2] Papers, V. 46.
[3] Cf. Douglass, Discourse, 304; Belknap, III. 225.
[4] Papers, III. 564.
[5] *Idem*, III. 586, 589, 591, 592, 605.

issues outstanding were reduced to about £8200,[1] and the price of silver remained at 9s. for the year 1715. During 1716, the legislature reissued £1500 of bills[2] instead of burning them, so that the currency remained stationary. At the same time, taxes to the amount of £1000 were suspended.[3] The price of silver rose to 10s. per ounce for 1716, the increased depreciation being due perhaps to larger issues of paper by other provinces. Although the colony now had a paper circulation of about $27,000,[4] and a marked depreciation of twenty-five per cent had set in, the legislature had complained of "a very great scarcity of Money," and had resorted to a repeal of part of the taxes levied to sink the bills of credit. This action was prophetic of the events of the ensuing year.

Early in 1717, it was proposed to make a new and much larger emission,[5] and by May it was voted to issue £15,000 on loan for eleven years at ten per cent interest.[6] The money was to be

[1] The total issues had been £9200 after the emission of 1714.

[2] Papers, III. 643, 644, 646, 647.

[3] Idem, III. 647.

[4] The circulation must have remained at about £8200, or $27,330. The population of New Hampshire was estimated at only 10,000 in 1730. Coll. of N. H. Hist. Soc., I. 229. The money in circulation in 1716 must have amounted to about three dollars per capita, a large sum for a province with so few industries and so little commerce as New Hampshire had. In 1730, the imports into the province were estimated at only £5000 sterling. Idem, I. 228.

[5] Papers, III. 671, 675, 687.

[6] Idem, III. 688–689. Cf. Belknap, II. 20–21; Hildreth, II. 311.

lent upon mortgages on land double the value of each loan, and the various towns were to receive shares proportioned to their quotas of the province taxes. The annual payments of ten per cent of the loan were to be burned in the presence of the assembly each year, and bills issued by other provinces were to be accepted in such payments only at five per cent discount. It is evident that the New Hampshire inflationists were unwilling to be outdone by their brethren in Massachusetts and Rhode Island, where public loan banks had been created in 1714 and 1715.[1] None of the bills of former emissions were burned this year,[2] so that the currency of the province must have been increased to about £23,000. As a result, the price of an ounce of silver rose to 11s. in 1718, and 12s. in the following year.[3]

For the next few years the inflationists seem to have been content with what they had accomplished. In 1718, the assembly voted to burn £900 of old bills,[4] but the records do not state distinctly that this event took place. In 1720, £964 was actually burnt.[5] Thus, at the most, the currency was decreased by only £1864 between 1718 and the end of 1720. Meanwhile counter-

[1] Felt, 67; Potter and Rider, 11.

[2] The records show no further burning of bills until 1718. In January, the lower house of the legislature passed an act intended to reissue all the bills of credit in the treasury. Papers, III. 667.

[3] Belknap, III. 225.

[4] Papers, III. 736, 737.

[5] *Idem*, III. 786.

feiters had been at work in the province,[1] so that
the governor recommended that some of the bills
should be exchanged for new currency.[2] In 1721,
the governor received instructions from England
to consent to no more laws for issuing bills of
credit unless they contained a clause providing
that they should not go into operation until approved by the home government.[3] By this time
the depreciation had increased so greatly that an
ounce of silver was worth 13s. in paper;[4] yet it
appears that £1500 of money that had been
drawn into the treasury was "misapplied," so that
the governor had to urge the assembly to "consider of ways and means to bring it into the treasury again."[5]

During 1721, bills to the amount of £1188 were
burned,[6] but the currency did not improve. In
spite of this fact, the legislature attempted to emit
£20,000 and then £15,000 of new paper, and
desired to reissue money that had been paid into
the treasury.[7] Thus the appetite for a cheap currency had not been satisfied, although $67,000 of
paper was in circulation.[8]

[1] Papers, III. 797. [2] *Idem*, III. 830.
[3] *Idem*, III. 813-814. Cf. Bancroft, II. 263 ; Green, 163.
[4] Belknap, III. 225. [5] Papers, III. 830.
[6] *Idem*, III. 810, 819, 829.
[7] *Idem*, III. 802, 807, 815, 835, 838.
[8] Subtracting the sums already stated to have been burned from
the total emissions, it appears that £20,148 was in circulation or in
the treasury. This would amount to more than six dollars per
capita.

The colony now became involved in an Indian war which lasted for three years.[1] This furnished a pretext for renewed issues of paper; and another was found in a proposition "for Striking bills of Credit in this province for the encouragement of raising naval Stores,"[2] for which the royal assent was desired. The result was that in May, 1722, the legislature voted to issue £2800;[3] and in the following October decided to emit £2000 more.[4] These were used for province expenses, and were to be redeemed by taxes payable in bills of credit or naval stores. No paper seems to have been burned this year; and, by its close, silver was selling for 14s. 6d. per ounce. Besides making these two new issues, the legislature voted[5] to emit £5384 of bills of credit to be exchanged for the worn and defaced paper issued prior to 1716.[6] These new bills were to be redeemed in five equal instalments by taxes that should begin in 1724 and continue to 1728.[7]

[1] See Belknap, II. 43–83 ; Papers, IV. 148.
[2] Papers, IV. 40, 317.   [3] *Idem*, IV. 35, 36, 38, 39, 315.
[4] *Idem*, IV. 74, 76.   [5] *Idem*, IV. 35, 36, 315, 339, 340.
[6] The issues prior to 1716 amounted to £9200. Of these I find that no more than £2000 were burned prior to 1722. *Idem*, III. 592, 605, 737. The other bills that were burned were a part of the £15,000 emitted on loan in 1715. This would make it seem that £7200 of the early bills must be in circulation, whereas the law of 1722 proposed to exchange only £5384. The legislature may have assumed that all of the £4052 of bills burned prior to 1722 were of the emissions prior to 1716. On this assumption it would have been calculated that £5148 were in circulation.
[7] The old bills were replaced only gradually by the £5384 emis-

The province had, at the beginning of 1723, a currency amounting to about £25,000.[1] This was equivalent to at least eight dollars per capita,[2] and the price of silver soon advanced to 16s. per ounce. During 1723, the records show that £321 of the bills were retired,[3] while no more issues were made. But, in 1724, the governor had to ask for additional funds for conducting the campaign against the Indians,[4] and a new issue of £2000 was authorized.[5] These bills were to remain in circulation for a period of ten years, since the taxes levied to redeem them were not to be collected until 1733 and 1734. During 1724, £626 of the currency was burned,[6] so that the net

sion. I find that £2281 of old bills were exchanged between 1723 and 1726. Papers, IV. 119, 122, 137, 162, 163, 181, 195, 196, 202, 211, 228. By 1737, the total number of bills exchanged was £4998. See Papers, IV. 246, 247, 299, 517, 598, 618, 633, 652, 690, 704, 710, 718, 732. In 1742, £85 more was exchanged. Papers, V. 182. This raised the amount exchanged to £5084.

[1] This is the total of the £20,148 issued and in circulation prior to 1722, and the £4800 emitted in that year.

[2] The province could not have had a population much in excess of 10,000 before 1730. See Coll. of N. H. Hist. Soc., I. 229.

[3] Papers, IV. 348. Besides this, £789 of the bills issued prior to 1716 were burned after being exchanged for bills of the £5384 emission. Idem, IV. 119, 122. This, however, did not effect any change in the amount of money in circulation. In subsequent statements no account will be taken of the bills exchanged for those of the £5384 emission.   [4] Idem, IV. 156.

[5] Idem, IV. 157, 158, 167, 395, 398; V. 29. The house of representatives desired to emit £3000, but the council refused. Idem, IV. 156, 157. This is perhaps an indication of a desire for a conservative policy upon the part of the council.

[6] Idem, IV. 381.

increase of the paper money for the year was only £1374.

In May, 1725, Governor Wentworth informed the assembly[1] that the clergy of the province had been sorely distressed by the depreciation of the paper currency, since salaries of £100 established a dozen years before had been reduced to about one-half of their original worth.[2] The assembly, in the same month, abolished the five per cent advance that had been allowed for province bills received in payment of taxes.[3] Shortly after this, bills issued by the other New England colonies were made receivable for the taxes of the current year.[4] This last action is explained probably by the desire of the assembly to make the retirement of the New Hampshire bills as difficult as possible, for any bills of the other provinces that might come into the treasury were sure to be reissued. In December, an issue of £2000 of paper was authorized[5] in order to defray the expenses of the war. This emission, like the previous one, was to be redeemed by taxes due only after ten years. The paper burned during this year amounted to £1377,[6] so that the net increase of the currency was £607.

[1] Papers, IV. 169.
[2] Silver was at 8s. per ounce in 1710, and at 15s. or 16s. in 1725. Belknap, III. 225.
[3] Papers, IV. 175, 178, 401.
[4] *Idem*, IV. 407. See also law of 1729. *Idem*, 522, 529.
[5] *Idem*, IV. 194, 205, 411, 417, V. 30.
[6] *Idem*, IV. 181, 405.

At the opening of 1726, the province must have had about £26,624 of paper in circulation.[1] In January, £500 was issued in order to replace worn or defaced bills of any issue since 1715.[2] Then in December two new emissions, aggregating £2000, were authorized.[3] One-half of these was to be redeemed by taxes in 1737, and the other half in 1738. In this same month the legislature had to appropriate £150 of currency in order to purchase a bill of exchange for £50 sterling.[4] During the course of the year bills amounting to £940 were burned,[5] so that the legislation of 1726 resulted in a net addition of £1060 to the currency of the province.[6]

In 1727, a further emission of £2000 was authorized, and the bills were to be redeemed in 1739 and 1740.[7] Thus the period of redemption, which at first had been five years, had now been lengthened to thirteen. During this year £1099 of the former issues was retired,[8] so that the real increase

[1] This equals the £24,948 circulating at the end of 1722, plus the £4000 emitted in 1724 and 1725, and minus the £2324 burned in 1723, 1724, and 1725.

[2] Papers, IV. 201, 205, 416, 417.

[3] Idem, IV. 232, 239, 438, 443, V. 30.

[4] Idem, IV. 233–234. This corresponds very closely to the figures of Belknap. The latter gives 16s. as the price of silver in 1726. Belknap, III. 225. The sterling price of silver was 5s. 2d.

[5] Papers, IV. 237, 422, 442.

[6] In May of this year the house desired to issue £2000 for public buildings, but the council refused. Idem, IV. 430.

[7] Idem, IV. 250, 251, V. 30.

[8] Idem, IV. 246, 445.

of the currency was £901. In the spring of 1728, the lower house of the legislature proposed to issue £30,000 upon the same terms as the loan of 1717, but the council objected on the ground that this was too large a sum.[1] A similar proposal was made a month later, and met with the same fate.[2] Upon the first of June, two projected issues were under discussion, but neither one seems to have been authorized.[3] During this entire session the two houses of the legislature had been engaged in a series of disputes over various matters,[4] and it is not strange, therefore, that the council felt inclined to object to a proposal to add £30,000 to a currency that was already depreciated. The legislature was dissolved in June, and did not meet again until April 22, 1729.[5] During the entire year no bills seem to have been destroyed, and the price of silver had now advanced to 17s. per ounce.[6]

When the legislature met in 1729, several attempts were made to reissue bills that had been drawn into the treasury in payment of taxes.[7] In the end, £1776 of the currency was reëmitted,[8]

[1] Papers, IV. 289, 490.

[2] *Idem*, IV. 298. Meanwhile, a proposition to issue £3000 had failed to receive the approval of the council. *Idem*, IV. 491.

[3] *Idem*, IV. 502.

[4] On this dispute see Belknap, II. 90–93.

[5] Papers, IV. 308.   [6] Belknap, III. 225.

[7] Papers, IV. 529, 553.

[8] This was in two issues of £1076 and £700. *Idem*, IV. 516, 517, 530, 546, 550, 557, V. 30.

after a discussion in which the instructions of the governor played a part.[1] The salary of the chief magistrate was now fixed at £600 in the paper money of the province, a sum which was declared to be worth £200 sterling.[2] By this time the £15,000 issued on loan in 1717 was due, but only £5797 had been actually paid in and destroyed.[3] The legislature was unwilling to retire this currency, but finally provided that it should be withdrawn in three instalments in 1729, 1730, and 1731.[4] During the entire year, £3108 of old bills were burned;[5] but the outstanding currency still amounted to about £25,477, while the price of silver advanced to 19s. 6d. per ounce.[6]

In 1730, Governor Belcher informed the assembly that he had "a liberty to emit from time to time what Bills of Credit may be necessary to defray the expense" of the province.[7] Accordingly no time was lost in preparing a bill for issuing £1300,[8] which received Belcher's assent after the assembly had made alterations desired by him in the bill granting his salary.[9] Encouraged by its success in this matter, the legislature, later in the year, passed a bill for issuing £6000 for repairing forts

[1] Papers, IV. 517.

[2] *Idem*, IV. 513. For Belcher's salary in 1730 see *Idem*, IV. 570, 760, 761.

[3] See *Idem*, III. 786, 810, 819, 829, IV. 181, 237, 246, 349, 381, 526.

[4] *Idem*, IV. 516, 537, 544, 624.

[5] *Idem*, IV. 497, 517, 526.

[6] Belknap, III. 225.

[7] Papers, IV. 566.

[8] *Idem*, IV. 571, 572, 761.

[9] *Idem*, IV. 571-572.

and building a state house.[1]   This time, however, the governor objected,[2] and " produced his Instructions prohibiting his assent to any bill for the Emission of any more paper currency, except for the support of the government." Besides this measure, the assembly sought also to postpone to a later period the redemption of the outstanding bills ; but here again Belcher's veto was encountered.[3]   No paper money was burned during this year, so that the currency of the province must have increased to about £26,777.

In 1731, the legislature brought forward repeated projects for issuing more paper, one of these taking the form of a £40,000 loan,[4] but these efforts proved fruitless.   No bills were burned in this year, however, so that the currency remained unchanged.   In 1732, Governor Belcher, whose instructions required him to have the outstanding currency retired punctually according to the law,[5] called the attention of the legislature to the £15,000 loan emitted in 1717.[6]   He said that, although all of the loans ought to have been paid by 1731, not half of the issue had actually been collected. When the legislature desired to emit £1000 of bills to be redeemed by a tax in 1744, he informed it that his instructions required him to have all the money retired by 1742.[7]   During the year, the

[1] Papers, IV. 583.

[2] *Idem*, IV. 771–772.

[3] *Idem*, IV. 771.

[4] *Idem*, IV. 593, 607, 608, 777.

[5] *Idem*, IV. 772.

[6] *Idem*, IV. 624.

[7] *Idem*, IV. 621, 622, 786.

currency was diminished by burning £1311 of old bills,[1] so that it stood at about £25,466.

In 1733, the house of representatives twice attempted to emit £20,000 upon loan for a period of sixteen years, but the council objected to the project, stating finally that it would be "diametrically opposite" to the governor's instructions.[2] The representatives then desired to petition the King for his assent to this project,[3] and a deadlock ensued which was ended by the governor, who dissolved the assembly.[4] In January, 1734, a new legislature was convened, and Belcher urged it to place the defences and public buildings of the province in proper condition, and to provide for the public debts.[5] Within a few days the lower house proposed to issue £3000 of paper that should not be retired until after 1742, and the council passed an act to emit £3000 which should be cancelled in 1740, 1741, and 1742.[6] This ultimately led to another deadlock,[7] which called from Governor Belcher a sharp message stating that he would not under any conditions extend the time of the currency beyond 1742.[8] The representatives then declared their intention of appealing to the Board of Trade, and defied the governor.[9] They

[1] Papers, IV. 598, 622.

[2] Idem, IV. 634, 635, 636, 637, 640, 791.

[3] Idem, IV. 641-642.   [4] Idem, IV. 644-645.

[5] Idem, IV. 647-648. On this dispute see Belknap, II. 109-110.

[6] Papers, IV. 655, 799.   [8] Idem, IV. 662.

[7] Idem, IV. 657-661.   [9] Idem, IV. 663-664.

next discussed plans for reissuing interest money
due on the £15,000 loan, until Belcher finally dissolved the assembly a second time.[1]   Belcher then
issued a proclamation ordering the commissioners
in charge of the £15,000 loan to enforce strictly
the payment of the amounts still outstanding.[2]

In the fall of 1734, a new assembly was convened,
and urged by the governor to provide the funds
needed for meeting public debts and supporting
the government.[3]   But the members showed no
disposition to comply with his request, and were
soon sent back to their homes.   Between January 1,
1733, and December 31, 1734, the bills of credit
burned amounted to £2035,[4] so that the currency
of the province now stood at the sum of £23,431.
Yet the large issues made by the other colonies in
New England and the unwillingness of the New
Hampshire legislature to fulfil its own promises
had discredited the paper, so that silver was now
selling [5] at 27s. per ounce.   Under such conditions
the house of representatives had passed an act
making the paper issued by the province a tender
even in special contracts,[6] and had the assurance
to send over for the consideration of the English
authorities a scheme for emitting £60,000 of new
bills of credit.[7]

In April, 1735, Governor Belcher called the

---

[1] Papers, IV. 666–667.   [5] Belknap, III. 225.

[2] *Idem*, IV. 668.   [6] Papers, IV. 659.

[3] *Idem*, IV. 671–680.   [7] *Idem*, IV. 834–835.

[4] *Idem*, IV. 633, 652.

assembly together again. He informed them that no taxes had been laid to supply the treasury for four years, and that the needs of the province were extremely urgent.[1] The house of representatives prepared a supply bill, which provided for the emission of £4000 of bills of credit[2] that were to be redeemed in 1742 by taxes payable in hemp, flax, and bills of credit issued by the other New England provinces as well as those emitted by New Hampshire. The council objected to this measure, pointing out, among other things, that a tax payable in this manner would not call enough province bills into the treasury to make it possible to retire the paper by 1742.[3] The representatives insisted upon their original measure, and the governor then dissolved[4] the assembly. During the session Governor Belcher had called the attention of the legislature to the fact that certain citizens of New Hampshire had presumed "to strike and Issue paper notes or Bills to pass in lieu of money." He said that, since the province was restrained by express instructions from doing such a thing, "private persons ought not to presume upon it."[5] The house of representatives replied[6] that it was "not sensible wherein such an attempt is unwarrantable unless some notorious Fraude or Cheat might be designed and discovered therein," since the instructions from the English authorities did not

[1] Papers, IV. 681, 685.
[2] Idem, IV. 694.
[3] Idem, IV. 695.
[4] Idem, IV. 696-698.
[5] Idem, IV. 685.
[6] Idem, IV. 688.

extend "to negotiable Notes amongst Merchants and Traders." Belcher proceeded to issue a proclamation warning people against receiving the notes; and desired to have the legislature pass an act outlawing these private issues,[1] as Massachusetts had been induced to do.[2] He asserted that complaints had been received[3] that "some of the Principle founders or undertakers in the scheme have Refused to give credit to those their own notes." This seemed to close the incident.[4] During 1735, bills were burned to the amount of £1023,[5] so that the currency amounted to about £22,408.

In 1736, a new assembly was called together, and the old quarrel was resumed; but the grounds of dispute were slightly changed. The house of representatives finally drew up an address to the governor,[6] which the council pronounced "so full of first Principles of Nature and void of those of Grace" as to justify a refusal to join with the lower house in any further acts of legislation.[7] Governor Belcher called the answer of the representatives indecent, and once more dissolved the

---

[1] Papers, IV. 688, 697.

[2] In 1735, Massachusetts passed an act forbidding any person to receive the bills issued by these New Hampshire merchants. Acts of Mass., II. 743–744.

[3] Papers, IV. 697.

[4] On this private issue in New Hampshire see Belknap, II. 110; Felt, 91–92.

[5] Papers, IV. 690.

[6] *Idem*, IV. 707–708.   [7] *Idem*, IV. 711–712.

assembly.[1]   During 1736, paper to the amount
of £1000 was retired,[2] and the currency was
reduced to £21,408.   Toward the close of the
year the price of silver fell from 27s. 6d. to 26s.
6d.,[3] so that the resolute course of Governor
Belcher[4] was resulting in a slight decrease of the
depreciation.

Early in 1737, a new assembly convened, and
the governor stated that it was now six years since
"any supply of money to the Treasury" had been
provided.[5]   The representatives then proceeded
to discuss the advisability of issuing £3000 to
replace worn and defaced bills.[6]   Finally the governor consented to the issue of £6500 of new bills,
in order to defray the accumulated debts of the
last five or six years.[7]   These debts included £970
of arrears on the salary of the governor, six years
arrears of salary due to the treasurer, six and one-
half years salary due to the clerk, and arrears due
to other persons for periods of similar length.
These new bills[8] were to be redeemed by taxes[9] of
which £4000 were payable in 1741, and £2500[10]

[1] Papers, IV. 712–713.   [2] Idem, IV. 704.

[3] Belknap, III. 225.

[4] The council bore the brunt of the contest with the representatives, but it was probably reflecting the governor's wishes.   This
often happened in colonial politics.   See Greene, 87.

[5] Papers, IV. 716.   [6] Idem, IV. 717, 822, 824.

[7] Idem, IV. 722–724, 732, 734.

[8] A copy of one of these bills may be found in Winsor, V. 174.

[9] Papers, IV. 724.

[10] In Idem, V. 30, this issue appears as two issues, one of
£4000 and the other of £2500.   The date is erroneously stated 1736.

in 1742. Thus Belcher nominally adhered to the letter of his instructions; but the taxes seem to have been made payable in hemp, flax, and bar iron, as well as in paper, so that they would not suffice to call in all of the bills emitted.

The assembly now succeeded in securing the passage of a bill for the issue of £3000 in order to exchange old and worn bills.[1] Not content with this, efforts were made, upon various pretexts, to issue £500, £1000, and then £1500 more paper; but all of these seem to have failed.[2] During 1737, bills to the amount of £963[3] had been burned; so that the currency of the province had received a net increase of £5537,[4] and now equalled £26,945. In the following year, silver rose to 28s. per ounce.[5] In reviewing this long contest, Belknap justly concluded[6] that the real reason why the representatives refused for so long to supply the funds needed for the debts of the province was "that they wanted emissions of paper money, to be drawn in, at distant periods," which was contrary to the instructions of the governor as well as to his well-known principles.

In 1738, the legislature was not convened until November. For once it seems that no propositions

[1] Papers, IV. 732, 734. In 1738, it was reported that the £3000 had been exchanged and burned. *Idem*, V. 7.

[2] *Idem*. IV. 733, 734, 748, 750, 753, 829, 830, 831, 832.

[3] *Idem*, IV. 718.

[4] This is £6500 minus £963. The £3000 issued for exchanging old bills would have made no addition to the currency.

[5] Belknap, III. 225.   [6] *Idem*, II. 109.

were made for the issue of more bills of credit.[1] The governor called the attention of the assembly to the fact that the officials of Boston had arrested counterfeiters who had a plate for manufacturing bills like those emitted by New Hampshire in 1737.[2] Other indications of the activity of counterfeiters were not wanting,[3] and a law was passed[4] making the penalty for this offence "the pains of death without benefit of clergy." The governor and assembly received at this time a petition from Rev. Hugh Adams, praying for relief.[5] He stated that his nominal salary of £104 was now worth no more than £36, on account of "the altered prices of all necessaries for livelihood"; and asked that his stipend "be made good in full value as really as in name," and that his parish be required to make the payments punctually. During 1738, the records show that £4334 of currency was burned,[6] so that the outstanding paper now amounted to about £22,611.

During 1739, no additions were made to the currency, and no bills were burned. In June of

[1] See Papers, V. 1–9.

[2] *Idem*, V. 2.   [3] *Idem*, V. 55–56.

[4] *Idem*, 2, 4, 5, 8, 9. Cf. also *Idem*, V. 212. This law may be found in Acts and Laws of New Hampshire, 171–172.

[5] This petition is a most curious one. See Belknap, III. 350–358.

[6] Papers, V. 7. At the same time £3000 of old bills, exchanged for the new issue authorized in 1737, were burned before the assembly. This did not affect the amount of money in circulation, and is neglected here.

this year, the House of Commons requested the Privy Council to demand from each of the colonies a statement of the amounts of bills of credit issued and redeemed since 1700.[1] In accordance with this resolution, the secretary of New Hampshire prepared a statement concerning the bills of credit emitted by that province.[2] He said that some of the records had been lost through the destruction of his house by fire, and that the books of the office in former times had not been kept "with a due exactness." He stated that, as nearly as he could ascertain, £56,384 of bills of credit had been emitted by the province, of which £16,730[3] were issued upon loan. He estimated that all of these bills had been retired except £10,576 of the bills issued for public expenses and "about" £2000 of those emitted upon loan; and stated that the paper in circulation would all be retired by 1742.

This report will be found to differ very materially from the statements made in the preceding pages, but the points of difference admit of a partial explanation. According to the data given by the writer, the emissions of new bills had amounted to £44,800. The report of 1739 places the total at £56,384; but this figure includes at least some of the bills reissued,[4] which are excluded

[1] 23 Journals of House of Commons, 379.   [2] Papers, V. 45–46.

[3] In this sum he included the £15,000 issued in 1717, and the £1730 loaned out in 1714 and 1716.

[4] Thus the report of 1739 expressly includes the £1730 loan, which was made by reissuing bills paid into the treasury. We have a statement of the province accounts for the years between 1722 and

from the writer's statement.[1]   The total amount of currency reissued from 1709 to 1739 was £17,390.[2] Some of these bills must have been included, besides the £1730 expressly mentioned, in the total of £56,384 stated by the secretary.   In the second place, it will be remembered that the writer placed the currency in circulation in 1739 at £22,600 ;[3] while the report of 1739 states that the outstanding bills amounted to about £12,576. It is impossible to account for this difference.   The writer feels certain that his account of the bills emitted and bills cancelled[4] is complete, and that

1740, in which £1076 and £700 reissued in 1729 are included. Papers, V. 30. The report of 1739 undoubtedly includes other reissues besides the £1730 expressly mentioned.

[1] This method of procedure is simplest and most satisfactory. By subtracting the bills destroyed from the new issues, from which reissues are rigidly excluded, one can readily ascertain the amount of currency outstanding.

[2] This includes £7276 issued in 1711, 1712, 1715, 1716, 1725, and 1729 in order to pay province expenses, as explained in previous paragraphs.   It includes £1730 issued on loan in 1714 and 1716; £5384 issued in 1722 to exchange old bills; and £3000 issued for the same purpose in 1737.

[3] This is the difference between the £44,800 of new emissions and the £22,189 of such bills burned.   The records show that £4998 of old bills was burned before 1729 in exchange for the £5384 issued in 1722, and that £3000 was burned in 1738 in exchange for the £3000 issued in 1737.   But these transactions did not alter the amount of currency in circulation, and therefore the £7998 of paper thus burned is not included in the amount subtracted from the £44,800 of new bills issued.

[4] Thus the list of bills burned, which the writer secured from the records, is more complete than one found in a report of the treasurer in 1740.   See Papers, V. 23–33.

the report of 1739 is based upon data that were
not wholly accurate, as the secretary of the province admitted.[1]

In 1739, William Douglass wrote[2] that the
" Publick Bills " of New Hampshire " are so much
counterfeited they scarce obtain a Currency." For
this reason, and on account of the instructions of
the governor, he said that the " outstanding Bills
of publick Credit, some on Funds of Taxes, some
on Loan, do not exceed £12,000, gradually to be
cancelled by December 1742." It is possible that
Douglass secured his information from the same
person who prepared the report of 1739 for the
English authorities. He tells us finally that the
ordinary expenses of government for the province
of New Hampshire were £1500 New England
currency. This gives us the basis for an interesting comparison. The £22,600 of currency in circulation amounted to fifteen times the annual
public expenditures, so that the practice of receiving the bills in payment of taxes could do but little
to maintain the credit of the paper money.

This closes what we may call the first chapter
of New Hampshire's experience with a paper currency. The bills of credit had depreciated so that
the price of silver had risen from 8s. to 29s. 6d. per
ounce;[3] but the amount in circulation had been

---

[1] Moreover, since the interference of the English authorities was
feared, the author of the report of 1739 had every inducement to
place the outstanding bills at the smallest possible figure.

[2] Douglass, Discourse, 302–303.   [3] Belknap, III. 225.

diminished from £26,777 in 1730 to £22,611 in
1739, and the situation would improve if Belcher's
firm policy should be continued. Yet it must be
remembered that the results would have been much
worse than they actually were in 1739, if the legislature had been able to consult its own wishes in
issuing paper. The policy of the house of representatives had been manifested with sufficient
clearness, and the evident desire of this branch
of the legislature was to provide for all province
expenses by the emission of bills of credit that
were supposed to be redeemed by taxes after long
periods of ten or twelve years. Such a policy
would surely lead to bankruptcy unless restrained
by the governor and council, especially since, after
the bills had once been emitted, the assembly was
extremely disinclined to enforce the withdrawal of
the paper at the end of the periods contemplated
by the law.

CHAPTER II

COLONIAL ISSUES (1740–1774)

In 1740, news reached the province that England had declared war against Spain. Governor Belcher called the assembly together, and urged that Fort William and Mary should be strengthened.[1] The house of representatives replied that this could not be done[2] unless bills of credit could be issued and made to run beyond the year 1742. In a few days the governor dissolved the assembly, after it had become evident that he could not secure the passage of such measures as he desired.[3] It was reported at this time that a considerable part of the £15,000 loan of 1717 was still outstanding.[4] In August, another session was called, in order to provide for the equipment of soldiers to take part in an expedition against the West Indies. After some recrimination it was voted to issue £2000 for this purpose, and the bills were to be redeemed at the end of 1742 by taxes payable in paper money, flax, hemp, and bar iron.[5] During 1740, bills of credit were burned to

---

[1] Papers, V. 11.

[2] *Idem*, V. 18–19.

[3] *Idem*, V. 28, 67.

[4] *Idem*, V. 28.

[5] *Idem*, V. 52, 70, 71. Winsor gives a copy of one of these bills. Winsor, V. 175. In Papers, V. 30, the bills issued in 1740 are

the amount of £1197,[1] so that the currency of New Hampshire now stood at £23,414.[2]

The printed records for 1741 are exceedingly meagre,[3] but no mention is made of new emissions of paper. Governor Belcher at this time submitted a message[4] complaining that he had lost £3240 since 1730 through depreciation of the bills in which his salary was paid. The representatives replied[5] that the law fixing the salary made no provision for changes in the value of the bills, and that the governor would have to be content with what he was then receiving.

Late in 1741, Governor Belcher had been succeeded by Benning Wentworth, who convened the legislature in January, 1742.[6] The new governor congratulated[7] the assembly because "the Publick faith has been so Religiously kept in regard to past Emissions of paper money," and because "all former Emissions will be complyed with in the yeare 1742." He also asked to have his salary fixed in such a manner that "it may not be liable

---

placed at £2700. This sum may include the £700 mentioned in *Idem*, V. 72, 77. But, as the records do not show that this passed the council, I shall omit it from the list of issues.

[1] Papers, V. 17, 18, 23.

[2] This allows for the £2000 emitted and the £1197 cancelled in 1740. If the additional £700, mentioned in a previous note, was actually emitted, then the currency would amount to £24,114.

[3] See Papers, V. 73-86.

[4] *Idem*, V. 84-85.　　　　　[5] *Idem*, V. 85.

[6] On Wentworth's relations with the legislature at this time, see Belknap, II. 183-186.　　　[7] Papers, V. 136.

to vary or subject to depreciate by the uncertain value of paper Currency," which is an indication that his faith in the good intentions of the assembly was not over strong. The representatives proceeded to request that Wentworth should inform them concerning the nature of his instructions on the subject of issuing bills of credit,[1] and soon had under way a bill for emitting £6000.[2] The governor insisted that he could not assent to any such measure unless ample provision was made for his support ;[3] and a bargain was finally arranged upon this basis, Wentworth receiving a present of £125, and an annual grant of £250 out of the interest of the money that was soon issued upon loan.[4] As a result, we find him assuring the legislature of his "hearty concurrence" in any measure that would "expedite" the emission of the loan bank.[5]

The net result of the bargain concluded in 1742 was the issue of £4720 of paper money in order to pay public expenses,[6] and the emission of £25,000 upon loan.[7] Both of these issues were to be of a new tenor, and were declared equal to proclamation money, *i.e.* silver at a rating of 6*s*. 8*d*. per ounce. The bills of former emissions, now to be known as old tenor, were to pass in all payments

---

[1] Papers, V. 139, 141, 146.
[2] *Idem*, V. 142, 143, 145, 150.
[3] *Idem*, V. 669.
[6] *Idem*, V. 159, 212, 284, 619, 654.
[7] *Idem*, V. 160, 161, 164, 208-213, 620, 654.

[3] *Idem*, V. 151, 152.
[4] *Idem*, V. 152, 153, 155.

at one-fourth of the value of the new money.[1] Both of these acts received the approval of the English authorities.[2] The assembly desired to authorize another issue of £1280, but to this the governor objected.[3] During this year the bills that were cancelled amounted[4] to £1332; so that £22,082 of old tenor bills probably remained in circulation. At the nominal rating of 4 for 1, these would be equivalent to £5520 in bills of the new tenor.

In 1743, the legislature of Massachusetts proposed[5] to the other New England colonies that commissioners should be sent to Worcester to devise a plan for common action in retiring the outstanding bills of credit. We do not know, however, whether such a conference ever occurred. The £25,000 loan authorized in 1742 was not placed in circulation until after the assent of the home government was received in August of the following year.[6] Silver soon rose[7] from a price of 28s. in the middle of the former year to 32s. per ounce at the close of the latter. When the legislature met in May, 1743, the governor, being under the impression that the taxes of the previous year would call in all of the old emissions, urged that "a nice Enquiry" be made as to the exact condi-

---

[1] Papers, V. 143, 145, 157, 159, 615, 620.

[2] *Idem*, V. 654. A copy of one of these bills is given by Bryant and Gay, III. 133.

[3] Papers, V. 159, 616, 629.

[4] *Idem*, V. 161, 165, 181, 182.

[5] Felt, 115.

[6] Papers, V. 94, 654.

[7] Belknap, III. 225.

tion of the old currency.[1] He also said that provision had been made for "exchanging all money
of the old Tenor," if the taxes levied for sinking the
old bills should prove insufficient.[2] During 1743,
bills of credit were emitted to the amount of
£1280,[3] and bills of old tenor amounting to £3052
were burned;[4] so that the currency of the province must have equalled £19,030 in old tenor
and £31,000 in new.[5]

In 1744, renewed military expenses were incurred, and the assembly clamored loudly for
further emissions of paper, demanding at one time
£10,000 in a single issue.[6] In order to persuade
the governor to consent to further emissions, a
joint committee of the house and council was
appointed[7] to draw up resolutions showing the

[1] Papers, V. 652.

[2] This contradicts his first statement that the taxes for 1742
would call in all of the bills. He evidently doubted whether they
would suffice for that purpose.

[3] These were in two issues of £300 and £930. Papers, V. 209,
212, 670, 672. They seem to have been the £1280 of blank bills
which the legislature wished to emit in 1743. *Idem*, V. 159, 616,
629. This made £6000 new tenor issued for province expenses.
See *Idem*, VI. 223.   [4] *Idem*, V. 204.

[5] The £19,030 old tenor was equal to £4757 in new. Therefore the whole amount of currency was equivalent to £35,757 in
new tenor bills, or $119,190. The population of the province at
this time could not have been far from 20,000. In 1749 or 1750
Douglass estimated it at 24,000. Summary, II. 180.

[6] Papers, V. 239, 240, 248, 249, 720.

[7] *Idem*, V. 238–239. Wentworth seemed at one time to be
about to consent to the issue of bills in violation of his instructions.
Idem, V. 242–243.

necessity for such action. In the end, Wentworth consented to an act providing for the issue of £5500, on the condition that it should not go into operation until the consent of the English authorities should be secured.[1] The writer is unable to find whether such consent was secured and the bills actually emitted. Wentworth had positive instructions not to consent to the emission of more than £6000 of bills for the expenses of government,[2] and brought these out in a controversy in 1745, during which there was no mention of a violation of instructions in the previous year. Moreover, no issue of £5500 is included in a statement prepared by the assembly in 1753 concerning the paper issued during the previous decade.[3] For these reasons the proposed emission will not be included in the writer's list of actual issues.

During 1744, bills of the new tenor to the amount of £1122 were burned by the assembly,[4] so that the new tenor money was reduced to £29,878.[5] Of the old tenor bills, £771 was cancelled in this year.[6] It will be well at this point to complete the story of the bills of credit of the old emissions. The reader will remember that the writer's figures showed that £22,611 of old tenor money was in circulation in 1739, and

[1] Papers, V. 236, 251, 252, 551, 716, 722.
[2] *Idem*, V. 279.
[3] *Idem*, VI. 223–226.   [4] *Idem*, V. 250.
[5] This is on the assumption that no bills were issued in 1744.
[6] Papers, V. 250.

£19,030 at the end of 1743; whereas the report of 1739 placed the outstanding bills at only £12,576, and Governor Wentworth thought that all the bills would be brought in by the taxes of the year 1742. The records show that, between 1744 and 1754, inclusive, bills of credit of the old tenor were burned to the amount of £21,301.[1] This is a complete demonstration that the writer has not overstated the amount of old currency outstanding in 1739 and 1743.

At the opening of 1745, the price of silver was 35s. per ounce, and it steadily increased as the year progressed.[2] Preparations for the expedition against Louisbourg were now under way,[3] and New Hampshire was called upon to furnish her quota of men. In order to raise funds, the representatives proposed[4] to issue £10,000 of bills which should be redeemed by taxes in ten annual instalments beginning in 1755. The council objected that the bill did not appropriate all of the money

---

[1] The list is as follows : 1744, £771 ; 1746, £1397 ; 1747, £473 ; 1748, £342 ; 1753, £6733 ; 1754, £11,585. See Papers, V. 250, 416, 526, 919, VI. 221, 222, 250, 251, 252, 256, 257, 258, 259, 261. The writer's figures showed that £19,030 was outstanding at the end of 1743. The fact that a larger sum than this was actually burned between 1744 and 1754 may have been due to the presence of counterfeit bills. If it is true that the issues of 1740 amounted to £2700, as stated in Papers, V. 30, instead of £2000, as given in the writer's statement, then £700 of this excess of bills cancelled is accounted for.

[2] Belknap, III. 225.

[3] See Winsor, V. 410 ; Belknap, II. 198–200.

[4] Papers, V. 276–277 ; Belknap, II. 201.

issued to the purpose of defraying the charges of the expedition, and that the taxes for redeeming the bills ought not to be postponed longer than 1751.[1] Then the governor sent the assembly the text of one of his instructions,[2] by which he was ordered to consent to the emission of no more than £6000 of bills of credit. Wentworth sought counsel from Governor Shirley, of Massachusetts, and was advised to consent to the issue of paper without waiting for the royal approval, because the great emergency would justify his conduct in the eyes of the home government.[3] After considerable wrangling concerning the terms of the bill,[4] an act was finally passed[5] providing that £13,000 should be emitted, and that these bills should be redeemed by taxes between 1751 and 1760.[6]

The Louisbourg expedition proved more expensive than was expected, and more money was soon needed. In July of the same year, £6000 was issued.[7] Then, in September, the house of representatives voted to emit £12,000 more, but this time the council refused to assent to such a measure.[8] In October, however, the governor consented

---

[1] Papers, V. 278.   [2] Idem, V. 279.   [3] Idem, V. 933.

[4] Idem, V. 281, 282, 284–291.

[5] Idem, V. 290, 291, 296, 742 ; Belknap, II. 201–202 ; Barstow, 165.

[6] In the address of 1753, the date of this issue is given as February, 1744. The year of 1744–45 is undoubtedly meant.

[7] Papers, V. 334, 336, 338, 348, 756, 757, 763, 767.

[8] Idem, V. 377, 380, 773.

to an issue of £8000 that was to be redeemed by taxes in the four years following 1762.[1] This last act contained a pledge that, if England should reimburse the colony for the expenses incurred in the last undertaking, the money thus granted should "be put into ye Treasury as a fund for the immediate calling in and sinking said Bills." The three emissions of 1745 aggregated £27,000,[2] and the new tenor money now in circulation amounted to £56,878;[3] so that the price of silver rose to 37s. per ounce.[4]

In 1746, new expeditions were projected.[5] Early in the spring it was proposed to issue £1500 of new bills which should be redeemed out of the interest received on the £25,000 loan,[6] but the records do not show that such action was authorized. In June it was decided to issue £60,000 for the purpose of defraying the expenses of an expedition against Canada; and the assembly pledged that at its next meeting provision would be made for the redemption of these bills.[7] This enormous emission more than doubled the

---

[1] Papers, V. 383, 384, 387, 405, 776, 779.

[2] These are all mentioned in the report of 1753, in *Idem*, VI. 223–226.

[3] No bills of the new tenor were burned in this year. The £56,878 now in circulation amounted to seven or eight dollars per capita.

[4] Belknap, III. 225.

[5] *Idem*, II. 226–228.

[6] Papers, V. 407, 412.

[7] *Idem*, V. 432, 433, 813, 817, 821, VI. 224–225.

quantity of new tenor money in circulation,[1] and the price of silver quickly jumped from 37s. to 50s. per ounce.[2] In December, Governor Wentworth was constrained to request the legislature to "make ample satisfaction for the Deficiency" in his "sallary" caused by "the Depreciating of the Paper currency."[3] Without much delay an act was passed[4] granting Wentworth £1000 for this purpose, which shows that the governor's complacency in allowing bills of credit to be issued secured for a time the good will of the assembly.

The £60,000 emitted in 1746 seems to have been left without any provision for its redemption except that the legislature promised[5] that, if Parliament should reimburse the province for its expenses, the money thus granted should be applied to sinking the bills. During 1747, the currency continued to fall in value; and the price of silver rose from 53s. to 60s. per ounce,[6] as the full effects of the £60,000 emission began to be felt. Thus silver had risen from 27s., at the beginning of Wentworth's administration in 1742, to 60s. in the year 1747. In the face of this decline of the credit of the paper, the legislature proceeded to devise schemes for emitting more currency,[7] and

---

[1] No bills of the new tenor were burned this year, and the currency must have increased to £116,878, or $389,000, — more than $16 per capita.

[2] Belknap, III. 225.

[3] Papers, V. 846.

[4] *Idem*, V. 855.

[5] *Idem*, V. 435.

[6] Belknap, III. 225.

[7] Two projects were for emissions that should be redeemed solely

finally authorized the governor to issue enough bills to pay off the troops of the province.[1]

In 1742, when the bills of the new tenor were emitted, an act was passed which provided that the new currency should be accepted in all payments at 6s. 8d. for an ounce of silver, and that in future years the value of the money should be regulated by the assembly in the fall of each year.[2] It was also enacted that a severe penalty should be imposed upon any one who should offer to receive the bills at a lower rating, or to pay a premium for silver. In 1746, the judges of the superior court seem to have rated the bills at less than their nominal value, and in the following year the house of representatives ordered all the courts to adhere strictly to the rating established in 1742.[3] Soon after this, an act was passed by the lower house reaffirming the valuation established in 1742 for the bills of credit, but to this the council objected.[4] During 1747, only £2110 of new tenor

out of funds that might be granted by Parliament. A third contemplated the issue of £4000 redeemable by taxes to be levied in 1761 and 1762. Papers, V. 546, 551, 556, 560, 561, 901.

[1] Papers, V. 562, 563, 901. I am unable to determine whether any such bills were issued. They are not mentioned in the address of 1753. *Idem*, VI. 223–226. Therefore I shall omit them.

[2] *Idem*, V. 620. The provisions of this act may be inferred from the references in V. 501, 531, 554.

[3] *Idem*, V. 501–502. This was probably not accepted by the council, otherwise the subsequent measures introduced into the house would have been needless.

[4] *Idem*, V. 531–532, 553–554.

bills was burned,[1] so that £114,778 of paper money was still in circulation.[2]

In 1748, it appears that the affairs of the £15,000 loan authorized in 1717 were not all settled, and the committee in charge of this business was ordered to hasten the adjustment of its accounts.[3] Early in this year Governor Wentworth received from Governor Shirley a communication[4] stating that Massachusetts was considering a plan for retiring its outstanding bills of credit by means of the funds that Parliament intended to grant the colony in return for its expenditures during the late war. Shirley desired to have a conference appointed, by which all the New England provinces might devise "one general method or scheme"; but New Hampshire was not willing to consider the subject of redeeming its currency at this time.[5]

Douglass estimated the amount of New Hampshire currency outstanding in 1748 at £450,000 "of old tenor value."[6] Since the ratio of old tenor to new was four to one, this sum would

---

[1] Papers, V. 525.

[2] This makes no allowance for the possible issue in 1747, concerning which the author was unable to reach a definite conclusion.

[3] Papers, V. 585.

[4] *Idem*, V. 565–569.

[5] See Felt, 119–120.

[6] Summary, II. 528. Douglass converted the new tenor bills of New Hampshire into old tenor in order to have a common basis for comparison of New Hampshire's issues with those of other colonies.

equal £112,500 in new tenor. The writer's figures show that £922 of new tenor bills were cancelled during 1748,[1] so that the currency of the province was reduced to £113,856, an amount which agrees very closely with the estimate given by Douglass. This was a large enough figure to justify the remark of Douglass[2] that New Hampshire was "always inclinable to a depreciating fraudulent paper currency." In 1748, the price of silver fluctuated from 54s. to 58s. per ounce.[3]

In 1749, the governor and assembly became involved in a bitter dispute over the question of the representation of certain towns and the election of a speaker.[4] This lasted for several years and prevented all legislation; so that the representatives were "incapable of augmenting their paper currency," to use the words of Douglass.[5] By this time the London agent of New Hampshire had received about £30,000 of money granted by Parliament to reimburse the province for its expenses in the late war. This money could not be invested because the agent had no authority to do so, and the province lost about £900 sterling of interest money during each year that the quarrel lasted.[6] Since the price of silver now

[1] Papers, V. 586.　　　　　[2] Summary, II. 193.

[3] Belknap, III. 225.

[4] On this quarrel see Papers, VI. 69–126; Belknap, II. 267–276; Douglass, Summary, II. 35–38; Greene, 151.

[5] Summary, II. 193.

[6] Belknap, II. 273. The governor, of course, attributed the blame to the assembly. Papers, VI. 125.

varied from 56s. to 60s. in old tenor money, the bills of the new tenor must have exchanged for silver at about 15s. in paper for one ounce of that metal.[1] At this rate of exchange, the money granted by England would have been sufficient to retire a little less than £90,000 of the outstanding new tenor bills,[2] and the province could easily have withdrawn the rest by its regular taxes.

In 1750, Massachusetts prohibited the further circulation within her borders of any bills of credit issued by New Hampshire, Connecticut, and Rhode Island.[3] In the following year Parliament passed an act that forbade[4] any of the New England colonies to emit bills of credit and make them a legal tender. At length, in September, 1752, the dispute between the governor and assembly was terminated, and the business of law-making was resumed.[5] It was decided[6] to have the reimbursement money invested in public stocks, and to apply the interest realized from this investment to the redemption of the paper money.[7] As no bills had been retired since 1748, and the currency amounted to £113,856, this could not be considered a violent measure of contraction.

In 1753, the legislative mill was once more in

---

[1] Old tenor was worth one-fourth of the new tenor.

[2] The sterling rating of silver was 5s. 2d.

[3] Felt, Massachusetts Currency, 122.

[4] Stat. at Large, 24 George II. c. 53.

[5] See Belknap, II. 276–277; Papers, VI. 127 et seq.

[6] Papers, VI. 143, 147.

[7] Idem, VI. 227, 273.

working order and ready for further experiments with the paper currency. The imperial statute of 1751 had required that all outstanding bills should be punctually retired at the times appointed in the existing laws, and that none of them should be reissued. This called forth a protest from the legislature of the province, and an address to the King was adopted upon the subject.[1] In this the members protested that the province was unable to redeem its paper as rapidly as required by Parliament, and petitioned that the time for retiring the £60,000 issued for the Canada expedition should be extended to 1766. They stated also that the taxes laid for redeeming bills of former emissions amounted to £3800 annually. The assembly voted[2] at this session to reissue[3] £12,500 of bills that were then in the treasury. This money was to be used for defraying debts that had been accumulating during the late interregnum, and taxes were levied to call in the bills in five annual instalments, beginning in January, 1754. The new tenor bills cancelled in this year amounted to only £193,[4] so that the currency stood at £113,663.

During 1754, the lower house of the legislature seems to have desired to get £6000 of the bills

---

[1] Papers, VI. 223–226.

[2] *Idem*, VI. 210, 211, 212, 225.

[3] The discussions on p. 211 seem to make it clear that this was a reissue, although on p. 225 it seems to be mentioned as a new issue.   [4] *Idem*, VI. 285.

out of the treasury.[1] The assembly proceeded to draw upon the interest of the funds in London in order to secure money to defray current expenses,[2] but levied taxes that were intended to retire an equivalent amount of currency. At this time the bills of the £25,000 loan began to be cancelled, and the whole amount of new tenor money burned in the course of the year was £14,132.[3] This left £99,531 of new tenor bills in circulation. The province now reverted to the old practice of receiving commodities in payment of taxes,[4] although its paper currency was large enough to depreciate to only one-third of its original value. For the year 1754 twenty different commodities were made receivable at fixed ratings, and the practice was continued for a dozen years longer.[5] The confusion in which the paper money had involved the province was increased by the unusual activity displayed at this time by those persons who were engaged in manufacturing counterfeit bills.[6] In 1755, counterfeiters who were operating with New Hampshire money were arrested in Rhode Island.

In January, 1755, preparations were commenced

---

[1] I assume that this was the purpose of the act for granting £6000 mentioned in Papers, VI. 285.

[2] *Idem*, VI. 285, 334.

[3] *Idem*, VI. 270, 271, 272, 273, 274.

[4] See *Idem*, V. 622, 684, VI. 151, 274.

[5] *Idem*, VI. 378, 516, 591, 669–670, 712, 751, 870, VII. 39, 80, 107.

[6] *Idem*, VI. 14, 20, 28, 338, 352–353, 372, 417, 453, 457, 641.

by Shirley for an attack upon Crown Point,[1] and
New Hampshire was called upon for her quota of
men.[2] The imperial statute of 1751 had expressly
provided [3] that paper money might be issued
"upon sudden and extraordinary emergencies of
government," and Governor Wentworth finally
assented to the emission of £40,000 of new currency in order to meet the expense of this expedition.[4] These Crown Point bills were issued at a
rating of fifteen shillings of paper [5] for one "Spanish mill'd Dollar," [6] so that they were practically
a currency of a new tenor; and they were to be
redeemed by taxes at the end of reasonably short
periods.[7] Yet they depreciated so rapidly that
silver rose from 60s. to 70s. per ounce in old tenor
currency during the course of the year,[8] and the

[1] See Winsor, V. 502.

[2] Papers, V. 355–357.

[3] Stat. at Large, 24 George II. c. 54, sec. 4.

[4] This was in two issues of £30,000 and £10,000. Papers, VI.
368, 376, 425. On these emissions see Belknap, II. 307; Hildreth,
II. 450; Winsor, V. 590–591. A copy of one of these bills may be
found in the work last mentioned.

[5] This was 3⅓ times the sterling value of the Spanish dollar,
which was worth but 4s. 6d. At this valuation an ounce of silver,
worth 5s. 2d. sterling, would be rated at a little less than 17s. 3d. in
new tenor.

[6] Thus the bill for five shillings, of which a copy is given by
Winsor, is declared equal to one-third of a dollar. Winsor, V. 590.
Cf. Belknap, II. 307.

[7] Thus the £10,000 issued in September was to be redeemed in
1760. Papers, VI. 425.

[8] Belknap, III. 225. When bills of exchange were drawn in this
year, the rate of exchange was at first £3.25 Crown Point money

pay of the soldiers had to be raised about eleven per cent.[1] The law of 1751 had absolutely forbidden any province to make bills of credit a legal tender;[2] and, therefore, the Crown Point bills were made receivable merely at the treasury of the province.[3]

Naturally enough, no old currency was cancelled during 1755; indeed, the records show that no more bills were burned until 1758. Governor Wentworth found that the paper money was useless for expenses incurred outside the province,[4] and was hard pressed to secure sterling money for such purposes. From time to time the assembly found itself in need of an exportable currency, and drew upon the funds invested in London. Thus during 1755 and 1756, bills of exchange were drawn for £2950 sterling; but in each case provision was made for retiring what was deemed an equivalent amount of provincial currency.[5] In 1756, Wentworth arranged[6] to borrow £3000 sterling from Governor Shirley of Massachusetts. Late in 1755, word was received from the governor of Connecticut that that province had outlawed all

for £1 sterling; and later in the year it rose to £3.75 for £1 sterling. Papers, VI. 376, 428.

[1] Belknap, II. 307. The pay was raised from £13.10 to £15.

[2] Stat. at Large, 24 George II. c. 54, sec. 7.

[3] See copy of bill given by Winsor.

[4] See his message of 1756. Papers, VI. 487.

[5] *Idem*, VI. 376, 385, 410, 419, 428, 434, 435, 486. Besides these sums, £300 was loaned at interest. *Idem*, VI. 339.

[6] *Idem*, VI. 487.

bills issued by New Hampshire, and had prohibited them from being received in any payments
whatsoever.[1]

In 1756, renewed efforts to raise troops were
called for, and £35,750 of new bills was printed
from the plates used in the previous year.[2] These
were to be redeemed by taxes levied in 1759 and
1761; and it was pledged that any money that
should be granted by the King to reimburse the
province for its expenses should be an additional
fund for sinking the bills.[3] The new money was
to have the same nominal value as that issued the
previous year, but silver continued to rise in price
until it reached 100s. per ounce.[4] As a result,
the pay of the soldiers had to be raised from fifteen
to eighteen pounds,[5] and the governor requested
the assembly to make good the depreciation of his
salary.[6]

In 1757, more men had to be raised; and the
governor, although fearing[7] " bad consequences,"

---

[1] Papers, V. 446.

[2] *Idem*, VI. 503, 516, 520. This was in two issues of £30,000
and £5750. The latter was made from blank bills printed the
previous year. *Idem*, VI. 516, 531.

[3] The text of this act may be found in Papers, VI. 506–508.

[4] Belknap, III. 225. Since the Crown Point money was given
a nominal rating of $3\frac{1}{3}$ times the value of sterling, the nominal
value of silver in bills of the new tenor was nearly 17s. 3d. In
bills of old tenor the price of silver would be four times as much,
or 69s. per ounce. The difference between 69 and 100 shillings
represents the depreciation of the new money.

[5] Belknap, II. 307.   [6] Papers, VI. 543.

[7] See his message. *Idem*, VI. 565.

felt obliged to consent to an issue of £20,000 of additional currency.[1] This was to be retired by taxes payable in 1761 and 1762, and any reimbursement money that might be received from the King was pledged as a second fund for its redemption. None of the £99,531 of new tenor bills outstanding in 1754 had been retired, and £95,750 of new currency had been issued in 1755, 1756, and 1757. The province had, therefore, about £195,280 of currency in 1757, while its population probably did not exceed 55,000.[2] The price of silver, therefore, increased to 110s., and this made it necessary to raise the pay of the troops for a third time.[3]

In 1758, £20,500 of additional paper was emitted,[4] and bills to the amount of £3536 were burned.[5] The result was a net increase of £16,964 in the currency of the province, while silver rose to 120s. per ounce.[6] In 1756, a second grant of money, amounting to £8000 sterling, had been received from England and brought to this country;[7] while in 1758 it was decided to draw upon the funds in London for £2000.[8] The sum thus drawn was to be made good by a tax of £12,500, payable in the Canada bills issued in 1746, which is

---

[1] Papers, VI. 569–571.

[2] For 1754, Mr. Bancroft estimated the population at 50,000 whites and a few blacks. Bancroft, II. 389–391.

[3] Belknap, II. 307, III. 225.

[4] Papers, VI. 663, 665. The printed records give no information concerning the character of this issue.

[5] *Idem*, VI. 640, 652.

[6] Belknap, III. 225.

[7] Papers, VI. 543–545, 578–579.

[8] *Idem*, VI. 643–645, 654.

a recognition of a depreciation of more than six to one for the Canada money.[1]   In one of the governor's messages of this year, the attention of the legislature is directed to the old £15,000 loan of 1717.   Wentworth urged that an act should be passed "to oblige delinquent borrowers of the £15,000 Loan to make speedy payment of the sums from them respectively due,"[2] which showed that fifty years had not proved long enough to settle the accounts of this enterprise undertaken by the province.

In 1759, the province issued £13,000, which was declared to be of sterling value, and was to be redeemed partly by bills of exchange drawn upon the funds in England and partly by taxes levied in 1762 and 1763;[3] and it is possible that further emissions were authorized during the course of this year.[4]   These new bills differed from previous issues in that they were emitted at sterling rates and supported by sterling funds.[5]   The province now had a rich variety of different kinds of money.   In 1760, the assembly made another issue

---

[1] These bills were issued at proclamation rates.

[2] Papers, V. 691.

[3] The amount authorized was £17,000. *Idem*, VI. 712. But only £13,000 was issued. *Idem*, VI. 774.

[4] *Idem*, VI. 717, 726. The editor of the Provincial Papers saw fit to omit large parts of the Journals, so that it is impossible to determine whether these were new issues or reissues of old bills. See editor's note in VI. 320.

[5] Note the plan outlined in resolutions of the assembly in 1758. *Idem*, VI. 679.

of £15,000 of sterling bills, bearing five per cent interest, and redeemable from the proceeds of taxes levied in 1763, 1764, and 1765.[1] In 1761, the heavy military expenses of the colony came to an end with the emission of £20,000, probably in sterling bills such as had been issued in the two preceding years.[2]

Thus New Hampshire, in a period of seven years, had issued no less than £116,250 of new tenor money,[3] and at least £48,000 of sterling bills.[4] We have little information concerning these sterling issues. But they seem to have been hoarded to such an extent that they entered into circulation less than the other bills,[5] and they were retired within a few years.[6] This fact, and the uncertainty whether the printed records contain a full account of the amounts of paper burned by the assembly, will make it impossible to form

[1] Papers, VI. 735, 744, 745, 752, 756, VII. 38.

[2] *Idem*, VI. 779, 786.

[3] £40,000 in 1755; £35,750 in 1756; £20,000 in 1757; and £20,500 in 1758.

[4] The writer's figures are £13,000 issued in 1759, £15,000 issued in 1760, and £20,000 issued in 1761. It is possible, as stated in a previous note, that there were two other issues or reissues in 1759, concerning which the records offer no certain information.

[5] *Idem*, VII. 65. The issue of 1760 certainly bore interest. Since all these issues were secured in whole or in part by sterling funds, they would naturally be hoarded to a considerable extent.

[6] Thus in 1760 the sterling bills were made receivable for province rates. *Idem*, VI. 733. By 1764 they had become so scarce that other bills were made receivable for taxes that had been payable originally in sterling bills. *Idem*, VII. 38.

any very definite conclusions concerning the number of bills circulating in this or in subsequent
years. Belknap's tables show that the price of
silver ranged from 120*s.* to 140*s.* per ounce in old
tenor money between 1761 and 1763.[1] In 1760,
Governor Wentworth stated that a silver dollar
exchanged for six pounds of the old tenor money,[2]
a figure which agrees exactly with Belknap's quotations for the ounce of silver for that year. In
1763, the assembly granted the governor £1250 of
new tenor money, which was declared to be equivalent to £200 sterling.[3] This is a rate of £6¼ new
tenor for £1 sterling, and would indicate a rate of
£25 old tenor for £1 sterling.[4]

But the bills were no longer a legal tender, and
their ability to do harm was infinitely diminished.
In 1762, the legislature authorized the issue of
£20,000 of sterling bills,[5] of which £10,000 was
to be used for sinking the Louisbourg and Canada
bills emitted in 1745 and 1746. These old issues
had aggregated £87,000, and had sunk to less
than one-sixth the value of sterling,[6] so that the
£10,000 of sterling money would probably suffice

[1] History, III. 225.   [2] Papers, VI. 744.   [3] *Idem*, VI. 878.
[4] This would give a price of about 129*s.* old tenor for an ounce
of silver.
[5] *Idem*, VI. 844. Of this amount, £20,000 was not issued until
1763. *Idem*, VI. 869. Of the entire issue, £10,000 was said to be
outstanding in 1765, when bills of exchange were drawn in order to
redeem it. *Idem*, VII. 65.
[6] *Idem*, VI. 655. They were made payable for a tax in 1758
at a rate of 6¼ for 1.

for exchanging all that now remained outstanding. In 1763, the records show that currency of various issues to the amount of £63,518 was burned.[1]

By 1764, the assembly seems to have learned something from the experience of the last few years, for we find[2] it expressing the opinion that "another Emission of a paper currency would . . . be fruitless and attended with mischievous consequences well known to every considering person the least acquainted with the circumstances of the Province." In a message written in 1765, Governor Wentworth informed the legislature[3] that all the paper money then outstanding must be retired "after the close of the year 1767"; and said that the province had incurred dishonor in the past by unreasonable neglect of its obligations. The assembly expressed the hope "soon to see an End of our Paper Currency."[4] Another sum of money recently received from England was devoted to the redemption of bills of credit;[5] and a balance of £12,000, remaining in London to the credit of the province, was devoted to the same purpose.[6] It was enacted, furthermore, that in the future no bills of credit should be reissued when once received at the treasury.[7] By the aid of the funds in England and the province taxes,[8] large

---

[1] Papers, VI. 859, 860.   Some of these amounts were sterling bills.

[2] *Idem*, VII. 30.   [3] *Idem*, VII. 85.   [4] *Idem*, VII. 94.

[5] *Idem*, VII. 53.   [6] *Idem*, VII. 52, 65.   [7] *Idem*, VII. 58.

[8] Statistics of taxes imposed between 1753 and 1766 may be found in Coll. of N. H. Hist. Soc., III. 152.

sums of paper were retired in 1764, 1766, and 1768.[1]

Mr. Belknap tells us that, at length, "sterling money became the standard of all contracts"; while the paper passed "as a currency," its value being regulated "by the price of silver and the course of exchange."[2] The records enable us to describe some of the details of this process, which gradually resulted from the action of Parliament in preventing the issue of more legal tender paper. In 1765, the legislature passed an act[3] "for ascertaining the value of coin'd silver and Gold," by which the dollar was rated at six and the guinea at twenty-eight shillings. These were the same rates that had been established in Massachusetts in 1750. The law of 1765 seems to have been disallowed by the home government,[4] but the rating of six shillings for a Spanish dollar continued to prevail in the province.[5] After the passage of this act, the outstanding paper was made payable for taxes at its "present value."[6]

---

[1] Papers, VII. 32, 117, 150, 193. These sums amount to £41,908 nominal value, but some of them are expressed in sterling and others in new tenor denominations. Hence the total just stated does not represent the true value.

[2] Belknap, II. 307–308.

[3] Papers, VII. 77–78.

[4] *Idem*, VII. 281. The assembly proceeded, nevertheless, to grant supplies and levy taxes "according to the present current value of money Passing among us." *Idem*, VII. 282.

[5] Belknap says that a dollar was rated at six shillings from 1765–1776. History, III. 225. Note especially Papers, VII. 282–283.

[6] *Idem*, VII. 80, 108.

But the provision made for redeeming the paper in 1768 did not prove sufficient to retire all of the currency. Accordingly the treasurer was authorized[1] to receive in public dues "any further Sum of said Bills that shall be offered," and the governor urged that another " Fund " should be established to redeem " the paper Bills of Credit of this Province that are yet passing as a currency solely upon the Reliance placed on the good faith of the Province, altho' they have some time since expired by law."[2] Early in 1770, £2092 of currency received at the treasury was burned in the presence of the legislature.[3] In December of the same year, the governor urged the assembly to consider ways and means of retiring the notes still outstanding;[4] and finally the treasurer of the province was authorized to borrow the funds needed to redeem the paper that still remained in the hands of citizens.[5] In 1791, Belknap wrote:[6] "The year 1771 was also distinguished by the abolition of paper currency. Silver and gold had been gradually introduced, and the paper had for several years been called in for taxes. The time limited for its existence being now come, it totally disappeared." In subsequent years small amounts of old bills were presented at the treasury.[7]

---

[1] Papers, VII. 152. [2] *Idem*, VII. 187.
[3] *Idem*, VII. 235-241. In 1769, £6000 of old tenor bills had been presented at the treasury. *Idem*, VII. 215-216.
[4] *Idem*, VII. 260. [5] *Idem*, VII. 263, 265.
[6] History, II. 355. [7] Papers, VII. 302, 319, 351.

After New Hampshire ceased to issue bills of credit, the use of treasury notes was introduced, as had been the case in Massachusetts some years earlier.[1] We have seen that the sterling bills issued in 1760 were really treasury notes, bearing interest at five per cent and redeemable out of the proceeds of taxes levied within a period of three or four years. Eight years later it was proposed[2] to authorize the treasurer "to issue Notes upon Interest to be Redeemed by the Province"; and this was actually done in 1770,[3] when such notes were issued in order to sink the paper then outstanding. In 1771, the treasurer was instructed to borrow £1500 for the use of the province,[4] probably in a similar manner. Later in the same year the governor informed the assembly that a grant of £6009 sterling had been received from Parliament in reimbursement of expenses incurred in the late war, and urged that this money be used for meeting the deficiencies of former years.[5] This advice seems to have been followed by the passage of an act[6] which provided for the redemption of treasury notes out of the proceeds of bills of exchange drawn upon the funds in London. In 1774, other notes then outstanding were redeemed with money that was in the treasury.[7]

[1] See Hutchinson's account of the introduction of treasury notes into Massachusetts. History, III. 9–10.

[2] Papers, VII. 156.

[3] *Idem*, VII. 263, 265.

[4] *Idem*, VII. 283.

[5] *Idem*, VII. 288.

[6] *Idem*, VII. 296.

[7] *Idem*, VII. 363.

COLONIAL ISSUES (1740–1774)

The experience of New Hampshire with her colonial bills of credit resembles so closely that of the other colonies, that it is unnecessary to present a summary of the results that flowed from these experiments with paper money. One thing, however, must impress the reader; and that is that, however disastrous the effects of New Hampshire's paper currency, the outcome would have been infinitely worse if the inflationists had not been controlled to a considerable extent by the royal governors and the statute of 1751. If these influences had not been felt, the issues of paper would have been swollen to a veritable deluge. Thanks to external pressure, the colony was finally restored to a specie basis, and the amount of paper circulating in 1774 had probably become small. In 1775, therefore, the standard of value in New Hampshire was the Spanish dollar, at a rating of six shillings; and £133 of the currency of the province was equivalent to £100 sterling.[1]

[1] Thus, in 1772, the legislature rated £140 provincial currency equal to 100 guineas. With the guinea rated at 21 shillings, as was the case after 1717, this gives an exchange of £133.33 for £100 sterling.

CHAPTER III

REVOLUTIONARY ISSUES

DURING the twelve years of peace and security that followed the close of the French and Indian War, New Hampshire enjoyed greater prosperity than had ever before fallen to her lot; and the population of the province increased until it amounted to about 82,000 souls in the year 1775.[1] The abolition of paper money had made it possible to introduce some degree of order into the finances of the colony, but it cannot be said that New Hampshire was prepared for the struggle that was now before her.

The annual expenses of the colony did not exceed £3500 sterling,[2] and taxation was proportionately light. The principal source of income was a tax on polls and estates,[3] which had existed in the province from the earliest times[4] and amounted in

[1] Belknap, III. 234.

[2] Adam Smith states it at this figure. Smith, W. of N., II. 154. In 1796, the expenses of the state were only $28,600, or £6440. In 1730, the ordinary expenses were stated at £1500 for the regular charges of government and £500 for contingencies. Coll. of N. H. Hist. Soc., I. 230.

[3] For the methods of assessment see Acts of New Hampshire, 29, 121, 172, 177, 178. The proportions of the various townships in a province tax in 1773 may be found in Papers, VII. 326–329.

[4] Note Papers, I. 448.

practice to an assessment of polls, real estate, and live stock.[1] Duties on imports [2] had met with little favor in the colonial period of New Hampshire's history,[3] and the only important branch of revenue besides the property and poll taxes was an excise on all liquors sold in the province.[4] In 1772, this was farmed out for £934.[5] It seems always to have been subject to a great amount of evasion.[6] Powder, or tonnage, duties were imposed upon foreign ships that entered the ports of the province,[7] but the receipts from this source were insignificant.[8]

Thus the burden of taxation in New Hampshire was extremely light, and the province had no revenue system [9] adequate to the necessities of a

[1] Thus, in 1796, polls were rated at £11,525, real estate at £15,531, live stock at £12,882, and all other items at £577.   State Papers, Finance, I. 442.

[2] The excise on all liquors sold in the province included all imported liquors, and may have been referred to sometimes as an impost. See Papers, VII. 129.

[3] Thus, in 1716, the governor had recommended an impost, " which every Government in ye world doth but we." Papers, III. 649. But the assembly replied that public charges could be met most conveniently by a tax on persons and estates. *Idem*, III. 651.

[4] For the laws imposing the excise see Acts of N. H., 168–170.

[5] Papers, VII. 236, 247, 261, 303.

[6] *Idem*, III. 449, 554 ; VII. 139.

[7] Acts of N. H., 64.   [8] Hill, 18–23.

[9] With some allowances, the following passage, written in 1730, gives a correct picture of the provincial finances at the outbreak of the Revolution : " The revenue arising within this province is three hundred ninety and six pounds, by excise, which is appropriated towards the Governor's salary, and about three or four

protracted war.   Such an emergency was certain
to be made the occasion for renewed issues of
paper money, especially since the restraining influence of the royal governor was now removed.
Belknap states correctly the cause of the difficulties
experienced by the state in the struggle for independence when he says:[1] "The war in which we
became involved with Britain, found us not des-
titute of resources, but unskilled in the art of
finance."

When the question of financial methods was
raised in 1775, the Provincial Congress resolved
that the war could not be carried on without paper
money; and wrote to the Continental Congress
urging that "some general plan for bills of credit"
should be adopted, or that the separate colonies
should adopt some common scheme for regulating
their own issues.[2]   Upon June 9,[3] before any continental bills had been emitted, New Hampshire
decided to issue £10,050 of treasury notes.   These
were not made a legal tender, but were receivable
at the provincial treasury.   They were to be redeemed by taxes in 1776, 1777, and 1778.   Before
the year closed, £30,000 of additional notes was
emitted upon a similar plan.[4]   Some of the bills

barrels of gun-powder, from the shipping, which is spent at the
fort.   There is no other revenue but by tax on polls and estates."
Coll. of N. H. Hist. Soc., I. 230.

[1] Belknap, II. 425.   Cf. also pp. 425–434.
[2] Papers, VII. 481, 483.
[3] *Idem*, VII. 510 ; Belknap, II. 396.
[4] Papers, VII. 549, 638 ; Belknap, II. 396.

thus issued bore interest,[1] but this provision was soon repealed.[2] Persons who should counterfeit the paper were to be punished as "Enemies to their Country."[3]

Upon the whole, during this year, the province seemed to desire to pursue a fairly conservative course respecting its paper issues. These treasury notes might not have depreciated if the war had proved to be of short duration, and the legislature did not at this time perpetrate wholesale robbery under the guise of a tender law. The regular province tax of £4000 was levied as usual,[4] and it was undoubtedly intended to collect punctually the taxes levied in order to redeem the paper. New Hampshire, unlike some of the other colonies, did not expect that the war could be carried on by the issue of paper money unsupported by taxation. Bartlett and Langdon, the delegates of the province to the Continental Congress, warned their constituents that ruin would result from " emitting paper on every occasion "; and regretted the course of the legislature in making the third emission of treasury notes.[5] In December, New Hampshire received from Congress a grant of $40,000 of continental money.[6]

In the opening days of 1776, a committee was appointed to devise " a Plan for sinking the Colony Debt,"[7] but before the end of January it was de-

[1] Papers, VII. 510, 550.
[2] Idem, VII. 575.
[5] Idem, VII. 615, 631.
[3] Idem, VII. 551.
[4] Idem, VII. 609.
[6] Idem, VII. 681.   [7] Idem, VII. 706.

cided to make a new issue of £20,008.[1] These bills were declared a lawful tender "at the Treasury and all other payments," and the taxes levied for their redemption were not to be collected until 1783 and the three subsequent years. It is worth while to call attention to the fact that the long postponement of the time of redemption and the first tender act came at the same time, and that this was just the period when the first difficulties were being encountered in maintaining the credit of the paper currency in most of the states.[2] Later in the year, the legislature made an attempt[3] to secure gold and silver in exchange for its notes. By June, it became necessary to pass more stringent laws against counterfeiting.[4]

During the month last mentioned, $10,000 was received from the federal treasury;[5] but the province voted to issue £3400 of fractional currency,[6] which was made a tender in all payments. At about the same time, the continental bills of credit and those issued by other colonies were made a legal tender,[7] and a refusal of the paper currency was made punishable by the forfeiture of the entire debt.[8] Thus, as Belknap says,[9] the "fraudulent

---

[1] Papers, VIII. 51, 60, 61.

[2] See Sumner, Financier, I. 48 *et seq.*   [3] Papers, VIII. 135, 176.

[4] *Idem*, VIII. 144, 184. For other references on counterfeiting see VII. 551; VIII. 404, 494, 525, 526, 532, 541, 546, 554, 558, 563, 569, 599, 600, 603, 694, 724.   [5] *Idem*, VIII. 168.

[6] *Idem*, VIII. 169.   [7] *Idem*, VIII. 144.

[8] This is Belknap's statement. History, II. 426.

[9] *Idem*, II. 427.

debtor took advantage of the law to cheat his creditor, under colour of justice"; while hawkers "who crept from obscurity and assumed the name of merchants, could even increase their substance."

In July, the legislature of the newly formed state of New Hampshire issued £20,160 of new bills of credit;[1] and two months later a state tax of £2500 was levied upon polls and estates.[2] Thus, at the end of 1776, the state had emitted £83,618 of paper currency,[3] practically all of which was in circulation;[4] while the volume of continental money had swollen to $25,000,000.[5] When the next year opened, this mass of paper had depreciated to about two-thirds of its nominal value.[6]

Price conventions and price regulations were now in order, and New Hampshire was represented at a conference of the New England states, which was held at Providence from December 25, 1776, to January 2, 1777.[7] By this convention, the rising prices of labor and commodities were attributed to avarice, and a price tariff for all New

---

[1] Papers, VIII. 190; Belknap, II. 407.

[2] Papers, VIII. 331. Cf. pp. 143–144.

[3] These figures of the writer agree exactly with a statement that may be found in *Idem*, VIII. 588.

[4] In January, 1776, the legislature voted to burn £1128 of interest-bearing treasury notes, but the records do not enable us to determine whether this was actually done. *Idem*, VIII. 56.

[5] Cf. Bullock, 130.   [6] *Idem*, 133.

[7] Papers, VIII. 406–407; Sumner, Financier, I. 55; Bullock, 127; Hildreth, III. 181.

England was prepared. Soon after this, New Hampshire established a legal scale of prices;[1] and, later on, laws were enacted against " monopoly and extortion."[2] Congress now asked the states to issue no more paper, and to withdraw the bills already issued.[3] New Hampshire voted to call in "all the Bills of Credit issued in 1775";[4] and, in September, reorganized her system of taxation.[5] It was decided also to ask from Congress a loan sufficient to enable the state to withdraw all the bills issued in 1775 and 1776.[6]

But in January, 1777, it was considered necessary to authorize the treasurer to issue interest-bearing notes to the amount of £30,000,[7] so that the currency was increased to about £111,800.[8] The depreciation of the paper continued until, by the close of the year, the currency was worth but one-third of its nominal value,[9] and this, too, despite the fact that other price conventions were convened to remedy the evil.[10] In November, a tax

---

[1] Papers, VIII. 455–456, 471.   [2] Belknap, II. 427–428.

[3] Journals of Congress, Feb. 15, Nov. 22, 1777.

[4] Papers, VIII. 587.   [5] *Idem*, VIII. 685.

[6] *Idem*, VIII. 588, 589.   [7] *Idem*, VIII. 454, 465, 588.

[8] The total issues now amounted to £113,568. But £1744 of the bills had been burned in April, 1777, so that no more than £111, 824 could have been in circulation. *Idem*, VIII. 537. If the £1128, mentioned in a previous note, was actually burned in 1776, the amount of outstanding bills would be slightly less than £111,800.

[9] See official rates adopted in 1780. *Idem*, VIII. 858. Cf. Bullock, 133.

[10] Sumner, Financier, I. 60, 65; Hildreth, III. 227, 232.

of £40,000, payable "in all bills of this State," was levied; and it was resolved that the "paper bills shall not be legal tender for debts after the first day of March next ensuing."[1] Finally, on November 22, Congress made its first requisition upon the states, and called upon New Hampshire for $200,000.[2]

At the opening of 1778, the paper money had sunk to rather less than one-third of its nominal value;[3] but, in March, the legislature voted to issue £40,000 of the treasurer's notes, payable in four years with interest at six per cent.[4] At the same time a tax of £80,000 was levied,[5] and £60,000 of this amount was appropriated to the payment of the requisition made by Congress in the previous year. But the sum thus set aside for federal purposes could not have been collected at the appointed time, for New Hampshire made its first payment into the federal treasury at the very end of 1779.[6] At the close of 1778, the state must have had about £151,000 of its paper outstanding;[7] and the depreciation of the paper currency had reduced its value to eleven or twelve cents on the dollar.[8]

---

[1] Papers, VIII. 722, 723, 724.

[2] *Idem*, VIII. 728–729; Journals of Congress, Nov. 22, 1777.

[3] Papers, VIII. 858; Bullock, 133.   [4] Papers, VIII. 779.

[5] *Idem*, VIII. 778–779.   [6] State Papers, Finance, I. 59.

[7] This includes the £40,000 of treasurer's notes authorized in March. During 1778, some bills were burned, but the printed records do not enable us to determine the amount. Papers, VIII. 762.

[8] *Idem*, VIII. 858; Bullock, 133.

During 1779, the treasurer was authorized to borrow £70,000 for the use of the state.[1] The writer has been unable to ascertain the character of the obligations issued at this time,[2] but it seems probable that the legislature was attempting to find some financial device[3] that would prove less dangerous than the emission of more bills of credit. In 1780, a loan of £300,000, at interest, was authorized.[4] From what we know of the manner in which the interest-bearing certificates of the federal government found their way into circulation,[5] it seems certain that New Hampshire's currency must have been increased by the obligations issued in 1779 and 1780.

Congress made three requisitions for money during 1779.[6] In March, New Hampshire levied a tax for £250,000;[7] and, in the following December and January, the state paid into the federal treasury $600,000 of continental currency, for which a credit of $54,512 in specie was received.[8]

[1] Papers, VIII. 823, 842.

[2] The writer has had access only to the Provincial and State Papers.

[3] The first of these two loans was to be contracted for one year, and was to bear interest.

[4] Papers, VIII. 868. Since the currency was then worth about one cent on the dollar, this sum amounted to no more than £3000 in specie.

[5] E.g., note the manner in which the loan office certificates found their way into circulation. Bolles, I. 260–261.

[6] Journals of Congress, Jan. 2, May 21, Oct. 6, 1779; Bullock, 158.   [7] Papers, VIII. 823.

[8] State Papers, Finance, I. 59.

In March, 1780, $500,000 more of the paper was paid in by New Hampshire, and an additional credit of $12,500 was obtained.[1] Thus, on these early requisitions, the state furnished the federal government with $1,300,000 of depreciated paper, which was rated at $123,948 in specie.[2]

In 1780, when Congress passed the 40 for 1 act,[3] New Hampshire voted to redeem its quota of the continental bills and to repeal its tender acts.[4] Within eighteen months the state paid into the federal treasury $5,200,000 of continental paper, the whole amount of its quota, for which a credit of $130,000 in specie was received.[5] Hamilton's report of 1790 leads us to infer that the state issued $145,000 of bills of the new tenor, in place of the old money turned over to the federal authorities.[6] In April, 1780, a table of deprecia-

[1] State Papers, Finance, I. 59.

[2] This was more than its real value, since the tables of depreciation established by Congress did not tell the whole truth. Bullock, 132.

[3] Journals of Congress, March 18, 1780; Finances of the United States, 136–138. This act called upon the states for taxes to redeem the continental money, which was declared to be worth only one-fortieth of its face value. When the old money was paid in, bills of a new tenor were to be issued to an amount not exceeding one-twentieth of the face value of the old emissions, "on the funds of individual states." Six-tenths of the new bills were to be at the disposal of the states, and the rest were to be "subject to the orders of the United States."

[4] Papers, VIII. 856.

[5] State Papers, Finance, I. 58.

[6] This states that the bills of the new tenor issued on the funds of New Hampshire, and appropriated to the use of the United

tion was adopted for use in the settlement of army accounts.[1]

The old currency now disappeared from circulation. In August, 1781, the state imposed a tax of $100,000, payable in "bills of the new emission."[2] A month later an act was passed[3] "for making Gold and Silver a Tender for all Debts" and for settling the depreciation of the paper currency. This rated the dollar at six shillings.[4] Early in 1782, the treasurer was authorized "to hire £20,000 in specie, and to give Notes on Interest for any sums demanded of him by virtue of an order from the President."[5] This was probably the same plan that was followed in the loans of 1779 and 1780. In June, Robert Morris's notes and the bills issued by the Bank of the United States were made receivable for all taxes as the equivalent of specie.[6]

New Hampshire had become dissatisfied with the apportionment of her quota of the requisitions, and claimed that she was made to bear more than her just share of the public burdens.[7] For this cause, or for some other, her compliance with the financial demands of Congress now became partial and reluctant. From 1781 to 1788, the state paid

States, amounted to $58,000. This was four-tenths of the total. State Papers, Finance, I. 58. See resolutions adopted in 1780. Papers, VIII. 876–877.

[1] Papers, VIII. 858. [2] *Idem*, VIII. 913.
[3] *Idem*. [4] Dip. Corr. of Rev., XII. 91.
[5] Papers, VIII. 931. [6] *Idem*, VIII. 945.
[7] Journals of Congress, April 1, 1782.

into the federal treasury $35,630 in specie, and
$86,474 in indents, leaving unpaid balances of
$216,625 in specie and $253,146 in indents.[1]

The Revolution had left New Hampshire with
a debt that was considered a heavy burden. One
estimate, probably unreliable, places it at $500,000
in 1784.[2] In 1782, it was decided to allow holders
of the obligations of the state to bring them to the
treasury and have them liquidated according to the
legal scale of depreciation.[3] When this should be
done, the treasurer was instructed to issue specie
certificates for the principal of the debts and for
accrued interest. In the course of six or eight
years a considerable part of the indebtedness was
paid off,[4] so that in 1790 the remaining debt
was estimated at $300,000.[5] Of this, $282,595
was finally assumed by the United States.[6]

New Hampshire did not escape the paper-money
mania that raged in so many of the states in 1785
and 1786.[7] In the former year various conferences
that were held to consider the subject demanded
"a new emission of paper bills, funded on real
estate, and loaned on interest." And this happened, be it noted, when so much of the paper

[1] State Papers, I. 56–57.
[2] Ford, Writings of Jefferson, IV. 139.
[3] Papers, VIII. 926.
[4] Barstow, 269, 293; Belknap, II. 461.
[5] State Papers, Finance, I. 29.
[6] Tenth Census, VII. 327.
[7] On this subject see Belknap, II. 461–477; Barstow, 269–272;
Hildreth, III. 473; Libby, 7–11, 52–54.

formerly issued was in circulation that the depreciation was sixty per cent on the notes and twenty
per cent on certificates of indebtedness.[1] As a
remedy for the discontent, the legislature of the
state passed a law that enabled debtors to offer
real or personal property "at a fair valuation" in
satisfaction of their engagements. But this act,
which remained in operation for five years, did not
quiet the agitation for more paper money. On
the contrary, it simply made specie more scarce
than before.

A paper-money party was formed in 1786, and
the newspapers teemed with discussions of the
necessity of issuing more currency in order to
stimulate industry and relieve the poor. Concerning these fulminations, the *New Hampshire Mer-
cury* observed[2] that "there is no single trace of
any idea of redemption, or any one attempt to give
the currency a foundation; but the whole seems
predicated on a supposition that the general court
by a mere act of legislation . . . could impress
an intrinsic value upon paper." The inflationists
claimed that "Paper money, or even leather but-
tons, when stamped by authority and funded with
realities, will answer for internal commerce as well
as silver and gold."[3] Finally, Belknap wrote:[4]
"The same party who were so zealous in favor of
paper currency, and against laws which obliged

[1] Belknap, II. 462.
[2] Coll. of N. H. Hist. Soc., III. 117–118.
[3] Libby, 53.   [4] Belknap, II. 467.

them to pay their debts, proceeded to inveigh against Courts and lawyers."

When the legislature met in 1786, paper money straightway became the principal subject of consideration; and finally a plan was formed for the issue of £50,000 of paper, which was to be loaned upon mortgage security at four per cent interest, and should be a legal tender in all payments. This scheme was submitted to the various towns for consideration, but the inflationists were not satisfied with this concession. Accordingly, they proceeded to gather in Rockingham County, and to march to Exeter, where they tried to intimidate the legislature. This movement proved a ridiculous fiasco; and, in January, 1787, the towns voted against the projected issue of paper money. Recent investigations have shown[1] that in New Hampshire, as elsewhere, the men who conducted the agitation for paper money in 1786 were the opponents of the Federal Constitution, when the question of its ratification was under discussion in 1788.

[1] See Libby, 54.

273

BIBLIOGRAPHY

In the parentheses following each title the reader will find the abbreviated titles generally used in the footnotes of this book.

Acts and Laws of New Hampshire. 1771. (Acts of N. H.)

Acts and Resolves of Massachusetts. Boston, 1869–1886. (Acts of Mass.)

Acts of New Jersey. Edited by P. Wilson. Trenton, 1784. (Acts of N. J.)

Acts of North Carolina. Newbern, 1773. (Acts of N. C.)

Adams, H. C. Public Debts. New York, 1887. (Adams.)

Adams, J. Works of John Adams. Boston, 1856. (Works of Adams.)

Adler, S. L. Money and Money Units in the American Colonies. Pamphlet. Rochester, 1900. (Adler.)

American Historical Review. (Amer. Hist. Rev.)

American Museum. (Amer. Mus.)

American Naturalist. (Amer. Nat.)

American State Papers, Finance. Washington, 1832–1859. (State Papers, Finance.)

Andrews, E. B. Institutes of Economics. Boston, 1889. (Andrews.)

History of the Last Quarter Century in the United States. New York, 1896. (Andrews, Hist.)

Annals of American Academy of Political and Social Science. (Annals.)

Annals of Congress. Washington, 1834–1837. (Annals of Cong.)

Archives of Maryland, Proceedings of Assembly. Baltimore, 1883–1894. (Arch. of Md.)

Arnold, S. G. History of Rhode Island. Third edition. New York, 1878. (Arnold.)

Ashley, J. Memoirs concerning the Trade and Revenues of the British Colonies. London, 1740. (Ashley.)
Atlantic Monthly. (Atl. Month.)

Baird, H. C. Criticisms on the Financial Policies of the United States and France. Philadelphia, 1875. (Baird.)
Bancroft, G. History of the United States. Author's last revision. New York, 1884. (Bancroft, Hist.)
A Plea for the Constitution of the United States. New York, 1886. Reprinted in Sound Currency, V. (Bancroft, Plea.)
Bankers' Magazine. (Bank. Mag.)
Barry, J. S. History of Massachusetts. Boston, 1855–1857. (Barry.)
Barstow, G. History of New Hampshire. Concord, 1842. (Barstow.)
Basset, J. S. The Constitutional Beginnings of North Carolina. Baltimore, 1894. (Basset.)
The Regulators of North Carolina. In Annual Report of American Historical Association, 1894. Washington, 1895. (Basset, Regulators.)
Bates, F. G. Rhode Island and the Formation of the Union. New York, 1898. (Bates.)
Belknap, J. History of New Hampshire. Philadelphia, 1784. (Belknap.)
Benton, T. Thirty Years' View. New York, 1854–1856. (Benton.)
Blaine, J. G. Twenty Years of Congress. Norwich, 1886. (Blaine.)
Bolles, A. S. The Financial History of the United States. New York, 1879–1886. (Bolles.)
Bollman, E. Plan of an Improved System of the Money Concerns of the Union. Philadelphia, 1816. (Bollman.)
Bowen, F. American Political Economy. New York, 1870. (Bowen.)
Bradford, W. History of Plymouth Plantation. Boston, 1856. (Bradford.)

Breck, S. Historical Sketch of the Continental Paper Money. Philadelphia, 1843. (Breck.)

Bronson, H. Connecticut Currency. In Papers of New Haven Historical Society, I. New Haven, 1865. (Bronson.)

Bruce, P. A. Economic History of Virginia in the Seventeenth Century. New York, 1896. (Bruce.)

Bryan, A. C. State Banking in Maryland. Baltimore, 1899. (Bryan.)

Bryant, W. C., and Gay, S. H. A Popular History of the United States. New York, 1876–1881. (Bryant and Gay.)

Budd, T. Good Order established in Pennsylvania and New Jersey. Reprinted by W. Gowans, in Bibliotheca Americana, IV. New York, 1865. (Budd, Good Order.)

Bullock, C. J. The Finances of the United States, 1775–1789. Madison, 1895. (Bullock.)

Burnaby, A. Travels in North America. Third edition. London, 1798. (Burnaby.)

Butler, B. F. Butler's Book. Boston, 1892. (Butler's Book.)

Butler, M. History of Kentucky. Cincinnati, 1836. (Butler.)

Calendar of Virginia State Papers. Richmond, 1875. (Cal. of Va. Papers.)

Calhoun, J. C. Works of Calhoun. Edited by R. K. Crallé. Columbia, 1851–1879. (Calhoun.)

Carey, H. C. Letters on the Currency Question. Philadelphia, 1865. (Carey, Currency.)

Letters to McCulloch. Philadelphia, 1866. (Carey, McCulloch.)

Carroll, B. R. Historical Collections of South Carolina. New York, 1836. (Carroll.)

Chalmers, R. Colonial Currency. London, 1893. (Chalmers.)

Clarke and Hall. Legislative History of the Bank of the United States. Washington, 1832. (Clark and Hall.)

Cleaveland, J. Banking System of the State of New York. Second edition. New York, 1864. (Cleaveland.)

Coin's Financial School. Chicago, 1894. (Coin.)

Collections of the Massachusetts Historical Society. (Coll. Mass. Hist. Soc.)

Collections of the New Hampshire Historical Society. (Coll. N. H. Hist. Soc.)

Colonial Records of North Carolina. Raleigh, 1886–1890. (Col. Recs. of N. C.)

Colonial Records of Pennsylvania. Philadelphia, 1852–1853. (Col. Recs. of Penn.)

Conant, C. A. A History of Modern Banks of Issue. New York, 1896. (Conant.)

Congressional Globe. Washington, 1834–1873. (Cong. Globe.)

Congressional Record. Washington, 1873 ——. (Cong. Rec.)

Cooley, T. M. Michigan. Boston, 1885. (Cooley.)

Cooper, P. Ideas for a Science of Good Government. New York, 1883. (Cooper.)

Crosby, S. S. Early Coins of America. Boston, 1878. (Crosby.)

Curtis, G. T. Constitutional History of the United States. New edition. New York, 1889. (Curtis.)

Del Mar, A. Money and Civilization. London, 1886. (Del Mar.)

Diary and Letters of Thomas Hutchinson. Boston, 1884. (Diary of Hutchinson.)

Diplomatic Correspondence of the American Revolution. Edited by Jared Sparks. Boston, 1829–1830. (Dip. Corr. of Rev.)

Documents relating to the Colonial History of New York. Albany, 1856. (Docs. of N. Y.)

Douglas, C. H. Financial History of Massachusetts. New York, 1892. (Douglas, Fin. Hist.)

Douglass, W. A Discourse concerning the Currencies of the British Plantations in America. Reprinted in Economic Studies of American Economic Association, II. New York, 1897. (Douglass, Discourse.)

BIBLIOGRAPHY

Douglass, W. Summary of the British Settlements in North America. Boston, 1749–1751. (Douglass, Summary.)

Dunbar, C. F. Laws of the United States relating to Currency and Finance. Boston, 1891. (Dunbar.)

Eighty Years' Progress of the United States. Worcester, 1861. (Eighty Years.)

Eleventh Census, Report on Population. Washington, 1895. (Eleventh Census, Population.)

Elliot, J. Debates on the Federal Constitution. Second edition. Washington, 1836. (Elliot.)

The Funding System. Washington, 1845. (Elliot, Fund. System.)

Essays on the Constitution. Edited by P. L. Ford. Brooklyn, 1892. (Essays on Const.)

Felch, A. Early Banks and Banking in Michigan. In Sen. Ex. Doc. 38, Fifty-second Congress, Second Session. Washington, 1893. (Felch.)

Felt, J. B. Historical Account of Massachusetts Currency. Boston, 1839. (Felt.)

Fernow, B. Coins and Currency of New York. In Memorial History of the City of New York. New York, 1893. (Fernow.)

Force, P. American Archives. Fourth Series. Washington, 1837–1853. (Force.)

Franklin, B. Works of Franklin. Edited by Bigelow. New York, 1887–1888. (Works of Franklin.)

Gallatin, A. Writings of Gallatin. Edited by H. Adams. Philadelphia, 1879. (Gallatin.)

Gouge, W. M. A Short History of Paper Money and Banking in the United States. Philadelphia, 1833. (Gouge.)

Greene, E. B. The Provincial Governor. New York, 1898. (Greene.)

Greene, G. W. Historical View of the American Revolution. Boston, 1865. (Greene Hist. View.)

Hadden, C. B.   State Banks of Wisconsin.   In Transactions of Wisconsin Academy of Arts and Sciences, X.   Madison, 1894. (Hadden.)

Hamilton, A. Works of Hamilton. Edited by H. C. Lodge. New York, 1885–1886. (Hamilton.)

Harper's Weekly. (Harper's.)

Harvard Law Review. (Harv. Law Rev.)

Hawks.   History of North Carolina.   Fayetteville, 1858. (Hawks.)

Hazard, E.   State Papers of the United States.   Philadelphia, 1792, 1794. (Hazard.)

Hening, W. H.   Statutes at Large, A Collection of All the Laws of Virginia. New York, 1823. (Hening, Stat.)

Hickcox, J. H.   Historical Account of American Coinage. Albany, 1858. (Hickcox, Coinage.)

History of the Bills of Credit of New York.   Albany, 1866. (Hickcox, Bills of Credit.)

Hildreth, R. History of the United States. New York, 1856. (Hildreth.)

Hill, W.   First Stages of the Tariff Policy of the United States. Baltimore, 1893. (Hill.)

Historical Collections of the Essex Institute. (Hist. Coll. Essex Inst.)

Historical Magazine. (Hist. Mag.)

House Report, 278, Twenty-third Congress, First Session, Washington, 1834. (H. Rep. 278.)

Howard, J. Q. Life of Hayes. Cincinnati, 1876. (Howard.)

Hutchinson, T.   Collection of Papers relative to Massachusetts Bay. Boston, 1769. (Hutchinson Coll. Papers.)

History of Massachusetts, Third edition. Boston, 1795. (Hutchinson, Hist.)

Iredell, J. Laws of North Carolina. Edenton, 1791. (Iredell, Laws.)

James, E. J. The Legal Tender Decisions. Baltimore, 1888. (James.)

BIBLIOGRAPHY

Jefferson, T. The Writings of Jefferson. Edited by P. L. Ford. New York, 1892 ———. (Ford, Writings of Jefferson.)

Writings of Jefferson. Edited by H. A. Washington. Philadelphia, 1860–1869. (Writings of Jefferson.)

Jones, J. S. Defence of North Carolina. Boston and Raleigh, 1834. (Jones.)

Journal of Political Economy. (J. P. E.)

Journals of Congress. Philadelphia, 1777–1788. (Journ. of Cong.)

Journals of the House of Commons. (Journ. of H. of C.)

Kelley, W. D. Speeches and Addresses. Philadelphia, 1872. (Kelley.)

Kinley, D. The Independent Treasury. New York, 1895. (Kinley.)

Knox, J. J. United States Notes. New York, 1885. (Knox.)

Laughlin, J. L. History of Bimetallism in the United States. New York, 1886. (Laughlin.)

Laws of Maryland. Annapolis, 1787. (Laws of Md.)

Laws of the State of Delaware. Newcastle, 1797. (Laws of Del.)

Laws of the State of North Carolina. Raleigh, 1821. (Laws of North Carolina.)

Leaming and Spicer. Grants and Constitutions of New Jersey. Philadelphia, 1752. (Leam. and Spicer.)

Leavitt, S. Our Money Wars. Boston, 1894. (Leavitt.)

Lee, R. H. Life of Richard Henry Lee. Philadelphia, 1825. (Lee.)

Letters to Washington. Edited by Jared Sparks. Boston, 1853. (Letters to Washington.)

Lewis, L. History of the Bank of North America. Philadelphia, 1862. (Lewis.)

Libby, O. G. The Geographical Distribution of the Vote on the Federal Constitution. Madison, 1894. (Libby.)

Linderman, H. R.   Money and Legal Tender in the United States.   New York, 1879.   (Linderman.)

Macleod, H. D.   Dictionary of Political Economy.   London, 1863.   (Macleod, Dict.)
History of Banking in England.   In History of Banking in All Nations.   New York, 1896.   (Macleod.)
Macpherson, D.   Annals of Commerce.   London, 1805. (Macpherson.)
Madison, J.   Writings of James Madison.   Philadelphia, 1867. (Writings of Madison.)
Magazine of American History.   (Mag. of Amer. Hist.)
Marquis (François Jean) de Chastellux.   Travels in North America.   English translation.   London 1787.   (Chastellux.)
Martin, F. X.   History of North Carolina.   New Orleans, 1829.   (Martin.)
McCall, H.   History of Georgia.   Savannah, 1811.   (McCall.)
McCulloch, H.   Men and Measures of Half a Century.   New York, 1888.   (McCulloch, Men and Meas.)
McCulloch, J. R.   Dictionary of Commerce.   Second edition. London, 1835.   (McCulloch.)
McMahon, J. V. L.   Historical View of Maryland.   Baltimore, 1831.   (McMahon.)
McMaster, J. B., and Stone, F. D.   Pennsylvania and the Federal Constitution.   Philadelphia, 1888.   (McMaster and Stone.)
McMurtrie, J.   Observations on Mr. Bancroft's Plea.   Philadelphia, 1886.   (McMurtrie.)
McRee, G. J.   Life and Correspondence of Iredell.   New York, 1857–1858.   (McRee.)
McVey, F. L.   The Populist Movement.   New York, 1896. (McVey.)
Miller, S. F.   Lectures on the Constitution.   New York, 1891. (Miller.)
Minot, G. R.   History of Massachusetts.   Boston, 1798. (Minot.)

BIBLIOGRAPHY

Minutes of the Provincial Council of Pennsylvania. Philadelphia, 1852. (Min. of Penn.)

Moore, J. W. History of North Carolina. Raleigh, 1880.
(Moore.)

Muhleman, M. Monetary Systems of the World. Revised
Edition. New York, 1897. (Muhleman.)

Mulford, I. S. History of New Jersey. Philadelphia, 1851.
(Mulford.)

Newcomb, S. Critical Examination of our Financial Policy.
New York, 1865. (Newcomb.)

Niles, H. Principles and Acts of the Revolution. Baltimore,
1822. (Niles.)

North American Review. (N. A. R.)

Noyes, A. D. Thirty Years of American Finance. New
York, 1898. (Noyes.)

O'Callaghan, E. B. Laws and Ordinances of New Netherland. Albany, 1868. (O'Callaghan.)

Paine, T. Writings of Thomas Paine. Edited by M. C.
Conway. New York, 1894–1896. (Paine.)

Pamphlets on the Constitution. Edited by P. L. Ford. Brooklyn, 1888. (Pamph. on Const.)

Papers of Lewis Morris. New York, 1852. (Pap. of Morris.)

Phillips, H. American Paper Currency. Roxbury, 1865.
(Phillips.)

Pickering, O. Life of Timothy Pickering. Boston, 1867.
(Pickering.)

Postlethwayt, M. Dictionary of Trade and Commerce. London, 1751. (Postlethwayt.)

Potter, E., and Rider, S. S. The Paper Money of Rhode
Island. Providence, 1880. (Potter and Rider.)

Pownall, T. Administration of the British Colonies. London, 1774. (Pownall.)

Proceedings of American Antiquarian Society. (Proc. Ant.
Soc.)

Proceedings of the Massachusetts Historical Society. (Proc. Mass. Hist. Soc.)

Proud, R. History of Pennsylvania. Philadelphia, 1789. (Proud.)

Provincial Papers of New Hampshire. Concord, 1867. (Papers of N. H.)

Quarterly Journal of Economics. (Q. J. E.)

Raguet, C. Currency and Banking. Philadelphia, 1839. (Raguet.)

Ramsay, D. History of South Carolina. Charleston, 1809. (Ramsay.)

Records of Massachusetts Bay. Boston, 1853. (Mass. Recs.)

Records of the Colony of Connecticut. Hartford, 1850. (Conn. Recs.)

Records of the Colony of Rhode Island. Providence, 1856–1865. (Recs. of R. I.)

Report of the Comptroller of Currency, 1876. Washington, 1876. (Rep't Compt. Currency.)

Report of the Director of the Mint, 1896. Washington, 1897. (Rep't Dir. Mint.)

Report of the Director of the Mint upon the Production of the Precious Metals. Washington, 1896. (Rep't Prec. Metals, 1896.)

Report of the International Monetary Conference of 1878. Washington, 1879. (Rep't Mon. Conf.)

Report of the Monetary Commission of the Indianapolis Monetary Convention. Chicago, 1898. (Rep't Mon. Com.)

Report of the Secretary of the Treasury, 1897. Washington, 1897. (Rep't Sec. Treas.)

Reports of United States Supreme Court.

Ripley, W. Z. Financial History of Virginia. New York, 1893. (Ripley.)

Rogers, J. E. T. First Nine Years of the Bank of England. Oxford, 1887. (Rogers.)

BIBLIOGRAPHY

Roosevelt, T. Winning of the West. New York, 1889–1896. (Roosevelt.)

Ruding, R. Annals of the Coinage of Great Britain. Third edition. London, 1840. (Ruding.)

Scharf, J. T. History of Maryland. Baltimore, 1879. (Scharf.)

Schuckers, J. W. Finances and Paper Money of the Revolutionary War. Philadelphia, 1874. (Schuckers.)

Scott, W. A. The Repudiation of State Debts. New York, 1893. (Scott.)

Secret Journals of Congress. Boston, 1821. (Sec. Journ. of Cong.)

Sedgwick, T. Life of William Livingston. New York, 1833. (Sedgwick.)

Senate Executive Document, 38, Fifty-second Congress, Second Session. Washington, 1893. (Sen. Ex. Doc. 38.)

Senate Miscellaneous Document, 132, Forty-first Congress, Second Session. Washington, 1870. (Sen. Misc. Doc. 132.)

Shaler, N. S. Kentucky. Boston, 1885. (Shaler.)

The United States of America. New York, 1894. (Shaler's United States.)

Shepherd, W. R. Proprietary Government in Pennsylvania. New York, 1896. (Shepherd.)

Sherman, J. Recollections of Forty Years. Chicago, 1895. (Sherman.)

Sikes, J. W. The Transition of North Carolina from Colony to Commonwealth. Baltimore, 1898. (Sikes.)

Smith, A. Wealth of Nations. Edited by J. E. T. Rogers. Oxford, 1880. (Smith, W. of N.)

Smith, S. History of New Jersey. Second edition. Trenton, 1877. (Smith, N. J.)

Smith, W. History of New York. New edition. Albany, 1814. (Smith, N. Y.)

Smyth, J. F. D. Tour in the United States. London, 1784. (Smyth.)

Soetbeer, A. Edelmetall-Produktion. Gotha, 1879. (Soetbeer.)

Sound Currency.

Sparks, J. Life of Morris. Boston, 1832. (Sparks, Morris.)

Spaulding, E. G. History of the Legal Tender Paper Money. Buffalo, 1869. (Spaulding.)

Statistical Abstract of the United States, 1898. Washington, 1899. (Stat. Abst.)

Statutes at Large of South Carolina. Columbia, 1837. (Stat. of S. C.)

Stevens, W. B. History of Georgia. New York, 1847. (Stevens.)

Sumner, W. G. Alexander Hamilton. New York, 1890. (Sumner, Hamilton.)

   Andrew Jackson. Boston, 1882. (Sumner, Jackson.)

   History of American Currency. New York, 1874. (Sumner, Currency.)

   History of Banking in the United States. New York, 1896. (Sumner, Banking.)

   History of Protection in the United States. New York, 1884. (Sumner, Protection.)

   The Financier and the Finances of American Revolution. New York, 1891. (Sumner, Financier.)

Taussig, F. W. State Papers and Speeches on the Tariff. Cambridge, 1892. (Taussig, Papers.)

   Tariff History of the United States. New York, 1888. (Taussig, Tariff Hist.)

   The Silver Situation in the United States. Baltimore, 1892. (Taussig, Silv. Sit.)

Tenth Census, VII. Report on Valuation, Taxation, and Public Indebtedness. Washington, 1884. (Tenth Census, VII.)

The American Annual Cyclopædia. New York, 1861 ——. (Ann. Cyc.)

The Federalist. Edited by P. L. Ford. New York, 1898. (Federalist.)

BIBLIOGRAPHY

The First Century of the Republic. New York, 1876. (First Century.)

The Nation. (Nat.)

The Pennsylvania Magazine of History and Biography. (Penn. Mag.)

The Statutes at Large of the United States. Boston, 1850–1873; Washington, 1873 ——. (U. S. Stat.)

The Statutes (of England and Great Britain) at Large. Edited by Pickering and others. Cambridge, 1762. (Stat. at Large.)

Thomas, I. History of Printing in America. Worcester, 1874. (Thomas.)

Trumbull, J. H. First Essays at Banking in New England. Pamphlet. Worcester, 1884. (Trumbull.)

Tucker, G. Money and Banks. Boston, 1839. (Tucker, Money.)

Tucker, J. R. Constitution of the United States. Chicago, 1899. (Tucker.)

Tyler, M. C. Literary History of the American Revolution. New York, 1897. (Tyler.)

Upton, J. K. Money in Politics. Boston, 1884. (Upton.)

Von Hock, C. H. Die Finanzen der Vereinigten Staaten von Amerika. Stuttgart, 1867. (von Hock.)

Walker, F. A. Money. New York, 1878. (Walker.)
Bimetallism. New York, 1896. (Walker, Bimetallism.)

Washington, G. Writings of Washington. Edited by Jared Sparks. Boston, 1855. (Sparks, Writ. of Washington.)
Writings of Washington. Edited by W. C. Ford. New York, 1889–1893. (Writings of Washington.)

Watson, D. K. History of American Coinage. New York, 1899. (Watson.)

Watson, J. T. Annals of Philadelphia. Revised edition. Philadelphia, 1897. (Watson, Annals.)

Webster, P. Political Essays. Philadelphia, 1791. (Webster.)

Weeden, W. B.   Economic and Social History of New England. Boston, 1891. (Weeden.)

Wells, W. V.   Life of Samuel Adams. Boston, 1865. (Wells.)

Wheeler, J. H.   Historical Sketches of North Carolina. Philadelphia, 1851. (Wheeler.)

White, H.   Money and Banking. New York, 1895. (White.)

Whitney, D. R.   The Suffolk Bank. Cambridge, 1878. (Whitney, Suffolk Bank.)

Whitney, E. L.   The Government of South Carolina. Baltimore, 1895. (Whitney.)

Willcox, W. F.   Density and Distribution of Population in the United States. In Economic Studies, II. New York, 1897. (Willcox.)

Williamson, H.   History of North Carolina. Philadelphia, 1812. (Williamson.)

Winsor, J.   Editor.   Narrative and Critical History of America. Boston, 1887. (Winsor.)

Winthrop, J.   History of New England. Boston, 1825. (Winthrop, N. Eng.)

Witherspoon, J.   Works. Edinburgh, 1805. (Witherspoon, Works.)

Wright, J.   The American Negotiator. Third edition. London, 1767. (Wright.)

Wynne, M.   History of the British Empire in America. London, 1770. (Wynne.)

Yale Review.   (Yale Rev.)

INDEX

289

INDEX

290